S0-FBP-420

THE DECLINE OF THE PROGRESSIVE MOVEMENT IN WISCONSIN

THE DECLINE *of* the PROGRESSIVE MOVEMENT *in* Wisconsin 1890-1920

Herbert F. Margulies

1968
THE STATE HISTORICAL SOCIETY OF WISCONSIN
MADISON

To my Mother and Father

COPYRIGHT © 1968 BY
THE STATE HISTORICAL SOCIETY OF WISCONSIN
ALL RIGHTS RESERVED

LIBRARY OF CONGRESS
CATALOG CARD NUMBER
LC 68–63073

EUROPE: W.S. HALL & CO., INC., LONDON, AMSTERDAM, NEW YORK
CANADA: HARVEST HOUSE, LTD., MONTREAL
INDIA: THACKER & CO., LTD., BOMBAY

MANUFACTURED IN THE UNITED STATES OF AMERICA BY
WORZALLA PUBLISHING COMPANY
STEVENS POINT, WISCONSIN

Preface

REFORM MOVEMENTS have been accorded a prominent place in American history; none more so than the progressive movement. Much of progressivism's achievement occurred on the national level, where the movement is associated with men like Theodore Roosevelt, Woodrow Wilson, and Robert M. La Follette. Yet it is a suggestive coincidence that each of these three served first as a reform governor before moving on to the White House or the Senate chambers. The fountainhead for the progressive movement was the state. When that source of vitality ran dry, the national movement withered.

While the progressive movement was expressed in greater or lesser degree in every state of the union, La Follette's Wisconsin won the greatest reputation as the pioneer progressive state and showcase of the movement. This honor, first conferred by journalists such as Lincoln Steffens and Frederic C. Howe, has been confirmed by historians. During the La Follette administrations, 1901 through 1905, the Wisconsin legislature passed thoroughgoing and effective railroad taxation and regulation laws, created a comprehensive system of direct primary elections, and adopted a model civil service law. After a period of quiescence through 1909, reform experienced a renaissance in the years 1911 through 1914, during the administrations of Francis E. McGovern, and a host of progressive measures were passed, including a state income tax law, a workmen's compensation law, a corrupt practices act, various laws designed to benefit farmers, and laws regulating the hours of labor of women and children and establishing a state insurance system. The legislation was unusually well drawn by Charles McCarthy and his Legislative Reference Library and by experts like John R. Commons or B. H. Meyer from the University of Wisconsin. Experts manned the commissions that blossomed in these years—the Industrial Commission, the Railroad Commission, the Tax Commission, the Insurance Commission, and the Dairy Commission, among others—and they competently administered the reform legislation.

Even in Wisconsin, however, the progressive movement proved vulnerable. The political underpinnings of the movement were eroding throughout the period of progressive ascendency, and in 1914 the progressives sustained a defeat from which the movement never recovered. Along the way, La Follette had made many bitter enemies who were implacably dedicated to his overthrow. The progressive ranks were weakened by constant factionalism, by rival interests and ambitions; many of La Follette's lieutenants had fortresses of personal power from which they could emerge to tilt with one another; some drew on ethnic support, some on regional, and some on personal wealth or business connections. La Follette's efforts to keep order in this heterogeneous camp were inhibited by his own expressed commitment against anything suggestive of boss rule. Above all, the progressive movement was anchored by its Jeffersonianism, which prohibited an alliance with the strong socialist element; and when the progressive legislature exceeded the limits imposed by this philosophy on spending, bureaucratization, and welfare measures, it put the movement as a whole in mortal danger.

This book is focused on the causes of the decline of the progressive movement in a single state, in the belief that a clear and coherent view of national progressivism is attainable only after a great many such studies have been done. Thus, though I hope this work will contribute to a general understanding, I do not here attempt to draw conclusions about progressivism nationally. As yet, the number of extensive works on state politics is limited. Among them, George Mowry's *The California Progressives* is outstanding. Other books that will be especially useful to the synthesizer include Hoyt L. Warner's *Progressivism in Ohio, 1897–1917,* Winston A. Flint's *The Progressive Movement in Vermont,* Richard Abrams' *Conservatism in the Progressive Era: Massachusetts Politics, 1900–1912,* Irwin Yellowitz's *Labor and the Progressive Movement in New York State, 1897–1916,* and Albert D. Kirwan's *Revolt of the Rednecks: Mississippi Politics, 1876–1925.* Biographies of many progressive leaders offer insights into state politics. But many more full-scale political studies will be needed before general theories become verifiable. In any case, when the time for synthesis comes, it should be done on the basis of a balanced overview of all the states, not from the vantage point of a closely focused state study. To draw general conclusions from Wisconsin's political history alone would be especially ill-advised, for while the politics of each state is unique unto itself, Wisconsin is perhaps (as George Orwell might have observed) more unique than others.

Understanding of the decline of the progressive movement in Wisconsin requires some preliminary study of its origins in the 1890's and its early development after the turn of the century. The first two chapters are devoted to this.

The erosion in progressive fortunes began in the 1906 primaries. My detailed study, relying chiefly on manuscripts and newspapers, begins with that contest and continues through the election of 1920. While I have sampled the primary sources for the background years, the late 1880's, the 1890's, and the years of La Follette's administration as governor, I have felt compelled to rely chiefly on secondary sources for this period, which is dealt with in chapters one and two.

A key question relating to the progressive movement concerns the date of its demise. The causes one ascribes to its decline and the role attributed to World War I will in large part be determined by the answer to this temporal question. It is my contention that Wisconsin's progressive movement had run its course before American entry into the war and that the causal factors were evidenced in the years prior to 1917. The situation was complicated by the fact that a strong reformist wave rose in the state in the immediate postwar period. In order to place the pre-war years in proper perspective, it is therefore incumbent on me to show that this postwar reformism was in fact a new and different phenomenon born of the war rather than a continuation of the pre-war movement. The last chapters are given to that task.

The study began as a dissertation, presented in 1955. From that sprang articles.[1] The present work is a further distillation of both, informed by the results of further rumination and by research in primary and secondary sources published since 1955. This book is, I hope, the latest but I trust not the last word on the decline of the progressive movement in Wisconsin.

I wish to express my thanks to the editors of the *Wisconsin Magazine of History* and of *Mid-America* for permission to use portions of articles verbatim in chapters 3 and 4. Thanks are due also to the University of Hawaii Research Council for facilitating my most recent research on this subject. I benefited from the advice of more people than I can practicably name. I do wish, however, to acknowledge my debt to Professor Merle Curti for his invaluable counsel and unfailing encouragement. My thanks also to

[1] Herbert F. Margulies, "Issues and Politics of Wisconsin Progressivism, 1906–1920" (doctoral dissertation, University of Wisconsin, 1955); "The La Follette-Philipp Alliance of 1918," *Wisconsin Magazine of History*, (Summer, 1955); "The Background of the La Follette-McGovern Schism," *Wisconsin Magazine of History* (Autumn, 1956); "Weaknesses in Wisconsin Progressivism, 1911–1914," *Mid-America*, (July, 1957); "The Election of 1920 in Wisconsin: The Return to 'Normalcy' Reappraised," *Wisconsin Magazine of History* (Autumn, 1957); "Weaknesses in Wisconsin Progressivism, 1905–1909," *Mid-America* (July, 1959); "Anti-Catholicism in Wisconsin Politics, 1914–1920," *Mid-America* (January, 1962).

Preface

Professor Vernon Carstensen and Miss Alice E. Smith, both of whom helped me with criticism on a number of occasions. Finally, I am indebted to the State Historical Society of Wisconsin and its personnel for gathering and organizing much of the source material for this study and for providing willing and informed aid in many ways.

HERBERT F. MARGULIES

Honolulu, Hawaii
January, 1968

Contents

	Preface	v
I.	THE RISE OF THE PROGRESSIVES	3
II.	PROGRESSIVES AND STALWARTS	51
III.	FACTIONALISM, 1906–1916	83
IV.	ACCOMPLISHMENT AND DISASTER, 1911–1914	124
V.	EMANUEL PHILIPP AND THE SURVIVAL OF CONSERVATISM	164
VI.	LOYALTY, LOYALTY, LOYALTY	193
VII.	RECONSTRUCTION AND THE NEW PROGRESSIVISM	244
	CONCLUSION	283
	Select Bibliography	291
	Index	300

I

The Rise of the Progressives

LOOKING BACKWARD from the vantage point of 1930, a longtime observer of Wisconsin politics remarked of the Harrison-Cleveland campaign of 1888 that "People at that time seemed to take their politics more seriously than they do today. There was a clearly marked line between Republicanism and Democracy."[1] Indeed there was. And although the issues of that day—the tariff, civil service, railroad rates, and the like—may seem inconsequential in the twentieth century, they meant the difference between success or failure, election or defeat, in the nineteenth.

The Democratic party was surprisingly vital in post-Civil War Wisconsin. It invariably polled more than 40 per cent of the major party vote for governor until 1896, and usually as much as 46 or 47 per cent.[2] The state's German-Americans, the largest single immigrant group, were mainly Democrats, and they wielded great power. When in 1889 a Republican legislature adopted the Bennett Law, requiring parents to send their children to schools which taught in English, both Catholic and Lutheran Germans were so offended by this blow to their parochial schools that they redoubled their support of the Democratic party, which consequently won the governorship in 1890.[3]

The seriousness of the Democratic challenge doubtless

---

[1] Ralph G. Plumb, *Badger Politics, 1836–1930* (Manitowoc, 1930), 88.
[2] Leon D. Epstein, *Politics in Wisconsin* (Madison, 1958), 35.
[3] Plumb, *Badger Politics,* 91.

contributed to the zeal and the unity of Republicans, many of whom were New England or upstate New York Yankees and who, apart from other considerations, were predisposed towards the Republican party as heir to the Whigs, Know Nothings, Free Soilers, abolitionists, and advocates of temperance and prohibition. The Civil War, which equated Republicanism with patriotism, cemented and fortified the attachment.[4]

The bulwark of the Republican party in Wisconsin, as in other northern states in the late nineteenth century, was the Union veterans, many of them organized in the Grand Army of the Republic.[5] Their normal association with the Grand Old Party was given fresh impetus by President Cleveland's satirical vetoes of 228 private pension bills and by his veto of a bill to broaden the basis for claims. To make matters worse, Cleveland ordered the return of captured Confederate flags to the appropriate Southern states. Commander-in-chief Lucius Fairchild, a Republican and ex-governor of Wisconsin, led in arousing national protest. The G. A. R. was at the height of its power in this period. Peak membership in Wisconsin, 13,944, was achieved in 1889. Benjamin Harrison, Republican beneficiary in 1888 of the veterans' wrath against Cleveland, deferred to the old soldiers and solidified their Republican attachment in 1890 by signing a liberalized pension bill.[6]

It was difficult to get very far in Republican politics without G. A. R. support. Robert M. La Follette, as a young aspirant for Congress in 1884, reached the veterans of his district through his most important early backer, General George Bryant, who had been an intimate of Ulysses Grant

---

[4] Epstein, *Politics in Wisconsin*, 35–36.

[5] Albert O. Barton, *La Follette's Winning of Wisconsin* (Des Moines, 1922), 198.

[6] Mary Dearing, *Veterans in Politics: The Story of the G. A. R.* (Baton Rouge, 1952), 330–402; for the role of Fairchild, see Sam Ross, *The Empty Sleeve, a Biography of Lucius Fairchild* (Madison, 1964), 206–209; *Wisconsin Blue Book, 1917*, 397.

and was popular with the veterans of his district, many of whom had served under him.[7] The veterans were a conservative lot by modern standards. They were easily impressed with appeals to crush "treasonable" radical doctrines. During the Milwaukee labor riots of 1886, Wisconsin posts of the G. A. R. "tendered their services to the state administration; and General Fairchild proposed that the governor summon the whole department to suppress the disorder."[8]

Leaders of the Republican party, young and old, coming and arrived, were not uncomfortable in this kind of company during the 1880's. Even the young La Follette, a man innocent of Civil War experience and destined to lead the progressive rebellion, felt quite at home within the Republican party. It was not because he was a conservative on clearly defined issues, but rather that the issues that would later divide conservatives and liberals, while already on the scene, had not yet come to center stage. La Follette, reflecting on his own background in politics, wrote in 1912 that "Few young men who entered public life thirty years ago had any wide outlook upon affairs, or any general political ideas. They were drawn into politics just as other men were drawn into the professions or the arts, or into business, because it suited their tastes and ambitions."[9] La Follette was, in the seventies and eighties, a bright young man on the make, an ambitious, self-made man of the American dream. A farm boy who by his own energy and enterprise worked his way through college while supporting his mother and sister, La Follette had no reason to question the conventional wisdom. The righteous would find their just reward in the land of opportunity. During the seventies, neither

---

[7] David Paul Thelen, *The Early Life of Robert M. La Follette, 1855–1884* (Chicago, 1966), 66–70; Belle Case La Follette and Fola La Follette, *Robert M. La Follette, 1855–1925* (2 vols., New York, 1953), 1: 58.

[8] Dearing, *Veterans in Politics*, 325.

[9] Robert M. La Follette, *La Follette's Autobiography: A Personal Narrative of Political Experiences* (Madison, 1913), 3.

mugwumpery nor grangerism attracted him.[10] His first campaign for public office, that of Dane County district attorney, in 1880, and his maiden speech in Congress both turned on the old-time virtue of economy in government.[11] La Follette shared his party's devotion to the tariff and was an influential defender of it in 1888 and after. He accepted the view that "it made little difference how high the duties were because competition between domestic manufacturers within the tariff wall would ensure to the consumer the lowest price commensurate with American wages for American workingmen."[12]

La Follette perceived that the lines between the progressive and standpat elements were being drawn in the eighties, and he thought he knew where the leaders stood. Speaker Thomas B. Reed was in the standpat camp, but it was he who gave La Follette a key appointment on the Ways and Means Committee. On the side of the people, in La Follette's view, and one with whom the young representative worked in close harmony, was William McKinley. But La Follette had kind words not only for McKinley but also for Blaine and Sherman, among others, even in retrospect. His wife recalled later how, in observing congressional proceedings from the gallery during the eighties, she was gladdened when Joseph Cannon entered the fray, "because I felt sure 'our side' would have the best of it."[13] In time, of course, La Follette and Cannon would be political opponents, and McKinley would be symbolic of an almost pre-industrial and certainly pre-progressive era. And pre-progressive it was, despite the Henry Georges and the Edward Bellamys. Alert and educated young Republicans of good conscience could still share with their elders a party feeling and loyalty that, in La Follette's words, "partook in some measure of the zeal and fervor of the days following the war."[14]

[10] Thelen, *Early Life of La Follette*, 27, 49.
[11] Belle and Fola La Follette, *La Follette*, 1: 47, 69.
[12] *Ibid.*, 1: 80.
[13] *Ibid.*, 1: 63.
[14] La Follette, *Autobiography*, 70.

The Rise of the Progressives

Given the zeal of the partisans, the relative closeness of the division between the major parties, and the fact that the issues of the progressive era had not yet emerged to cause internal schism within the parties, it was not surprising that each party was dominated by a few leaders and a statewide "machine." Since the progressives were later to attack the machines of either party, identifying them as servants of trusts, it is worth recalling that political bosses and machines antedated industrialism in America, and, in their Jefferson-Jackson phase, were associated with the rise of the common man. The political machine was also associated with the unwillingness of the people to delegate authority to their representatives and a consequent hamstringing of state governments by detailed and restrictive state constitutions. Machines filled this vacuum, to do the things that individuals and groups wanted done.

The Republican machine leaders of Wisconsin performed all the traditional services of the pre-industrial era and some new ones as well. Federal and state patronage was usually available to them, since their party elected most of the Presidents and governors. Senator Philetus Sawyer was especially adept in securing federal patronage, as well as pensions and river and harbor aid, which in turn generated business and jobs.[15] Railroads did not bring the machine into existence, but their advent did provide co-operative politicians with additional tools. The railroads were able to help young lawyers by throwing business their way; and railroad passes, distributed liberally to legislators, their families, friends, and constituents, were exceedingly potent political weapons.[16]

Nevertheless, trouble of unimagined dimensions was brewing for many of the old leaders and their system. The machines, characteristically serving powerful constituents in order to use them, had themselves gradually become tools of those they had set out to use. The swift rise of the railroads, the development of lumbering, and the advent of

---

[15] Richard Nelson Current, *Pine Logs and Politics: A Life of Philetus Sawyer, 1816–1900* (Madison, 1950), 214, 237–238.
[16] Barton, *La Follette's Winning of Wisconsin*, 95–96.

other forms of big business produced the change. The railroads became more than merely patrons of the machines whose services were incidentally useful to these machines—instead, they developed their own direct lines of communication and coercion and to a degree replaced the old machines in the political arena. A. O. Barton, an astute young Madison newspaperman, noted during the nineties that following the defeat of the Granger movement the railroad lobby "had grown increasingly strong and arrogant with time." Corporation lobbyists, led by the well-known railroad group, were frequently regarded as the real powers in the legislature. They maintained lavishly equipped apartments, serviceable for lobbying; but often the conventional roles were reversed and it was they who were courted, dined, and deferred to by legislators eager for railroad passes for themselves or their friends and constituents. Many legislators used passes during legislative sessions to take four-day weekends for the pleasures of travel or to attend to business back home. The lobbyists were left in Madison, where they cheerfully prepared new legislation.[17]

Meanwhile, the political machine was itself changing. Enactment of a Granger law in 1874 had alerted the railroads to the fact that old-line politicians were not reliable. Soon leaders in the business world assumed the top political positions. The Democratic party was dominated in the eighties by the Milwaukee Bourbon, Alexander Mitchell, and in the nineties by William Vilas and E. C. Wall, the one a high-minded hard-money man, corporation attorney, and investor in pine lands and paper mills, the other a Milwaukee electric utility executive of varied and extensive economic interests.[18] In the Republican party, ex-governor Lucius Fairchild and the veteran boss Elisha Keyes were shunted aside into positions of only local power during the eighties as a business-oriented triumvirate took their place.[19]

[17] *Ibid.*, 94–95, 97.
[18] See especially Horace S. Merrill, *William Freeman Vilas, Doctrinaire Democrat* (Madison, 1954).
[19] See especially Ross, *The Empty Sleeve*, 184–200; Thelen, *Early Life of La Follette*, 55–60; Richard W. Hantke, "Elisha W. Keyes, the Bismarck of

The Rise of the Progressives

Heading the group was Philetus Sawyer, a crusty old lumber baron who as representative and later United States Senator proved as shrewd and determined in politics as in business. (Actually, in Sawyer's case the two were not easily separated, for his wealth rested in large part on pine lands secured from the federal government at very low cost and used without conservationist scruple.[20]) He was ever concerned also for the financial welfare of his political friends, informing them of land and other opportunities and helping to secure federal favors of every sort. His fellow lumberman John Strange regarded this attribute of loyalty as Sawyer's strongest political asset. But it was in connection with one of the land deals, a piece of legislation designed to open up certain Wisconsin Indian lands to public purchase, that young Representative La Follette first fell out with the old Senator.[21]

The second member of the Republican triumvirate was Henry C. Payne. Born in Massachusetts in 1843, Payne involved himself in Milwaukee business and civic life in the sixties and became President of the Young Men's Library Association. He began organizing Milwaukee Republicanism in the seventies. In 1890, Payne was Secretary of the Republican State Central Committee, and, according to La Follette, "political manager of the Wisconsin machine, lobbyist for the St. Paul Railroad and the Beef Trust, and had the backing of the important corporate interests of the state." Possessed of "A fine head and figure, meditative, introspective eyes, a quiet, clear-cut, convincing way of stating his views, he was certainly the most accomplished rail-

---

Western Politics," *Wisconsin Magazine of History*, 31:29–41 (September, 1947); and Herman J. Deutsch, "Railroad Politics," *Wisconsin Magazine of History*, 15: 391–411 (June, 1932).

[20] John Strange, "The Autobiography of John Strange" (unpublished manuscript, *ca.* 1919), 25, in the John Strange Papers, State Historical Society of Wisconsin; Current, *Pine Logs and Politics*, 103–236. Unless otherwise indicated, all manuscript collections cited herein are at the State Historical Society of Wisconsin.

[21] Strange, "Autobiography," 25; La Follette, *Autobiography*, 27.

road lobbyist I ever knew," La Follette later recalled.[22] Through the nineties, Payne was involved with the management of the Milwaukee Electric Railway and Light Company, which owned and operated the street railway system in Milwaukee and several suburban cities. He was for a time president of the Milwaukee and Northern Railroad Company, director of the First National Bank of Milwaukee, one of the receivers for the Northern Pacific, and involved in other enterprises as well. For Payne, as for Sawyer, business, politics, and personal life blended together. Payne was something of a liaison man for the group. As national committeeman, he established contact with eastern political and business elements. Within Wisconsin, he was on friendly and co-operative terms with his Democratic counterpart, E. C. Wall, and the two had offices in the same building.[23]

The latest addition to the Republican leadership was John C. Spooner. A railroad attorney of considerable talent, Spooner did not care for the rough-and-tumble of politics. Elected to the United States Senate in 1885, Spooner quickly proved himself a master constitutionalist, debater, and orator. He was less frequently associated with the unsavory aspects of politics and business than Sawyer or Payne, but he believed that business opportunity was the key to popular felicity, so with complete good conscience he was able to assist in the business of opening up Indian lands, securing favorable franchises, winning tariff protection, and guarding railroad interests.[24]

But while railroaders, lumbermen, utilities magnates, and manufacturers were gaining in political influence, farmers, especially dairymen, were becoming more numerous and better organized. So too were laboring men and noncorporate middle-class elements. A new generation of potential leaders was coming on the scene, with college degrees

[22] Alexander M. Thompson, *The Political History of Wisconsin* (Milwaukee, 1902), 448; La Follette, *Autobiography*, 33.
[23] Plumb, *Badger Politics*, 102.
[24] Dorothy Ganfield Fowler, *John Coit Spooner, Defender of Presidents* (New York, 1961).

The Rise of the Progressives

and new-fangled ideas. And immigrants, especially Germans and Scandinavians, were becoming more numerous and better accustomed to American ways. In the unwillingness and inability of the Old Guard to come to terms with these groups lay the precondition for a major political explosion in the state.

Wisconsin had developed as a wheat-growing state. Those who pioneered Wisconsin in the middle of the nineteenth century profited by the new and cheap land of the state, lake transportation to the east coast, and a thriving European market. The New Englanders, New Yorkers, and Germans who plowed Wisconsin's fields brought forth their largest crop of wheat in 1860, 27,000,000 bushels. But wheat growing was most profitable on cheap and fresh land, and Wisconsin soon lost these advantages to a new group of frontier states, Iowa, Minnesota, Kansas, Nebraska, and the Dakotas. The older, earliest settled, and most fertile counties of Wisconsin, in the south and east of the state, were the first to reduce wheat production. In these areas, wheat growing was coming to an end by 1879.[25]

Fortunately for Wisconsin, dairying arose as a lucrative substitute for wheat growing. While wheat production declined from 22,680,000 bushels in 1870 to 6,665,000 bushels in 1900, the number of milch cows on Wisconsin pasture rose from 251,000 to 696,000 during the thirty-year period. By 1900, income from dairy herds totaled 38 per cent of Wisconsin farm income, while wheat yielded 16 per cent. Oat, corn, and hay growing developed to complement dairying. Barley and tobacco growing helped to round out the diversified agricultural economy that was developing.[26]

Wisconsin farmers, with other western farmers, suffered from the prolonged post-Civil War decline in agricultural prices. Only greatly expanded production sustained cash income per farm at a relatively even level between 1870 and

---

[25] Joseph Schafer, *A History of Agriculture in Wisconsin* (Madison, 1922), 92–94.
[26] John S. Bordner, "The Use of Wisconsin Land," *Wisconsin Blue Book, 1935* (Madison, 1935), 59–90, 61.

1896. Average income per farm was somewhat higher during the eighties and nineties than in the seventies, however.[27] And dairying offered a bright future for many.

Populism had relatively little impact in Wisconsin, due in part to the fact that Wisconsin dairymen did not share many of the complaints of Plains states wheat growers. As their product was of relatively slight bulk, and their production conditions were stable, they had less concern about freight rates and credit conditions, though these were by no means matters of complete indifference. A Farmers Alliance unit did exist in the state and did move into the People's Party during the 1890's, as in other states; but in Wisconsin labor, not farmers, formed the nucleus of the party.[28]

The dairy farmer did make certain demands with respect to state action, however. "What he asked of government was mainly low taxes, protection against substitutes, and aid in the never ending search for greater production at lower cost."[29] Considering the growing importance of the dairymen, politicians would ignore these modest expectations at their peril.

The danger was the greater because the Wisconsin farmer was heir to a strong anti-railroad tradition that might at any time help to kindle the fires of reform. While wheat was still king, bitterness against the railroads for shady practices in their construction operations, unfavorable freight rates, and low-quality service gave rise in 1874 to the famous Potter Law, designed to control freight rates. The law was soon scuttled by railroad counteraction, but the anti-railroad tradition survived.[30] It mingled with a generalized anti-

[27] P. E. McNall, W. P. Mortenson, and R. D. Davidson, "Development of Wisconsin Agriculture," *Economic Information for Wisconsin Farmers* (Madison, 1934), 5: 6.
[28] See especially Milton M. Small, "The Biography of Robert Schilling" (master's thesis, University of Wisconsin, 1953).
[29] Theodore Saloutos and John D. Hicks, *Agricultural Discontent in the Middle West, 1900–1939* (Madison, 1951), 12.
[30] During the 1850's, railroad entrepreneurs sold stock in their projected roads to farmers along the route and then passed the farmers' notes to

The Rise of the Progressives

corporation feeling among farmers that found expression in protests against the protective tariff in the elections of 1888, 1890, and 1892.[31]

The industrial growth of Wisconsin was in an early stage of development in 1890. Even so, Milwaukee already boasted a budding machine-tool industry as well as brewing, tanning, and other industries. Elsewhere in the state, especially along the Fox River, flour milling, lumber manufacturing, and paper milling thrived. The dairy industry was rising and railroads employed significant numbers throughout the state.

In Milwaukee, the one big city of the state and sixteenth most populous in the nation, with 204,468 residents in 1890,[32] labor organization had progressed to the point where the Knights of Labor had fifty lodges and at least sixteen thousand members by 1886. Labor elsewhere in the state was almost wholly unorganized. Laborers were not so numerous as farmers, nor were they, in fact, always distinguishable from farmers, for in the smaller mill towns laborers switched between town and country with bewildering rapidity.[33] Workers were nevertheless to be reckoned with in politics. Their interests were hardly identical with those of their employers, and many were ready to back a new element in politics. A good deal of labor discontent in Milwaukee was to be channeled through the socialist movement and third parties, culminating in the Social Democratic party in the late nineties. Outside of Milwaukee, however, workers were potentially useful to reformers within the two old parties.

---

eastern investors. When the roads collapsed in the panic of 1857, foreclosure on the farm mortgages was threatened. An authority on railroad history who grew up in Wisconsin, Professor George R. Taylor, believes that the anti-railroad tradition in Wisconsin was unmatched in any other state. Conversation with Taylor, February, 1954.

[31] Merrill, *Vilas*, 151–197.

[32] *Eleventh Census of the United States, 1890* (Washington, 1891), 15: lxvii.

[33] Gertrude Schmidt, "History of Labor Legislation in Wisconsin" (doctoral dissertation, University of Wisconsin, 1933), 13–14.

Professional people—doctors, lawyers, ministers, teachers, and small businessmen—were most evident in Milwaukee, where they spearheaded a reformist movement directed primarily against the street railway monopoly and concerned themselves with honest and efficient government and increase in services.[34] In the smaller cities and towns, middle-class elements were growing proportionally with the growth and maturation of the state. Some were becoming restive as they saw economic and political power concentrated in the small Milwaukee coterie known as the Milwaukee Regency or simply The Ring.[35]

Meanwhile, a new generation of educated young men was rapidly coming on the scene. By 1890, the state had eighty high schools qualified to prepare students for university study. The number had almost doubled by 1900. Enrollment at the University of Wisconsin was 539 in 1886–1887. By 1892 it passed the thousand mark and in the academic year 1899–1900 enrollment reached 2,400 and the trend remained strongly upward.[36]

In the same period immigrant groups, especially the Germans and Scandinavians, were more than ready for full political recognition. Those of German birth or parentage numbered 626,030 in 1890 in a total population of 1,693,330; of these, 259,819 had been born in Germany. Among Norwegians, 130,737 were of Norwegian birth or parentage, and 65,696 of these were Norwegian-born. First- and second-generation Swedes totaled 29,993; 20,157 of them were born in Sweden.[37] First adjustments having been made, these people were prepared now to receive the recognition that went with high political office. The Old Guard leaders, Yankees all, while by no means oblivious to the ethnic groups, were yet slow to open the door to them.

Basic underlying sources of trouble for the Old Guard were present, then, by 1890. When certain incidents oc-

---

[34] Bayrd Still, *Milwaukee: The History of a City* (Madison, 1948), 307–311.
[35] Ross, *The Empty Sleeve*, 177.
[36] Merle Curti and Vernon Carstensen, *The University of Wisconsin, 1848–1925: A History* (2 vols., Madison, 1949), 1: 662, 659–660.
[37] *Eleventh Census, 1890*, 15: clxvi, cxxxix.

The Rise of the Progressives

curred that worked against the entrenched leaders, they triggered a prolonged and consequential chain reaction in Wisconsin that came to be called the progressive movement. Some of these incidents resulted in part from the overconfidence and carelessness of the Old Guard leaders.

Before La Follette had come forth as a reformer, the arrogance of one of the Republican triumvirate, Henry C. Payne, paved the way for a fateful rebellion of the state's dairy leaders. Payne had the temerity to lobby in Washington and Madison for oleomargarine interests, and farmers, alarmed by the oleo challenge and resentful of Payne's activity, "walked to the caucuses and conventions with cornstalks over their shoulders, making an organized fight to nominate and elect as governor William Dempster Hoard."[38] Hoard was a pioneer of scientific dairying, a founder of the Wisconsin Dairyman's Association, and editor since 1885 of *Hoard's Dairyman*. He was also a loyal Republican, and the Old Guard accepted him without a major struggle. He justified their faith in his soundness when, in his inaugural message to the legislature, he urged continued co-operation between farmers and the railroads and decried radical measures.[39] In the same message, however, he called for creation of a Dairy and Food Commission, to enforce laws against impurity and adulteration. He deemed such a commission essential to the improvement of Wisconsin's dairy products, the key to the eastern market. But Payne brazenly intervened with the legislature on behalf of the oleo manufacturers in an effort to block the bill. Finally Hoard could contain his anger no longer. He summoned Payne to his office and said, "Mr. Payne, you either keep your hands off this bill and retire from the field, or I will message the legislature, telling them that you, as Republican State Chairman, are a paid lobbyist in the employ of P. D. Armour, the packer. . . ."[40] When Payne tried to block Hoard's renomination in 1890, the resentment of the governor and

---

[38] Belle and Fola La Follette, *La Follette*, 1: 86.
[39] *State of Wisconsin Assembly Journal, Thirty Ninth Session, 1889*, 18–19.
[40] George William Rankin, *William Dempster Hoard* (Fort Atkinson, 1925), 93; Belle and Fola La Follette, *La Follette*, 1: 102.

his friends increased further. Payne yielded the state chairmanship to a Hoard supporter in 1892, but this gesture of conciliation was insufficient.

The storm of controversy provoked by the Bennett Law — which Governor Hoard sponsored — resulted in a Democratic victory in 1890. Finding themselves in power for a change, the Democrats promptly began prosecuting former state treasurers, mainly Republicans, for pocketing the interest on state deposits. These cases focused attention on an unsavory practice that had become all too ordinary and habitual, and the attendant publicity benefited not only the Democrats but Republican reformers as well throughout the 1890's.

The link between state treasurers and the Republican leadership was dramatized by the La Follette-Sawyer bribery incident in 1891, which began when Judge Robert Siebecker, La Follette's brother-in-law and former partner, withdrew from a pending treasurer case. Rumors soon circulated about a bribe attempt. On October 27 the leader of the Republican party, Senator Philetus Sawyer, startled the state with a prepared interview in the *Milwaukee Sentinel*. In it Sawyer explained how, as one of the bondsmen for the treasurers, he had innocently arranged a meeting with La Follette and, still not knowing of the relationship between La Follette and Siebecker, had offered La Follette a $500.00 retainer for participating in the case. Upon learning of the relationship, Sawyer said, he had withdrawn the offer and there the matter ended. La Follette, after some soul searching and consultation with friends, who warned against a reply, issued his own version of the incident to the *Sentinel*. In it he gave a long and detailed account culminating in the accusation that Sawyer had offered him a bribe to influence the Judge.[41]

The immediate reaction of politicians and press was

---

[41] Barton, *La Follette's Winning of Wisconsin*, 42–49. For other accounts, see especially Belle and Fola La Follette, *La Follette*, 1: 95–100; La Follette, *Autobiography*, 61–71; and Current, *Pine Logs and Politics*, 255–269.

largely adverse to La Follette, though the truth of his account was not the main point at issue. More relevant to many was that by besmirching the reputation of its leaders, he had dealt a severe blow to the Republican party, the savior of the Union and sole repository of political virtue. This reaction was not unanticipated by La Follette. In publicly responding to Sawyer, La Follette had deliberately crossed his Rubicon. And a momentous crossing it was for an ambitious, gregarious, energetic man of thirty-six years, already a three-term congressman, but relegated to state activity by the Democratic sweep of 1890 and the subsequent gerrymander of his district,[42] and now blocked from the normal channels of preferment within the state by the leaders of his own party. The choice was between retirement or rebellion, and young La Follette, "burning for achievement,"[43] was not ready to retire from politics.

Thus, just as the top leadership of the Republican machine began to deteriorate, a new leader who was to display remarkable abilities emerged on the state scene; a leader, moreover, whose only opportunity for power and office lay not in the normal processes of succession but in rebellion. That La Follette was estranged from the top party leaders by his own sense of honesty and courage would be a decided political asset in the years to come.

The incidents that triggered the revolt — Payne's actions vis à vis the oleo question and dairying interests, the treasury cases, and Sawyer's alleged bribery attempt — all had moral as well as economic overtones. The almost universal virtue of honesty was at issue, and on such a basis men of various persuasions might be aroused to common protest and common action. For many, perhaps most of those who joined La Follette, the commitment to reform did not involve a complete break with past ideas and party associations. Rather, theirs was an effort to purify and restore basically sound but temporarily corrupted institutions.

[42] Barton, *La Follette's Winning of Wisconsin*, 52.
[43] *Idem.*

La Follette himself continued as the conventional Republican in many aspects of his thought and action.

The contest between party men and progressives was prolonged and momentous. Much about it was ordinary, much was extraordinary. The reforms sought during the nineties were conventional enough: honesty, economy, benefits to dairymen; the battle occurred within one of the major parties, not through third-party action; La Follette relied on patronage, ethnic recognition, and other common coin of politics. In many ways, though, the battle was unusual. The reformers brought to it far more idealism, crusading zeal, and sheer energy than was common in factional politics; the populace was drawn into the contest far more fully than usual; and the ill-will generated on both sides reached unusual intensity and duration. Above all, La Follette was extraordinary. His oratorical talents, energy, dedication, and inspirational qualities were unmatched. Increasingly, he disregarded party welfare and pursued a strategy of constant factional warfare. Though his immediate ends and many of his methods were prosaic, the fight that he led sometimes took on the aura of a crusade.

Already experienced in state and national politics by 1891, La Follette understood that the roots of Republicanism in Wisconsin went deep, tapping more than corporate coffers or patronage. Nor is there reason to believe that his own devotion to leaders like McKinley or measures like the tariff had declined since the eighties. Hence, following the break with Sawyer, he was not prepared to read himself out of the party, and proposed instead to defend his claims to political legitimacy against the efforts of Sawyer's group to brand him a renegade. When the party machinery of his home county was switched from his friends and the chairmanship went to John Spooner's brother, La Follette had to attend the 1892 Republican national convention as a spectator, and was excluded from consultations. As campaign arrangements began, no request came for his services as an orator. But La Follette fought back. When his explicit offer to speak was rejected, he declared that he would

The Rise of the Progressives 19

make his own speaking arrangements. At this point the state chairman backed down and placed him on the Republican speakers list.[44]

Having salvaged a place for himself in the mother party, La Follette turned his efforts to the overthrow of that party's leadership. The campaign began in 1894, and though success was not immediate, this campaign did lay the basis for future successes. La Follette had a variety of personal assets that fitted him for the task ahead. Oratorical talent, developed and demonstrated at the University of Wisconsin, was not least of these. Another was willingness to work hard and attend to detail, to the point of complete exhaustion and illness. This willingness to work himself without stint, harnessed to seemingly worthy purposes, contributed to yet another major asset: an inspirational quality that helped him to enlist the efforts of others in his cause.

La Follette was strong among the young men of the state. His fellow graduates of the University of Wisconsin and students at the University were always especially susceptible to his idealistic appeal and example, as he proudly acknowledged.[45] The nature of their university training was part of the explanation.

American education has been associated with religion and morality throughout the nation's history. Despite the existence of sectarian opposition to the University of Wisconsin, it was not strange that the Madison institution was nursed, if not mothered, by religion. Representative of the continuity of the religious tradition was John Bascom, a learned New England ex-seminarian who became president of the University of Wisconsin in 1874. The moral emphasis that Bascom gave to education at Wisconsin was made possible, perhaps, by the large Yankee population of the state, which provided a firm and natural foundation for a type of education that was usual in the East. Far from being watered down by the fact of state support, the moral content of edu-

[44] *Ibid.*, 51–52.
[45] La Follette, *Autobiography*, 207.

cation at the University of Wisconsin was accentuated by it. Bascom stressed to students like Robert M. La Follette the moral debt that they owed the state that had given them their college education.[46] And while generally conservative, Bascom was ahead of his time in his opinions about labor, his fear of growing corporate control, and the environmentalist slant to his moralism.[47] At a time when the president was a teacher and faculties were small, the impact of such a man was great.

Graduates of the University of Wisconsin were prominent in reform ranks from the beginning. La Follette settled on popular Congressman Nils Haugen to lead the revolt, and began his rebellion in 1893 by writing to men throughout the state asking their opinion of the prospects for Haugen should he seek the Republican gubernatorial nomination. The more than twelve hundred responses — mainly from politically inactive young men, many of them graduates of the University of Wisconsin — proved sufficiently enthusiastic and Haugen entered the contest.[48]

La Follette's confidence was based on experience. As a collegian, he had won great popularity with his classmates and occasionally had earned their votes.[49] In his first bid for public office, for Dane County district attorney, the young college men were important to him. And when he ran for the Republican congressional nomination in 1884, bucking the waning machine of "Boss" Elisha Keyes, it was again "the young fellow that did it," as Keyes observed at one of the caucuses.[50] At the time, a significant concentra-

---

[46] La Follette, *Autobiography*, 12–13. Thelen stresses the impact of Bascom's personality on La Follette in reinforcing the latter's "moral earnestness." Thelen, *Early Life of La Follette*, 47–48.

[47] Curti and Carstensen, *The University of Wisconsin*, 1: 275–295; Henry May, *Protestant Churches and Industrial America* (New York, 1949), 20, 49–50, 145–146.

[48] Belle and Fola La Follette, *La Follette*, 1: 106; La Follette, *Autobiography*, 80.

[49] Thelen, *Early Life of La Follette*, 43.

[50] Belle and Fola La Follette, *La Follette*, 1: 59; Thelen, *Early Life of La Follette*, 68.

tion of university graduates resided in La Follette's district, which included the city of Madison.

For large numbers of enthusiastic volunteers to have much impact is rare though far from unknown in American politics. They did in Wisconsin in 1894 and in the years that followed. A. O. Barton wrote that "The devotion which La Follette inspired in the young collegians who fell under his sway amounted almost to fanaticism." And part of the explanation for it was La Follette's own patent sincerity and disinterestedness.[51] La Follette's supporters were more than ordinarily young, enthusiastic, and willing to endure some hardship by contributing money, time, effort, and sometimes even friendships and business to the cause.[52] The enthusiasm proved remarkably long lasting, so that when La Follette finally won his party's nomination for governor in 1900 Elisha Keyes could remark, "Never before were so many new faces seen in a Republican state convention in Wisconsin. The majority were young men whose enthusiasm has taken the place of experience."[53]

Yet the issues La Follette raised were more usual in politics. The 1894 appeal was not for a broadly constructive program, as La Follette himself acknowledged. He wrote only of overthrowing "corrupt machine control." Honesty and democracy were traditional American virtues, not calculated to dislodge men from their intellectual moorings. During the following decade of political strife, the La Follette appeal did not drift far from this anchor.

One of those who became a leader among La Follette's opponents, John M. Whitehead, a Yankee heir to Puritanism who practiced law in Janesville, agreed that La Follette appealed strongly to young university men. But he saw in this appeal something other than sheer idealism. Writing to the historian Ralph Gabriel in elaborate rebuttal

---

[51] Barton, *La Follette's Winning of Wisconsin*, 60.
[52] Belle and Fola La Follette, *La Follette*, 1: 88, 107; *Milwaukee Journal*, November 24, 1914, quoting William Hatton; John R. Commons, *Myself* (New York, 1934), 98.
[53] Barton, *La Follette's Winning of Wisconsin*, 160.

of La Follette's then recently published autobiography, Whitehead charged that "Mr. La Follette successfully appealed to these young men on the ground of self-interest, all the while, of course, putting up a show of very great seriousness and solemnity. . . . La Follette appealed to these young men and pushed them for local offices wherever he could, and told them that if they would join his standard they would break up the old ring and have a chance at the political crib themselves. . . ."[54] From the very start of his career, La Follette was able to win the support of "young men on the make, young men who were tired of professional politicians," because he was himself one of them.[55]

La Follette's extensive reliance on patronage throughout his career is beyond question. After he became governor, his use of state jobs for political purposes was notorious. Clerks, oil and factory inspectors, temporary personnel such as State Fair guards and ticket sellers, but especially game wardens — these were the political leg men.[56] Even before the big gubernatorial victory of 1900, La Follette had more than a worthy cause to offer the deserving. His awesome victory in prestigious Dane County in 1894, and especially his strength among farmers there, suggested to politicians that La Follette was a rare organizer and leader and that his favor might be of future value. Thus, at the 1894 state convention, "La Follette was pointed out and sought for in the convention."[57] Despite Nils Haugen's defeat at the convention, the fact that he secured almost a third of the delegates and that he and La Follette campaigned for the ticket suggested that, according to political usage, his manager, La Follette, would have substantial patronage at his disposal. Thus, in the weeks that followed the Republican

[54] John M. Whitehead to Ralph Gabriel, April 22, 1914, in the John M. Whitehead Papers.
[55] Thelen, *Early Life of La Follette*, 68–69.
[56] Robert S. Maxwell, *La Follette and the Rise of the Progressives in Wisconsin* (Madison, 1956), 63–64; Allen F. Lovejoy, *La Follette and the Establishment of the Direct Primary in Wisconsin, 1890–1904* (New Haven, 1941), 69.
[57] Barton, *La Follette's Winning of Wisconsin*, 67–80.

The Rise of the Progressives

victory of November, 1894, La Follette was besieged by office seekers. La Follette described the situation later that month: "If you imagine I have had time in the last two weeks to stretch my legs under the table you ought to take a look at the procession that files up to my office eight o'clock in the morning with petitions and prayers and papers and applications and recommendations. I never have seen the tailend of the procession. . . . Of course, I am glad to see them all for they are all right good fellows deserving the best in the shop. . . ."[58]

Though service to patronage seekers was burdensome, La Follette neither disparaged nor shirked the duty. To one applicant he wrote: "Of course you must know that I incurred many obligations in the contest last spring which I feel bound to discharge so far as possible."[59] Whatever principles might be involved in the contest, jobs and other favors were then and later the recognized coin for political service. The great majority of offices secured in the nineties and afterwards were too petty for the consideration of college men, but more responsible and better-paying offices were available, and to these La Follette always gave his fullest attention.

The La Follette-Haugen faction was represented on the 1894 state ticket by the candidate for state treasurer, Sewall Peterson, a Norwegian-born politician, and maintained friendly relations with the incoming secretary of state, Henry Casson.[60] Chiefly through these contacts, but in other ways as well, positions were secured that reflected well on the potency of the La Follette-Haugen faction.[61]

[58] La Follette to Charles S. Crosse, November 24, 1894, in the Robert M. La Follette Papers.

[59] La Follette to C. J. Rollis, November 24, 1894, in the La Follette Papers.

[60] Samuel Harper to Henry Casson, January 27, 1894; Casson to Harper, February 6, 1894; La Follette to Casson, November 14, 1894, November 15, 1894; La Follette to Minnie E. Gill, November 14, 1894; A. R. Hall to Harper, August 3, 1894; La Follette to C. M. Dow, August 6, 1895; Sewall Peterson to La Follette, August 13, 1896; all in the La Follette Papers.

[61] A. R. Hall to La Follette, November 29, 1894; C. S. Crosse to La Follette, November 19, 1894, in the La Follette Papers. The major offices gained were for Assistant State Treasurer and Deputy Railroad Commissioner.

Factional politics, based in part on rivalry for patronage, is ordinary in American politics. Prolonged selfless service by large numbers at considerable sacrifice is extraordinary. In which category does the La Follette movement of the nineties fit? There can be no definite answer, for to a considerable extent the paths of self-interest and selflessness were one. La Follette did have the capacity to rally men to the cause with his earnestness and eloquence; and the cause itself — simple honesty and democracy, the overthrow of a decadent and corrupt machine — seemed unquestionably worthy. More than that, it was respectable. And it was well within the familiar context of Republican ideology and the Republican party. And if the success of the cause required that its adherents take offices in party and government, what need was there for them to get introspective about it, to probe their psyches for symptoms of personal ambition? In retrospect, the only tenable though unspectacular conclusion is that the motives of most of the young reform leaders were mixed, that the ordinary and extraordinary were inextricably intertwined.

La Follette's relatively strong showing in 1894 was of course due to more than the help of the new young leaders whom he enlisted. Another factor was the backing of farmers and their leaders. La Follette was in a strong position to appeal to farmers, especially dairy farmers. Born and raised in a farm community, he had retained a strong sympathy and respect for the farmer. While Henry C. Payne was lobbying for the oleo interests, La Follette had, as a young representative in the eighties, spoken for a bill to tax oleomargine.[62] In 1888, he had loaned William D. Hoard his poll lists, and many of his close friends, such as General Bryant and H. C. Adams, had worked for Hoard. It was natural enough that Hoard, after being sidetracked as a result of the Bennett Law and the opposition of Payne, should have enlisted in La Follette's cause.

In 1894 Hoard and C. H. Everett, president of the State

---

[62] Belle and Fola La Follette, *La Follette,* 1: 69.

Dairymen's Association, joined in urging dairy farmers to get into politics. They pointed to the increased sale of oleo and the decline of the butter market in the mines and forests of the north; they charged that the packer-oleo interests maintained a $50,000-a-year lobby in Madison, and had forced the appointment of an assistant dairy commissioner who was hostile to the principles of the dairymen. Two years later the *Wisconsin Farmer,* the leading farm journal in Wisconsin, joined Hoard in supporting La Follette. The paper noted La Follette's support of anti-oleo legislation in Congress and Old Guard opposition to him as evidence that La Follette was a "friend of the farmer."[63]

Spearheaded by the dairymen, Wisconsin farmers finally achieved political integration. Opposition to the packers — the makers of oleo — provided a common cause for both dairymen and livestock raisers. Once Henry Payne and his political machine had come under attack, it was a simple matter to invoke other latent complaints among Wisconsin's agricultural community.

The state Grange had declined rapidly since the seventies. But though reduced to roughly two thousand members in 1890, its leaders continued to voice popular farmer protests. Among the measures advocated by Grange leaders between 1890 and 1895 were curbs on dealing in options and futures, an increase in the amount of currency in circulation, and better state regulation of railroads. Perhaps the most persistent theme involved taxation. In 1892 the Grange leader Washington Churchill said, "The unequal and unjust burden of taxation is a prolific source of discontent among farmers." The same complaint, accompanied by various reform proposals, reappeared constantly.[64]

La Follette had plenty of experience appealing to farmers. Beginning in 1880, he developed the practice of travel-

---

[63] *Hoard's Dairyman,* July 6, 1894; *Wisconsin Farmer,* July 24, 1896, quoted in Albert S. Harvey, "The Background of the Progressive Movement in Wisconsin" (master's thesis, University of Wisconsin, 1933), 81.

[64] Wisconsin Grange, *Report,* 1892, 1893, 1894, 1895, quoted in Harvey, "Progressive Movement in Wisconsin," 61–81.

ing by horse and buggy in the countryside, talking to farmers in their fields and homes, getting votes and making notations for mailing lists.[65] In 1894 he put his supporters to work in the same fashion: "Night riders galloped from farmhouse to farmhouse in Haugen's behalf, a new feature in campaigning."[66]

No less important than the farm vote was the ethnic vote, and the choice of Nils Haugen to lead the rebellion in 1894 was a happy one. A veteran of nine years of creditable service in Congress, the only member of the Republican congressional contingent to survive the Democratic sweep of 1890, Haugen was already well respected for his ability and courage, especially in the northwestern part of the state, his home area. La Follette described him as "a fine representative of the best Scandinavian type — tall, strong, virile, with something of the Viking quality in his character."[67] The fact of his Norwegian birth was not the least of his political assets.

La Follette, in securing the help of Haugen, was simply continuing and transferring to the statewide level a courtship of the Scandinavian voter that he had conducted successfully for years in his own locality. Raised in a heavily Norwegian area in rural Dane County, young La Follette had picked up a smattering of the language together with some sympathy and understanding for the people of that stock. His first campaign for office was successful partly because of help from an old Norwegian friend, Eli Pederson.[68] In 1893 La Follette knew that many of the western counties were "well settled by sturdy Scandinavian pioneers — an independent, liberty-loving people. I knew they felt a certain pride in Congressman Haugen's prominence and success, and I counted on their giving him very strong support."[69] By 1900 Wisconsin's Scandinavians numbered al-

[65] Belle and Fola La Follette, *La Follette,* 1: 47.
[66] Barton, *La Follette's Winning of Wisconsin,* 66.
[67] La Follette, *Autobiography,* 77.
[68] Belle and Fola La Follette, *La Follette,* 1: 47.
[69] La Follette, *Autobiography,* 288.

The Rise of the Progressives

most 200,000 (mostly Norwegians) in a population of 2,069,042.[70] The Scandinavians were centered primarily in the western part of the state, in the Mississippi River counties, and in a southern belt centering in La Follette's own Dane County. Though still far less numerous than those of German ancestry, who by 1900 numbered 709,969, the Scandinavians were much more cohesive politically. While the Germans were divided in religion, occupation, culture, and party, the Scandinavians were unified in the Lutheran church and their farm communities. They maintained their language and their own press, concentrated in the Republican party, and tended to act together in political matters.

Later, La Follette's hold on the Scandinavian vote was strengthened greatly when John Anderson's Norwegian-language paper *Skandinaven* swung in line behind him. The paper was published in Chicago but circulated in almost all parts of Wisconsin. Rasmus B. Anderson, publisher of a rival paper, *Amerika,* acknowledged that *Skandinaven* was found "in well nigh every home in Wisconsin" and that "its influence in moulding public sentiment among its thousands of readers was simply tremendous."[71] An anti-La Follette politician from rural and heavily Norwegian Trempealeau County wrote in 1901, "The Scandinavia is taken by about every one, and it is their political Bible."[72] John Anderson was won over by Haugen and others of his stock with a variety of arguments.[73] And although Rasmus Anderson was generally anti-La Follette, his *Amerika* was devoted mainly to nonpolitical topics.[74]

Scandinavian voters in Wisconsin, as elsewhere, were

[70] *Twelfth Census of the United States, 1900* (Washington, 1901), 1: clxxxii, xviii.
[71] Rasmus B. Anderson, *The Life Story of Rasmus B. Anderson* (Madison, 1917), 617.
[72] John C. Gaveney to Elisha Keyes, June 20, 1901, in the Elisha Keyes Letterbooks.
[73] Haugen to La Follette, April 11, 1894; La Follette to Haugen, June 2, 1894; Haugen to Sam Harper, December 4, 1896, in the Nils Haugen Papers; Barton, *La Follette's Winning of Wisconsin,* 57–58.
[74] Maxwell, *Rise of the Progressives,* 60.

moved by economic and political considerations.[75] Mainly farmers, they responded to La Follette's economic appeal. And the cultural baggage of the Norwegians prepared them for the anti-boss doctrines of the progressives. They came to the United States with experience under the revered democratic Constitution of 1814, and in the peasant party and labor movement.[76]

Though the ideological and economic factors that predisposed the Scandinavians toward the La Follette side were certainly significant, the desire for political recognition seems also to have been important. La Follette won the Scandinavian vote partly because he offered more positions of leadership and honor to Scandinavians.

The chief battleground in 1894 was La Follette's home county, Dane. This was also home for Elisha Keyes, for the Spooners and Horace A. Taylor, former chairman of the state central committee, editor of the *Wisconsin State Journal,* and now candidate for governor. All were determined to squash the incipient rebellion. A full slate of candidates ran with Taylor and it carried the cities of Madison and Stoughton, which would have ended the contest under normal circumstances. But La Follette had redoubled his efforts to carry the country districts for Haugen. This he did partly by arranging to have caucuses held in certain towns before the opposition could organize. The charge of "snap caucuses," familiar in later years, was now raised, and the La Follette supporters rejoined with charges of their own. Sharp practices of various sorts occurred at some of the caucuses, as when chairmen counted the "votes" of spectators and phrased questions in a biased way. Meanwhile, back in the city, the Madison press carried charges and countercharges of shady financial practices on the part of Taylor and two of La Follette's young supporters.[77]

[75] Theodore C. Blegen, "The Scandinavian Element and Agricultural Discontent," *Annual Report of the American Historical Association, 1921,* 219.
[76] B. J. Hovde, "Norwegian Americans," *Our Racial and National Minorities,* Francis J. Brown and Joseph Slabey Rousek, eds., (New York, 1939), 113.
[77] Barton, *La Follette's Winning of Wisconsin,* 65–66.

The Rise of the Progressives

La Follette flooded Dane County with thousands of personal letters, dictated and churned out in his law office. Meanwhile, his nightriders rounded up votes in the countryside.[78] Eventually these efforts were crowned with remarkable success: Haugen defeated Taylor in the latter's home county.

Haugen did not win at the state convention, the nomination going instead to William H. Upham of Marshfield. But the fact that he carried nearly one-third of the vote despite the brevity of his campaign and limited funds marked the campaign as something new and extraordinary. Volunteers, under able and implacable command, had done the job. The La Follette forces were heartened by the result, and they prepared to renew the bitter contest in 1896. The opposition was dismayed at this strange new kind of factionalism, which was somehow bringing discord into the Grand Old Party and by all appearances was not disintegrating with the dispersal of the 1894 convention.

Since the Democrats and the "half-breeds," as La Follette's supporters were often called, had a common foe during the 1890's, the efforts of each often benefited the other. The La Follette men had not reached the stage of bolting the Republican ticket in a general election, so after nominations had been made the burden of discrediting the dominant Republican group shifted to the Democrats. A major issue for the Democrats in 1894, and one that dovetailed nicely with La Follette's long-term drive for power, was the question of the prosecution of the ex-treasurers. Vigorous prosecution under Democratic Governor Peck had brought an initial court victory that was upheld by the state supreme court in 1893, calling for full recovery plus 7 per cent interest. Collections and judgments totaled $609,000 by early 1895.[79] Another quarter of a million dollars remained to be recovered. The Democrats warned the voters that if the Republi-

---
[78] *Ibid.*, 66.
[79] Current, *Pine Logs and Politics*, 286.

cans won the election, none of this would be collected from the bondsmen.[80]

The Republicans denied the charge, played up some minor corruption under the Democrats, repudiated the Bennett Law, and recited Major Upham's strong military record. This proved enough to restore them to favor and to office, ending the Democrat's hold on the governorship and legislature. A powerful lobby soon set to work in the legislature in support of bills to discontinue the treasury suits. Heading the lobby was Charles F. Pfister of Milwaukee, whose late father had been a bondsman for one of the state treasurers against whom a judgment amounting to $106,683.90 had been obtained.[81] Young Pfister, who had inherited several million dollars, derived mainly from a tanning business of international proportions, had already begun his rapid ascent in the Republican machine. Despite the fact that public attention had already focused on the issue, Pfister's efforts were successful; the bills passed. Governor Upham was more at home in business and G. A. R. affairs than in politics. He opposed the introduction of the bills, but, loyal to party, he signed them.[82]

The event was significant for the "half-breeds." The discontinuance of prosecutions in the treasury cases "aroused the people to a realization that something was radically wrong with the processes of government. The legislature did not represent the will of the people, but of the party bosses. . . . The time was ripe for a movement to reform the democratic processes; the people only wanted a leader."[83]

La Follette, whose falling out with Sawyer had made him a less desirable candidate than Haugen in the first assault, offered himself for governor in 1896. Since a campaign against the power of the machine, with its organization,

[80] Larry Gara, *A Short History of Wisconsin* (Madison, 1962), 173; Belle and Fola La Follette, *La Follette*, 1: 112.
[81] La Follette, *Autobiography*, 82.
[82] Thompson, *Political History of Wisconsin*, 261; Lovejoy, *Direct Primary in Wisconsin*, 27.
[83] *Ibid.*, 27.

its money, and the support of most of the press, was widely regarded as an act of self-sacrifice, La Follette did not have to worry about arousing the resentment of men like Hoard and Haugen. Indeed, it was Hoard who headed the group that issued the first call to Republican voters for La Follette's candidacy. Haugen remained loyal to him also. And the young leaders who had been enlisted in 1894 and heartened by that effort came forth once more.

While the half-breeds were united behind a strong leader, the opposition was in some disarray. There was talk of Sawyer for governor, but he was in his eightieth year and at long last enjoying a bit of leisure, occasioned by the Democratic capture of the legislature in 1892 and his failure to retain his senate seat. Though still the recognized leader of his party, Sawyer was content simply to exert a negative force against any accommodation with La Follette, who had rebuffed his conciliatory overtures in 1894. The following year, when the Republicans again had power to elect a senator, Sawyer was not a candidate, leaving the honor and office to Spooner, who had himself been displaced by a Democrat earlier in the decade.[84]

Governor Upham had been loyal to the party leaders, with his appointments and his action on the treasury cases, but he had thereby made himself unacceptable to many voters and to politicians who were fearful of voter reaction. He was unceremoniously denied support for renomination, and swiftly descended to relative obscurity in state politics.

Spooner and Payne remained, of course, but both had their attentions and ambitions fixed on Washington. Spooner, who had little taste for politics in any case, was looking forward to renewing his service in the Senate; Payne had reason to hope for a cabinet position and continued service on the Republican national committee. Charles Pfister had money, Milwaukee business connections, and a taste for political manipulation and "the fellowship of men in public

[84] Current, *Pine Logs and Politics,* 282, 300.

life,"[85] but his political capacity was not great, as even the anti-La Follette men admitted.[86]

The Sawyer group therefore chose Edward Scofield to oppose La Follette for the Republican gubernatorial nomination in 1896. Major Scofield had a respectable record as Civil War veteran, prominent lumberman, and party functionary. His was not a great political talent, however, and even after he became governor he did not assume party or factional leadership.

Characteristically, before renewing his attacks on the Old Guard, La Follette refortified his position in the party by participating as a delegate at the Republican national convention and making a seconding speech for his old friend William McKinley. He then launched a vigorous campaign in which he tried to build on the strong foundation of support that he had in southwestern Wisconsin.[87] Despite lack of organization in Milwaukee and some other places,[88] La Follette came into the state convention in August with what he believed to be a majority of delegates. He led in the first day's balloting against five opponents, but no decision was reached when the convention recessed for the night. That night, according to La Follette's subsequent public charges, some of his delegates were brought into a private room and offered bribes of from twenty-five to seven hundred dollars for their votes or the votes of others that they could deliver. La Follette based his charges on the statements of some twenty men who came to him and told him of it. By La Follette's account, Pfister visited him late that night and said that La Follette was beaten but that if he made no fuss, he would be taken care of later.[89] The next day La Follette was beaten and Scofield nominated.

[85] Plumb, *Badger Politics,* 109–110.
[86] John M. Whitehead to Ralph Gabriel, April 22, 1914, in the Whitehead Papers.
[87] La Follette to O. L. Wright, July 7, 1896, in the La Follette Papers.
[88] J. J. McGovern to La Follette, November 22, 1897, in the La Follette Papers.
[89] Barton, *La Follette's Winning of Wisconsin,* 71–72; La Follette, *Auto-*

The Rise of the Progressives

Here surely was war to the political death. Or was it? The La Follette men may have been tempted to press on with their righteous cause, to bolt the convention and set up an independent ticket, as La Follette later recalled that many of his young supporters urged.[90] But no bolt occurred. Instead, in the midst of the sixth ballot, as Scofield's victory became evident, a Dane County La Follette man interrupted the roll call to move that Scofield's nomination be made unanimous.[91] And in the campaign that followed, La Follette made twenty-five speeches for the party's national and state ticket, defending sound money and the protective tariff against the dangerous William Jennings Bryan.[92] In short, a large measure of ordinary politics remained to set off the extraordinary.

One of the major extraordinary factors in the Wisconsin situation was La Follette's uncompromising determination to remain his own man. President McKinley, grateful to his old friend and colleague for support at the national convention and in the campaign, and supported in the idea by Senator Spooner, offered La Follette the office of Comptroller of the Currency. La Follette, though financially embarrassed at the time,[93] turned it down. His wife Belle later commented, "His refusal of a $6000.00 job probably made a more profound impression on Wisconsin citizens than happenings of much greater importance."[94] His public refusal of the office was a bold, defiant trumpet call, signalling the beginning of the next campaign. In the words of the *Milwaukee Journal,* it would have been a "scandalous betrayal" to have accepted the office "while leaving to be

---

biography, 83–84; see also M. A. Hoyt to Gilbert Roe, August 15, 1896, and George P. Rossman to La Follette, March 8, 1897, in the La Follette Papers, for other allegations of bribery.

[90] La Follette, *Autobiography,* 84–85.
[91] Thompson, *Political History of Wisconsin,* 263.
[92] Barton, *La Follette's Winning of Wisconsin,* 75.
[93] La Follette to Dr. Harry Favill, September 23, 1896, in the La Follette Papers.
[94] Belle and Fola La Follette, *La Follette,* 1: 121.

crucified by the machine those who had dared to brave the rotten old organization and had given their trust to him as leader.... Now that La Follette has proved to his followers his trustworthiness, his influence will be greatly increased."[95]

For La Follette as political captain, it was not sufficient simply to renounce office at the hands of the enemy. It was equally important that some offices be secured for his followers and that his influence on patronage be demonstrated. Some state offices were available, but his well-publicized friendship with McKinley put thoughts of federal jobs into the minds of innumerable office seekers who pressed their claims on him from November, 1896, into the summer of 1897.[96] In reality, McKinley's victory was a source of some embarrassment, for it opened a prospect of federal patronage that La Follette was not in a position to exploit. Well-established custom, occasionally reinforced by the exercise of senatorial courtesy, put the non-classified jobs in the hands of senators and congressmen, and La Follette had no friends in the Wisconsin contingent. La Follette felt the urgency of the matter and made several trips to see McKinley, first in Canton, Ohio, and later in Washington, hoping to "break over the rule."[97] In this he failed.

La Follette did win a negative victory of some moment, however. Henry C. Payne was vigorously pursuing a cabinet post and Sawyer and Isaac Stephenson, another old lumberman in politics and wealthiest of the lot, made a pilgrimage to Canton to urge that Payne be named Postmaster General. But La Follette, with the help of Haugen and others, and by means of a counter-candidacy — William D. Hoard for Secretary of Agriculture — persuaded McKinley to reject Payne. While Hoard also had to be turned down in the interest of harmony, he was said to be "kindly and grateful," perhaps deriving consolation from the thought that

[95] *Milwaukee Journal,* July 10, 1897, enclosed in A. R. H. [Hall] to La Follette, July 10, 1897, in the La Follette Papers.
[96] See the La Follette Papers, Boxes 6 and 7, for this correspondence.
[97] La Follette to E. G. Mills, July 6, 1897; La Follette to William D. Hoard, August 11, 1897, in the La Follette Papers.

his candidacy had helped keep his bitter enemy Payne out of the cabinet.[98]

La Follette's rejection of a Washington job and his strong campaign for federal patronage reflected his determination to press on with the factional fight. Immediately after his convention defeat in August, he wrote to supporters throughout the state, urging loyalty to the ticket but renewal of the fight against "the machine."[99] At the same time, efforts were launched to establish a statewide newspaper that might serve as organ for the faction.[100] To keep his organization together, La Follette considered standing for the U.S. Senate in the 1897 legislative session.[101] Since political custom dictated that Scofield, if elected governor in 1896, be accorded renomination in 1898, these steps reflected and represented a marked and quite unusual escalation of the factional conflict.

In this same period, La Follette made known a new line of strategy that would so increase the stakes of the conflict as to take it almost beyond the bounds of existing political convention. To one of his allies he wrote: "Under any system which would have ensured the expression of the views of the Republicans of Wisconsin I would have been nominated three to one. The result of this contest but makes it more certain that some radical change should be made in the laws relative to nominations in order that machine methods and money domination no longer control. To this end I think we should bend our endeavors to secure the right men for the legislature this winter."[102] For La Follette, politics had been an after-hours job during the mid-nineties. The task of earning a livelihood at the bar in these depression years, as well as the extra money needed for serious politics, had rather fully occupied him. This experience

[98] Sam Harper to Nils Haugen, February 5, 1897, in the La Follette Papers.
[99] See the La Follette Papers, Box 5, covering August, 1896.
[100] La Follette to A. R. Hall, September 18, 1896, in the La Follette Papers.
[101] La Follette to James A. Stone, August 22, 1896, in the La Follette Papers.
[102] La Follette to George F. Cooper, September 7, 1896, in the La Follette Papers.

apparently played a part in directing his thoughts toward changes in political institutions. "The trouble is," he wrote a trusted ally, "we poor fellows who have to earn a living can only occasionally take a hand in politics. They keep at it all the while. Republicans generally are with us. We must solve the problem of making their sentiments control conventions. Difficult task but it must be done."[103] La Follette refined his thinking on this subject in the following months and in February, 1897, taking advantage of an invitation to give a Washington's Birthday address at the University of Chicago, he launched the movement to revamp party nominating procedures by scrapping the convention system in favor of direct primary elections. "Abolish the caucus and the convention," he urged. "Go back to the first principles of democracy; go back to the people."[104]

How a thoroughgoing primary system would work in practice, and what impact it would have on the structure of politics, was difficult to foresee. At the time, it clearly portended a revolution in the practice of politics. The primary system, seemingly involving much more of a direct appeal to the people than had been usual, threatened to render obsolete existing political institutions, methods, and customs. With that would come a downgrading in the importance of the old-style politician and possibly a thorough changing of the guard. It seemed, in short, that La Follette, not content simply to push his factional campaign well beyond customary bounds, was now proposing to change the rules of the game altogether.

The advocacy of the primary, beginning in 1897 and continuing until 1904, when the device was finally entrenched in law, was like the primary itself: it involved a direct approach to the people as the source of political power. Not content that La Follette's "Menace of the Machine" speech was published in several Chicago news-

---

[103] La Follette to George B. Clementson, September 7, 1896, in the La Follette Papers.
[104] La Follette, *Autobiography*, 196.

The Rise of the Progressives

papers and reprinted in some Wisconsin papers, Samuel Harper, La Follette's alter ego, arranged to publish a pamphlet including La Follette's speech, selected newspaper comments on it and a synopsis of a primary election bill introduced in the 1897 session. He asked La Follette men throughout the state to reach local editors with the offer of these pamphlets as free supplements to be distributed by the papers. To increase potential distribution, Harper suggested presentation of the supplement as "non-partisan" so that "the politics of the paper will cut no figure."[105]

The speech received much attention and favorable comment in the state. To capitalize on this situation, La Follette took another giant step away from political convention and toward a direct popular appeal on the basis of his attractive "non-partisan" issue. Though always pressed for time by his crowded case schedule, La Follette began to accept invitations to speak at county fairs in various parts of the state in late August and September, 1897. The speeches proved to be an important turning point in Wisconsin politics. Most of the fairs were managed by the county agricultural societies, whose leaders were generally favorable to La Follette. They knew, too, that La Follette's reputation as an orator and his prominence in politics, now reinforced by the Chicago speech, would be likely to attract good crowds. As word circulated in August that he was accepting invitations, the fair managers hurried to issue theirs.[106]

La Follette was at his best in this kind of situation, and his cause benefited from the effort. A *Milwaukee Journal* reporter describing his 1897 speeches probably did not exaggerate greatly when he wrote: "His words bite like coals of fire.... Disgust, hope, honor, avarice, despair, love,

---

[105] Samuel Harper to John Hume, March 5, 1897; Harper to James A. Stone, March 13, 1897, in the La Follette Papers.

[106] Frank W. Harland to La Follette, July 19, 1897; La Follette to A. F. Warden, August 12, 1897; D. O. Mahoney to La Follette, August 16, 1897; H. S. Comstock to La Follette, August 16, 1897; H. A. Bright to La Follette, August 26, 1897; Henry Miller to La Follette, August 28, 1897; George W. Werner to La Follette, August 31, 1897; all in the La Follette Papers.

anger, all the passions of man, he paints in strong words and stronger gestures. . . . He never wearies and he will not allow his audience to weary."[107]

The persistence of this grassroots campaign captured the popular imagination and brought a good deal of press coverage. The *Milwaukee Sentinel* and *Milwaukee Journal* published his state fair speech in full. La Follette believed that these speeches had great and lasting impact. As his wife pointed out, "They reached audiences well distributed over the state who listened without that prejudiced partisanship which characterizes political campaigns."[108]

La Follette was as effective in direct, personal contact as he was on the stump. A. O. Barton remarked, "There was about La Follette . . . a persuasive hypnotic power which it was difficult to resist."[109] A *Chicago Times-Herald* reporter wrote of him late in 1897: "His handshake is a grip that at once establishes a friendship. . . . The man is essentially democratic in his tastes. He deals neither in obsequious flattery nor vulgar sycophancy. He looks men straight in the eyes and talks to them slowly, deliberately, earnestly. His intense individuality compels magnetic response."[110] A related asset was a remarkable memory for names and faces.[111] With these assets, La Follette was able, in 1897, not only to sway mass opinion but also to make many personal friends whose help in future campaigns would be considerable.[112] He was especially successful with Scandinavians in this campaign, perhaps because the idea of the primary fitted well with their traditional veneration for political liberty.[113]

---

[107] *Milwaukee Journal,* October 2, 1897, cited in Belle and Fola La Follette, *La Follette,* 1: 124.
[108] Lovejoy, *Direct Primary in Wisconsin,* 40; Belle and Fola La Follette, *La Follette,* 122, 123.
[109] Barton, *La Follette's Winning of Wisconsin,* 54.
[110] *Chicago Times-Herald,* September 27, 1897, quoted in Barton, *La Follette's Winning of Wisconsin,* 86.
[111] *Ibid.,* 63; Edwin Gross, "A Political Grab Bag" (unpublished reminiscences), in the Edwin Gross Papers.
[112] Belle and Fola La Follette, *La Follette,* 1: 123.
[113] Lovejoy, *Direct Primary in Wisconsin,* 61.

The Rise of the Progressives

The state legislature and the governor had provided La Follette with fresh ammunition that winter, and this he effectively used in conjunction with his argument for the primary. During the early 1890's a farmer-manufacturer from rural Dunn County, in northwestern Wisconsin, had launched a persistent fight against the issuance and acceptance of railroad passes. In retrospect the people of Wisconsin, La Follette included, came to regard the anti-pass champion with a reverence usually reserved for founding fathers. Though he had been a lonely and ridiculed outcast among party politicians of his day, A. R. Hall had reflected the rising resentment of the Wisconsin electorate against the power, wealth, and abuses of the railroads. At long last, and not without a fight, Hall had seen his proposal included in the 1896 Republican platform. But the Republican legislature had not delivered on it, and, in the same session, the Republican governor reneged on another platform pledge by vetoing the Davidson bills relating to taxation of express and sleeping-car companies.[114]

La Follette linked these and other issues to his proposal for a primary, and in his famous "Fern Dell speech" said:[115]

> It is but just to say that no legislature has assembled in Wisconsin in many years containing so many good men as the last. But when a bill to punish corrupt practices in campaigns and elections is destroyed by amendment; when measures such as the Davidson bills requiring corporations to pay a just share of the taxes go down to defeat; when bills to compel hundreds of millions of dollars of untaxed personal property to come from its hiding place and help maintain government fail of adequate support; when republicans and democrats unite in defeating the Hall resolution to emancipate the legislature from all subserviency to the

---

[114] Wallace Sayre, "Robert M. La Follette, A Study in Political Methods" (doctoral dissertation, New York University, 1930), 95.
[115] Barton, *La Follette's Winning of Wisconsin*, 80–81.

corporations by prohibiting acceptance of railroad passes, telegraph and express company franks; when these things and many others of like character happen and are made matters of public record which no man may deny, then that man is untrue to his country, his party and himself who will not raise his voice in condemnation — not in condemnation of the principles of the political party in which he believes, or of the great body of its organization, but of the men who betray it and of the methods by which they control, only to prostitute it to base and selfish ends.

The remedy is to begin at the bottom and make one supreme effort for victory over the present bad system. Nominate and elect men who will pass a primary election law which will enable the voter to select directly candidates without intervention of caucus or convention or domination of machines. . . .

This kind of open criticism of his own party's record was relatively new and shocking. Belle La Follette recalled an Oshkosh Democrat saying: "That was the first time I had ever heard a man attack his own party and point out the sins it had been guilty of. . . ."[116]

But statewide campaigning at county fairs in an off-year was hardly usual either. These procedures, combined with the vastly broadened ideological appeal that La Follette was now making, reflected a change in La Follette himself. It was in 1897, A. O. Barton wrote, that La Follette "discovered himself and developed the master passion to which he was later so universally to give himself."[117] La Follette, in the midst of the decisive showdown contest of 1904, dated the beginning of the contest to 1897.[118]

La Follette's 1897 departure from political convention was great but far from complete. In some ways, the county fair speaking tour marked the beginning of a reformist cru-

---

[116] Belle and Fola La Follette, *La Follette*, 1: 122–123.
[117] Barton, *La Follette's Winning of Wisconsin*, 77.
[118] La Follette to A. Cornelison, May 24, 1904, in the La Follette Papers.

sade, in which righteousness would be engaged in selfless battle. At the same time, it fitted the established pattern of nonideological politics based on mutual self-interest. The primary device, while potentially disastrous to some, would be highly advantageous to others. The comptroller of West Superior, one of La Follette's young supporters, put the matter clearly enough: "Now all I want," he wrote, "is some measure that will break the ring and let young men who are not in favor with the present machine but who have merit and worth . . . get a chance at the helm of the state. I am of the opinion that a good deal of good and independent ability that will not bow to the machine is fully capable to fill the places now filled by the machine forces."[119]

There is another aspect to this matter of continuing self-interest. Even without a primary election system, La Follette's services as a campaigner had been greatly valued. Another of La Follette's West Superior backers urged La Follette to speak in his town in the fall of 1896. "Now there are personal reasons for this," he wrote. "A number of the people who supported you are candidates for county office, your humble servant among others. . . . We hold our convention in forepart of Oct. and have the utmost confidence that if you made one of your rousing speeches here it will turn the tide in our favor."[120] A local political leader also stood to gain in the esteem of friends, community, and self if he could land La Follette as a campaign speaker. If La Follette spoke in a locality, it was a big favor on his part to the local leaders. This was explicitly recognized by a party manager who offered La Follette an appropriate quid pro quo in seeking his services: "Now our people are all howling for you to come down. Please come if possible and will try to fix you up more than 4 delegates next time."[121]

When La Follette went directly to the people in all parts of Wisconsin in 1897, combining his oratorical skills

---
[119] H. E. Ticknor to La Follette, March 20, 1897, in the La Follette Papers.
[120] E. G. Mills to La Follette, September 18, 1896, in the La Follette Papers.
[121] R. W. C. to La Follette, October 23, 1894, in the La Follette Papers.

with an apparently popular and durable theme, he again demonstrated how useful a friend he might be and, by further popularizing himself and his message, became just that much more attractive as a political patron.

In the latter part of 1897 La Follette in effect levied assessments on some political friends in five key counties to raise money for a statewide newspaper, threatening to retire from politics if the money could not be raised.[122] It was, and *The State* was soon launched under the editorship of John M. Nelson, an active young La Follette supporter and University alumnus. Then, pressing his factional offensive, La Follette prepared to ignore party custom and contest Governor Scofield's renomination, partly as a means of keeping his organization together.[123]

La Follette's 1898 campaign against Scofield continued the broadened ideological appeal developed in 1897. La Follette announced his candidacy and his platform on July 15 in an address that was mailed to hundreds of thousands of voters. In this document he promised to make untaxed property pay its share; prohibit corrupt practices in campaigns and elections; secure all possible relief from trusts; prohibit use of passes and franks by public officials; and abolish the caucus and convention system and replace it with the direct primary.[124]

By 1898 La Follette had new support. The Republican Club of Milwaukee had been set up that year by prominent Milwaukeeans led by a group of young lawyers that included Theodore Kronshage and Francis E. McGovern. While the organization had formed to combat the corrupt bipartisan coalition that controlled Milwaukee politics in the interests of public utilities magnates, it quickly took an interest in statewide reform as well. Its encouragement and pressure, in fact, were partly responsible for bringing La Follette to seek

[122] La Follette to E. I. Kidd, November 6, 1897; La Follette to W. D. Hoard, November 10, 1897; La Follette to O. G. Munson, November 20, 1897, in the La Follette Papers.
[123] La Follette to Sewall Peterson, May 16, 1900, in the La Follette Papers.
[124] Belle and Fola La Follette, *La Follette,* 1: 126.

again the nomination for governor. The club endorsed his July statement of principles and secured its platform directly from La Follette.[125] The alliance was a natural one, for in Henry C. Payne, Charles Pfister, and the Democratic boss, E. C. Wall, the city and state reformers had common enemies. A twenty-four-page pamphlet issued by the club entitled "Governor Scofield's Record as Shown by His Official Acts" was unprecedentedly bitter, but it accorded with the crusading atmosphere that now permeated Republican politics.[126]

With the turn of the century, the Milwaukee reformers gained great political strength. Milwaukeeans became aroused in January, 1900, when Mayor David S. Rose, elected in 1898 as a sworn enemy of the Milwaukee Electric Railway and Light Company, put through a franchise extension favorable to the company. A series of disclosures of corruption involving aldermen and the city building inspector culminated in a large anti-graft meeting in September, 1903. The vigorous efforts of young Francis E. McGovern resulted in 260 indictments against twenty-four persons in 1904 and 1905, leading to thirty-three convictions by 1909.[127] The Milwaukee housecleaning projected the urban reformers into control of the Republican party in the county, and served to develop a leader of statewide reputation in McGovern, and to strengthen an important element in La Follette's coalition.

But all this was in the future. In 1898 La Follette was defeated in the convention—and again by bribery, he charged.[128] Still, the platform was substantially his, calling as it did for equal taxation, anti-pass and anti-lobby legislation, and modification of the nominating machinery. Too,

---

[125] Barton, *La Follette's Winning of Wisconsin*, 124–131.
[126] Robert C. Twombly, "The Reformer as Politician: Robert M. La Follette in the Election of 1900" (master's thesis, University of Wisconsin, 1964), 20.
[127] Frederick I. Olson, "The Milwaukee Socialists, 1897–1941" (doctoral dissertation, Harvard University, 1941), 136–142.
[128] La Follette, *Autobiography*, 95.

the La Follette faction was recognized on the regular ticket in the candidates for treasurer and attorney general. Though La Follette was becoming more daring, his effort remained conventional in some ways. A local historian and Wisconsin booster, writing a few years later, praised Governor Scofield's first administration, noted that he had been opposed for the 1898 nomination by "the brilliant and energetic ex-Congressman R. M. La Follette," that Scofield won renomination, and that "The friends of La Follette received full recognition in the makeup of the balance of the ticket. . . . The convention adjourned with all the elements of the party united and enthusiastic."[129] This was exaggerated, for when La Follette failed to campaign for the ticket, the chasm dividing the La Follette men from other Republicans widened. (He was kept out of the campaign by the onset of serious illness, but this was not generally known.[130]) It was true, however, that no open break occurred; the La Follette men gave no thought to bolting the ticket and Scofield was re-elected without difficulty, though with a reduced plurality as compared to 1896. And following the Republican victory, La Follette men promptly lined up for their share of the patronage.[131]

The Scofield administration fulfilled some of his party's platform pledges, including enactment of an anti-railroad-pass law—though not until the legislators had used and dispersed passes all winter. Laws were also enacted for *ad valorem* taxes on express, sleeping car, equipment, and freight companies, for inheritance tax, and for the establishment of a temporary tax commission. On the other hand, the legislature did not enact bills for a railroad commission, more equitable railroad taxation, or the primary election system.[132] So, despite the positive legislation adopted, the

---

[129] Thompson, *Political History of Wisconsin*, 266, 267.
[130] Twombly, "La Follette in the Election of 1900," 30.
[131] Gilbert Roe to Bryan J. Castle, November 15, 1898; George Bryant to Castle, November 30, 1898, in the Bryan J. Castle Papers; Twombly, "La Follette in the Election of 1900," 145, 153–156.
[132] Lovejoy, *Direct Primary in Wisconsin*, 49.

way was open for new attacks by La Follette and his supporters. But even as reformers began to sniff the sweet scent of victory, they realized that there would be no need to storm the walls. The gates would be swung wide for them if they stayed on the path of party harmony.

This fact was brought home by the accession to La Follette's ranks of a new group of allies. First and foremost of these was Isaac Stephenson, who, like Philetus Sawyer, was a rough-hewn millionaire lumberman who had gone into politics and served in Congress. He had played the political game according to the low ethical standards so widespread at the time,[133] had grown old in the service of his party, and expected in due course to be rewarded with a seat in the United States Senate. In 1899, in his seventieth year, Stephenson thought his turn had finally come. Instead, the place was given to one of the Milwaukee business-political group, a lawyer named Joseph Quarles. When the voting was over, the embittered Stephenson pointed his finger at one of Quarles' backers and said, "Some of these big fellows have got to look out." And the old man's family, "chagrined and mortified," told Stephenson "to spend all the money he wanted to in getting his revenge, but only to get it."[134] An alliance with La Follette was not unnatural in the circumstances.

Stephenson and La Follette had served together in Congress and had gotten on well. When Stephenson came over to the La Follette camp in search of revenge—and perhaps another approach to the coveted Senate seat—the La Follettes could greet him with unfeigned enthusiasm. In the new convert, the reformers had a man of influence and wealth who gave an estimated $400,000 to the cause between 1899 and 1908.[135]

Another of the Old Guard who joined La Follette for the 1900 campaign was Joseph Babcock, chairman of the

---

[133] Strange, "Autobiography," 32.
[134] Whitehead to Ralph Gabriel, April 22, 1914, in the Whitehead Papers.
[135] *Idem.*

House ways and means committee and luminary of the Wisconsin congressional delegation. Babcock, like Stephenson, had aspired to the Senate post. His alliance with La Follette was of some importance, for Babcock was a shrewd and influential Republican campaign manager.

A third unlikely newcomer to La Follette's ranks was Emanuel Philipp of Milwaukee. Large, suave, and swarthy, Philipp was at once a rising refrigerator car magnate and a trusted employee of the Joseph Schlitz Brewing Company.

It has been suggested that Babcock hoped to use La Follette to advance his own ambitions for the Senate and control of the party, and that Philipp, a new political leader of the Sawyer-Spooner-Payne faction, was trying to negotiate a truce between La Follette and the old Republican machine.[136] If these were the ends involved, it was the collapse of Old Guard leadership that made such means necessary. Sawyer had remained the leader of the party despite his advanced age, illness and semi-retirement from politics. He died in March, 1900, just as the nomination campaign was warming up. No suitable successor had been readied for this not improbable eventuality. Spooner remained preoccupied with national affairs and was little inclined towards active politicking; Payne, chronically ill and still ambitious for a cabinet position, apparently had no stomach for the kind of fight required to take over the leadership of the party in Wisconsin.[137] Early in 1900, he was engrossed with the approaching national party convention.[138] Scofield was never even considered, being a blunt man and not too adept politically. Charles Pfister, wealthy, close to Milwaukee business interests, and comfortable in political circles, was about to take over, but he was a heavy-handed tactician and did not command the complete respect of those who had followed Sawyer. John Whitehead, the upright conservative

---

[136] Maxwell, *Rise of the Progressives*, 16, 15.
[137] Robert S. Maxwell, *Emanuel L. Philipp, Wisconsin Stalwart* (Madison, 1959), 31.
[138] Barton, *La Follette's Winning of Wisconsin*, 142.

The Rise of the Progressives

Republican Yankee from Janesville, was always suspicious of "the Milwaukee crowd" and considered Pfister "something of a booby."[139] Some historians have agreed with that judgment.[140]

Given the weakened condition of the old machine, the power and determination already shown by the La Follette forces, and the new financial strength that Isaac Stephenson lent the reformers, it must have seemed to intelligent men like Babcock and Philipp that an accommodation with La Follette was the only feasible means to their several goals. They therefore threw in with him and offered to act as intermediaries between La Follette and the state's major business interests.

La Follette met with Milwaukee business leaders in Milwaukee and with Marvin Hughitt, President of the Chicago and Northwestern, in Chicago. At these meetings, La Follette gave assurances that he was not hostile to business and would be fair on such questions as the taxation of brewing and manufacturing corporations and railroads, and would oppose prohibition legislation. The response was satisfactory enough to permit some of his auditors to contribute to his campaign fund.[141] Written reassurances on the railroad taxation question addressed to Thomas H. Gill, attorney for the Wisconsin Central Railroad and a personal friend of La Follette's, won the neutrality of the Wisconsin Central and, according to John Whitehead, the financial support of the St. Paul railroad.[142]

Some negotiations took place with Henry C. Payne. Senator Spooner and others believed that La Follette and Payne agreed to a truce so that Payne would not oppose La Follette for governor and La Follette would not block Payne's appointment to McKinley's cabinet, as he had done in 1896.[143] A. O. Barton maintained that Payne rejected the

[139] Whitehead to Ralph Gabriel, April 22, 1914, in the Whitehead Papers.
[140] Maxwell, *Philipp*, 37; Barton, *La Follette's Winning of Wisconsin*, 37.
[141] Maxwell, *Philipp*, 33–34.
[142] Whitehead to Ralph Gabriel, April 22, 1914, in the Whitehead Papers.
[143] *Idem*; Barton, *La Follette's Winning of Wisconsin*, 142.

final terms proposed by representatives of the two sides, but acknowledged that the very effort may have lessened tensions between the factions.[144] Spooner and Whitehead believed that the negotiations had succeeded. In any event, Payne did not oppose La Follette in 1900 and later was appointed Postmaster General in McKinley's cabinet.[145]

La Follette's official announcement of his candidacy on May 16, 1900, was fully in the spirit of harmony that had been developing. He endorsed the work of the Scofield administration and disclaimed any designs on Spooner's seat in the Senate, a point that had concerned many Republicans.[146] When Spooner announced in July that he would not seek re-election, the cry that La Follette would dump the senator was silenced.[147] Meanwhile, *The State* was playing down ideological or personal differences and stressing instead the likelihood of victory.[148] The crusty old Scofield, last of the Civil War veteran governors of the state, was not mollified by kind words at such late date, having suffered more than ordinary vilification and ridicule at the hands of La Follette and his friends in past campaigns. He issued an open letter denouncing La Follette as a radical, a bolter, and a tool of railroads and special interests. But in this Scofield was alone among the major leaders of his party, and La Follette would not be provoked to abandon his new posture of sweet-tempered benevolence. He was widely praised in the Republican press for this new service to party harmony.[149] Later, he reassured state officeholders by urging that all who had been efficient be renominated.[150]

La Follette encountered some opposition, mainly from candidates of only local reputation, but these he treated with

---

[144] Barton, *La Follette's Winning of Wisconsin*, 142.
[145] The details of La Follette's negotiations with Stephenson, Babcock, Philipp, Payne, and the railroad executives are best described in Twombly, "La Follette in the Election of 1900," 70–110.
[146] Maxwell, *Rise of the Progressives*, 18–19.
[147] Belle and Fola La Follette, *La Follette*, 1: 132.
[148] Twombly, "La Follette in the Election of 1900," 39.
[149] Maxwell, *Rise of the Progressives*, 20.
[150] *Ibid.*, 18–19.

The Rise of the Progressives

courtesy. And as support mounted for him and he carried the caucuses and conventions in several key counties, his opponents quit the field. Thus, at the state convention, the new note of harmony that had been struck continued to sound, and Robert M. La Follette won his party's unanimous nomination for governor. (In good political fashion, he began a practice that was to be continued through the years of naming at least one prominent German to the ticket.[151])

La Follette's election campaign was notable only for its extent and the energy that he put into it. Beginning in Milwaukee on October 14, he traveled an estimated 6,433 miles, spoke ten to fifteen times a day six days a week, making 208 speeches in 61 counties to nearly 200,000 people. "This record," Belle La Follette claimed, "had never before been approached in Wisconsin."[152]

La Follette's indefatigable campaigning was remarkable; the burden of his message was not. He did not attack corporations and he stressed national rather than state issues for the most part, though he did give some attention to the primary and to railroad taxation. He spoke for Republicans from McKinley down and for Republican principles, one of which was economy. He offered equity but did not stress great expansion of state services, and in fact promised to reduce state expenses. After the Republican ticket won by about 100,000 votes, La Follette renewed the orthodox pledge of economy in his inaugural address.[153]

The circumstances of the harmony campaign of 1900 contributed mightily to the discordance that soon followed. Former opponents had come to La Follette out of temporary expediency, not abiding principle. He had accepted their support in the same spirit.[154] This temporary Republican unity, reinforced by the conventionality of La Follette's 1900

---

[151] *Ibid.*, 61.
[152] Belle and Fola La Follette, *La Follette*, 1: 134–135.
[153] Barton, *La Follette's Winning of Wisconsin*, 161; Maxwell, *Rise of the Progressives*, 89–90.
[154] Barton, *La Follette's Winning of Wisconsin*, 144; La Follette, *Autobiography*, 105–199.

campaign, was a reversion to a pre-La Follette kind of politics, a politics that could not long subsist. For while La Follette was perfectly willing to take advantage of party organization, partisan loyalty, and orthodox rhetoric, he was also dedicated to certain controversial ends and willing to use some highly offensive means.

In the years that immediately followed, La Follette would push for enactment of legislation that he had discussed in the 1890's, including the direct primary election and fuller railroad taxation and regulation. In the fight for these bills, and for political power, he would shuck off the niceties of party regularity, appealing directly to the people—to Democrats, even to Socialists—publicly condemning many fellow Republicans and privately conspiring against them. In all this, he would find justification in the notion that he had been betrayed by party regulars who had supported him in the election of 1900 only to knife his legislative proposals later. The regulars, the "stalwarts," would recall the harmony campaign even more bitterly. They would come to view La Follette not as a misguided zealot or a foolish visionary, but as a conscious hypocrite, a charlatan who would scruple at nothing to gain his ends. This common animus would help to mold the stalwarts into a solid anti-La Follette faction and sustain them through years of disappointment.

II

Progressives and Stalwarts

GOVERNOR LA FOLLETTE'S first message to the legislature, which, contrary to precedent, he delivered in person, surprised many by its vigorous and uncompromising advocacy of reform, notably a primary election law and ad valorem taxation of railroads. Coming so soon after the harmony campaign, it seemed like betrayal to those Republicans who were still wedded to archconservatism in government or to party unity in politics. A powerful railroad lobby at once set to work against the ad valorem tax proposal, using all the familiar tactics. Conservative elements secured control in the senate and blocked the thoroughgoing primary election bill. And Charles Pfister acquired the *Milwaukee Sentinel*, which had the largest statewide circulation of any morning paper in Wisconsin, and began to publish anti-La Follette stories. The governor was depicted as a tyrant who brow-beat legislators in a drive for executive domination.[1]

The Old Guard elements in control of the senate passed a watered-down version of the primary law, and the assembly, which had earlier passed a stronger bill, finally acquiesced. La Follette vetoed the bill, which surprised no one, but "the caustic and powerful message that accompanied the veto was scarcely looked for."[2] La Follette discussed the measure in

---

[1] Barton, *La Follette's Winning of Wisconsin*, 176–177; Maxwell, *Rise of the Progressives*, 38; La Follette, *Autobiography*, 106–107.
[2] Barton, *La Follette's Winning of Wisconsin*, 66.

detail, pointing to its many weaknesses, questioning its constitutionality, and characteristically chastising the opposition for its bad character and methods.[3]

La Follette's charges of bad faith and corruption, directed mainly against members of his own party, scarcely endeared him to the senate. Efforts to override the veto failed, but in a most unusual step the senate adopted by a vote of 18–8 a resolution "censuring the language of the veto message and the aspersions which it cast on the rectitude of the legislators. The resolution charged that the Governor had transcended all bounds of legislative propriety and constitutional rights in attacking the motives of the legislature."[4]

The railroad bill was in turn buried in the senate when La Follette insisted on ad valorem taxation instead of a simple increase in the license fee. The governor found an opportunity to comment on these proceedings when a minor measure to tax the ownership of dogs reached his desk. In a stinging veto, La Follette contrasted the willingness of legislators to tax the poor farmer for his dog to their reluctance when the powerful railroads were in question.

La Follette honestly viewed the conflict in these rather simple terms. Throughout his early manhood he tended to see life from a strongly moralistic perspective, in stark blacks and whites.[5] In his view, the battle was essentially part of a continuing conflict between the people, who wanted only justice, and the corporation-machine alliance, which sought special privilege. According to Mrs. La Follette, the Sawyer bribe incident caused him to reflect on isolated incidents of the past and now discern in them a grand pattern.[6]

In his *Autobiography,* published in 1913, La Follette wrote that in pursuance of this belief he had consciously adopted a strategy of constant simplification and dramatization of the underlying conflict. "It is my settled belief," he wrote, "that this great power over government legislation

[3] Lovejoy, *Direct Primary in Wisconsin,* 66.
[4] *Idem.*
[5] Thelen, *Early Life of La Follette,* 47–48, 104.
[6] Belle and Fola La Follette, *La Follette,* 1: 100.

can only be overthrown by resisting at every step, [and] seizing upon every occasion which offers opportunity to uncover the methods of the system."[7] Considering the "harmony campaign" of 1900, it may be difficult to believe that La Follette consistently pursued this philosophy. But it did square with his aggressive approach in 1901.

La Follette's view of his office was itself unusual for the time. As late as 1922, A. O. Barton was writing: "The governor's office is in the main a clerical position, by courtesy made ornamental." But La Follette strongly believed "that the executive should do more than merely recommend legislation; that he should assist and direct it wherever possible."[8]

La Follette later acknowledged that his use of his office and his approach to the legislature in 1901 was unusual. "I arraigned the legislature as derelict of duty. No normal condition would warrant any executive, state or federal, in calling the legislative department so sharply to account as I did in the veto of the Hagemeister [direct primary] bill and in the veto of the dog tax bill." His justification, of course, was that "in this case the situation was not normal. . . ." The legislature had violated Republican platform pledges of 1898 and 1900. "It was plainly the end of representative government in Wisconsin. It was the rule of a minority through trickery, bribery, and corruption. It was a state of revolt. The situation called for extraordinary, aggressive and strong action. . . . The legislators were the ones who were abusing their power. The executive was obeying the mandate of the people."[9]

In 1903, La Follette caused a sensation when he publicly charged that legislation was defeated in the 1901 session through bribery. The governor's remarkable use of the *reductio* fallacy was chronicled by A. O. Barton: "Governor La Follette did not charge wholesale bribery in the legisla-

---
[7] La Follette, *Autobiography*, 21.
[8] Barton, *La Follette's Winning of Wisconsin*, 168.
[9] La Follette, *Autobiography*, 118–119.

ture, but he drove home the point that, as in mathematics, things equal to the same thing are equal to each other; so the men who through political spite, or jealousy or sympathy, or whatever the motive, voted to ends and effects sought by bribery were equally guilty and dangerous, though not purchased, with the men actually bribed."[10]

This view was not simply retrospective, for it seems to have guided his actions in 1901. Whether La Follette lumped together those who opposed his legislation out of conviction or as a matter of strategy is not clear. Indeed, there was more than a little truth in La Follette's view. Powerful moneyed interests had in fact resorted to crass and subtle forms of corruption, and many in politics had promoted the same degradation in government. Milwaukee politicians had been especially susceptible to bribery through the years.[11] Why should this system have suddenly ended just because La Follette had become governor?

As strategy, it may have been sensible to tar the entire opposition with the same brush. But as history, presented in La Follette's influential *Autobiography*, it was oversimplified. It was the truth, but not the whole truth. La Follette's tactics gave to his opponents certain weapons that they might use against him—charges of tyranny, executive usurpation and the like. But more than that, La Follette's approach created genuine grievances. He not only armed existing enemies, but also made new ones. Barton, though a frank La Follette partisan, provided a fair description of the opposition:[12]

> It were a gross injustice to attribute ulterior motives to all the so-called stalwarts. As is the case over all issues and regarding all forceful men, there were honest differences of opinion. Many stalwarts were more honest and better patriots than many in the camp of reform; many opposed the

---

[10] Barton, *La Follette's Winning of Wisconsin*, 280.
[11] Strange, "Autobiography."
[12] *Ibid.*, 196.

governor because they did not know the man, misunderstood him or were misled regarding him. . . . Many also wearied of the long fight; many of hearing Aristides called just. A large class was actuated in its opposition by petty and sordid personal interests, while many of the older voters who believed in the fetish of party loyalty through good or evil report—whose vision was retrospective—frowned upon the departures which threatened to disrupt and divide the grand old party. The active and interested opposition came, however, from the big corporations who saw in La Follette's ascendency a menace to the continuation of their privileges, and from the old wheel horses of the party, the governmental agents of these interests who also foresaw their tenure of office and privileges in jeopardy.

Even among "the active and interested opposition" motives were probably not unalloyed, not wholly discreditable. Objections to La Follette's 1901 proposals were not untenable. Some members of the legislature "felt that it would be discriminatory to increase the tax burden of the railroads while the state's policy respecting the personal property tax was admittedly chaotic. . . ."[13] Moreover, the temporary tax commission, established in 1899, while arguing for higher railroad taxes, had not expressed a preference for the ad valorem system instead of the license fee tax, but instead mentioned both as acceptable. Senator John Whitehead had introduced a bill to raise the license fee from 4 to 5½ per cent for Class I railroads.[14]

The merits of the direct primary remained open to question. Senator Spooner's objections to the device, representative of the opinions of other highly respected leaders such as senators Whitehead and Andrew Kreutzer, were privately expressed to a political colleague during the 1903 battle over the primary: "I think a primary election law

---

[13] Maxwell, *Rise of the Progressives*, 38.
[14] *Ibid.*, 37–38.

as he [La Follette] wants it would destroy the party machinery, which is necessary in order to fight the political enemy of the party, and would build up a lot of personal machines, would make every man a self-seeker, would degrade politics to turning candidacies into bitter personal wrangles and quarrels, etc. I do not see how under such a scheme the office would be likely to seek the man."[15] Later experience brought some progressives to share Spooner's doubts.

Many Republicans remained concerned about party unity. Describing the situation following La Follette's vetoes of the direct primary bill and the dog tax to his longtime political ally "Hod" Taylor, Elisha Keyes gave vent to deep feelings when he wrote: ". . . It would seem as if the party was now driving out into the political sea without sail, anchor or rudder. Bob has split the party wide open, and there seems to be no getting together of the dissevered parts. . . ."[16] That La Follette was to blame for the split in the party Keyes had no doubt. Not only had La Follette vilified Republican legislators; he had also refused to consider any compromise on primary legislation. "He said to members of the legislature, take this bill. We will have no other. It is my bill. You shall pass it."[17] *Die Germania,* the leading German-language paper in the state, previously friendly to La Follette, criticized him strongly in a front-page editorial following his veto of the direct primary bill. The paper blamed him for the split in the Republican party and charged him with wanting to be a dictator.[18] This concern for party unity was not unusual in the German-language press, nor was it confined to the German element.[19]

---

[15] John Spooner to S. M. Booth, March 28, 1903, in the Spooner Papers, cited in Fowler, *Spooner,* 299–300.
[16] Keyes to H. A. Taylor, May 11, 1901, in the Keyes Letterbooks.
[17] Keyes to Col. John Hicks, August 21, 1901, in the Keyes Letterbooks.
[18] Lovejoy, *Direct Primary in Wisconsin,* 67.
[19] For a discussion of the political attitudes of the German-language press during the Progressive period, see Adolph G. Korman, "Political Loyalties, Immigrant Traditions and Reform: The Wisconsin German-American Press and Progressivism, 1909–1912," *Wisconsin Magazine of History,* 40: 2 (Spring, 1957).

The accusation of bossism against La Follette was not new. Back in 1897, the *Janesville Gazette* editorialized in response to La Follette's University of Chicago speech in favor of the primary: "What Mr. La Follette says about machine politics will receive reverent attention. The man who for five years has controlled the Dane County machine —the most mercenary, office-grabbing organization the state ever saw—should speak with authority when machine politics are under discussion."[20] More generally, many of La Follette's opponents in 1901 believed him and his supporters guilty of every dirty practice that they attributed to the stalwarts.[21] Under these circumstances, La Follette's attitude of supreme rectitude was infuriating to some.

Most aggravating of all in 1901 was the atmosphere of exclusion and conspiracy that surrounded the governor's office and seeped into the legislative chambers and hotel lobbies. Emanuel Philipp had participated wholeheartedly in La Follette's behalf in 1900; his relations with La Follette had been cordial, and La Follette at one time spoke of making him state campaign manager. But after La Follette's November victory, Philipp was not consulted on future policy.[22] Years later, Philipp showed continuing pique when he described the general atmosphere that set in early in 1901:[23]

> It had been the custom in the past for members to call at the executive chamber frequently for informal consultations and conferences on all subjects relating to legislation. . . .
>
> But conditions were changed now. As the days passed it was noticed that an air of mystery was beginning to gather about the capitol building. Men were called to the executive chamber for conferences, it is true, but they were carefully selected

---

[20] *Janesville Gazette*, February 25, 1897, quoted in Lovejoy, *Direct Primary in Wisconsin*, 37.
[21] Whitehead to Ralph Gabriel, April 22, 1914, and Whitehead to Max Farrand, May 11, 1914, in the Whitehead Papers; G. E. Vandercook to Keyes, December 14, 1901, in the Keyes Papers.
[22] Maxwell, *Philipp*, 34–35.
[23] Emanuel Philipp, *Political Reform in Wisconsin* (Milwaukee, 1910), 31.

from among their fellows and the consultations were always held behind closed, guarded doors. . . . There was an indefinable something in the atmosphere of the outer executive office that made it impossible for certain visitors to penetrate far beyond the portals with any degree of ease.

Long before any attempt was made to organize a faction in opposition to the governor there was a faction organized and disciplined to carry out his program. . . . The atmosphere of mystery that at first enveloped the executive chamber only, spread to the entire capitol—legislative chambers, committee rooms, corridors and even the cloakrooms and closets. . . .

There were little gatherings where whispered consultations were held; there was evasion, suspicion, secrecy on every hand. . . . Two men would be talking in a corridor and a third would approach; instantly there would be warning glances exchanged and the two would separate, to be seen a few minutes later continuing the conversation.

The general atmosphere of tension and suspicion was of course reflected in legislative debates. Thus, when objections were raised to the primary, the objectors were labeled "corruptionists," "corporation corruptionists" or "corrupt hirelings." "The spirit of the master was breathed into the members of the faction," Philipp recalled, "and it was bitter as gall." It was in reaction to this situation that outright opposition to the administration coalesced, Philipp claimed.[24]

Early in 1906, shortly after James O. Davidson, a progressive, had succeeded La Follette as governor, Elisha Keyes recalled the La Follette regime with some bitterness in a letter to John Spooner. "The atmosphere around the executive office has changed materially," Keyes wrote. "Anyone, high or low, rich or poor, black or white, can at once meet face to face the Chief Executive of this state without

[24] *Ibid.*, 41.

being trained through a cordon of outside guards."[25] Others wrote directly to Davidson in the same vein: "My association with the Stalwart movement in the state has been more as a protest against the bigotry and venom which La Follette has ever put in his campaigns, than against the measures he proposed...."[26]

A. O. Barton, still political reporter for Madison's *Wisconsin State Journal* and always sympathetic towards La Follette, frankly confirmed the stalwart complaint with respect to the general atmosphere and provided additional detail. "The rooms at the executive office," he wrote," "permitted the grading of callers into classes corresponding to their consequence or worth in the eyes of the governor and his kitchen cabinet. The large outer office, or reception room, was open to all. Here was the office of the private secretary and the executive clerk, and here were the newspaper men, politicians and all casual callers. Few stalwarts of consequence who had occasion to call ever got beyond this room."[27]

Commenting on Philipp's description of the situation, Barton added a significant explanation: "There is no great exaggeration in this picture, as observers of the period will remember, but it suggests the further fact that to espouse La Folletteism in the early days frequently proved a trial of men's souls. Too often it meant business reprisal and social ostracism."[28]

It may well be that the warlike and conspiratorial manner of the La Follette group was necessary. Certainly Philipp's rejoinder, which was, in effect, "You started it," was vastly oversimplified. The fact remains, however, that

---

[25] Keyes to Spooner, January 10, 1906, in the Elisha Keyes Letterbooks.
[26] O. W. Arnquist to James O. Davidson, May 9, 1906, in the James O. Davidson Papers. See also A. H. Reid to Davidson, May 17, 1906; A. H. Strange to Davidson, December 21, 1905; E. E. Sherwood to Davidson, December 4, 1905; Wallner J. Benedict to Davidson, January 3, 1906, all in the Davidson Papers.
[27] Barton, *La Follette's Winning of Wisconsin*, 263.
[28] *Ibid.*, 170.

many of La Follette's opponents were honest and independent men. The coalescence of these men with others into a dedicated "stalwart" opposition was in part a reaction to La Follette's aggressive approach, however necessary that approach may have been from a tactical standpoint.

As internecine Republican conflict became increasingly intense and personal, much stalwart venom was stimulated by and discharged against the members of La Follette's "inner circle." Until 1903, when he left the state, the chief *bête noir* within this select group was La Follette's private secretary, Jerre Murphy, a former political writer and editor who had looked for a reform leader to serve and found him in La Follette in the nineties. La Follette suffered a grievous blow with the untimely death of Sam Harper in 1898. Murphy came to supply the deficiency, in part. Belle La Follette wrote, "In appearance Jerre always reminded me of pictures of Edgar Allan Poe; he was of poetic temperament with a tinge of melancholy, had fine literary taste and a passion for collecting rare books and Oriental rugs." His conversation with opponents, she recalled, was peppered with satire and his shafts were "merciless and deadly."[29] In 1894, La Follette described Murphy's qualities as a political writer by saying: "No person upon the other side can claim that Jerre Murphy has been careless or indifferent as to his facts however much fault he may find with the sharpness of his arraignment."[30] The stalwart attacks against this sharp-tongued intellectual carpetbagger sprang as much from sincere feeling as from calculation.

The 1901 session marked the beginning of a new phase in Wisconsin politics. The non-La Follette element among Republican politicians, not really a coherent faction theretofore, now huddled together in fear and hatred of the governor and his allies.

In the short run, the stalwart effort was doomed to frustration and failure, and served only to aid La Follette in

---

[29] Belle and Fola La Follette, *La Follette*, 1: 141.
[30] La Follette to W. H. Upham, November 16, 1894, in the La Follette Papers.

his effort to simplify and polarize. The behind-the-scenes leadership remained largely reactionary, self-interested and inept. Nor did the stalwarts have anyone to head their ranks who could hope to match La Follette in stirring up faithful workers and rally the voters. The conservative Republican leaders in Washington —Taylor, who was Assistant Secretary of the Treasury, Spooner, and perhaps Payne—counseled caution. Best adhere to party usage and allow La Follette an unopposed renomination in 1903, relying on the legislature to minimize the damage, Taylor argued. In that way, Spooner would be brought to reconsider his decision not to seek another term in the Senate; and following La Follette's second term as governor, with Spooner and Quarles in the Senate, "the stalwarts would control the organization of the party."[31]

Cautious, tentative advice such as this was no substitute for the kind of firm leadership that Sawyer had once been able to give. It is doubtful whether "the boys" back in Wisconsin could have been controlled even by a Sawyer after the 1901 legislative session. The politicians and corporate managers, alarmed and aroused, were confident that they could defeat La Follette in an open fight. It was La Follette who had thrown down the gauntlet, stalwarts felt, so peace overtures must come from him, and given the nature of the man, that day would never come. On with the fight, then, whatever Henry Payne might say.[32]

An ill-conceived and poorly managed anti-La Follette organization ostensibly made up of eighteen senators and forty-one assemblymen established itself in August, 1901, with a statement that ". . . We view with alarm the persistent effort to strengthen the executive at the expense of

---

[31] H. A. Taylor to Elisha Keyes, August 8, 1901; see also Taylor to Keyes, April 15, 1901, and April 19, 1901, in the Keyes Papers.
[32] Keyes to H. A. Taylor, May 13, 1901; Keyes to Taylor, July 5, 1901; Keyes to W. H. Stennett, July 26, 1901; Keyes to Taylor, August 6, 1901; Keyes to William Bissell, August 15, 1901, in the Keyes Letterbooks; Dan B. Starkey to Keyes, August 20, 1901, in the Keyes Papers.

the legislative department of the state."[33] Sumptuous headquarters, "well stocked with good things," were set up on the eleventh floor of a Milwaukee building, and the organization was soon dubbed by its detractors the Eleventh Story League, though it called itself the Wisconsin Republican League. Charles Pfister, whose prestige and power had grown appreciably with the acquisition of the *Milwaukee Sentinel,* superintended the League's well-financed activities, chief of which was to flood the local press of the state with attacks on La Follette as a socialist bent on dictatorship.[34] Meanwhile, in June, Isaac Stephenson had established the *Milwaukee Free Press* to counter the *Sentinel* and had hired a *Sentinel* reporter, H. P. Myrick, to edit it. The *Free Press,* with its limited circulation, was no match for the *Sentinel.* But it did serve as a vehicle for attacks on the Eleventh Story League. In February, 1902, the campaign against the League reached a dramatic high point with a story prepared by John J. Hannan, charging the Eleventh Story League with the wholesale purchase of the editorial opinion of about three hundred state newspapers. The specifics, charges by Henry Roethe of the *Fennimore Times* that attempts had been made to buy up his editorial columns, soon backed up by like exposures by others, were the sensation of the year. Charles Pfister's blunder was an immediate boon to La Follette that carried long-run residual benefits, for reverberations of the shock echoed into the future.[35]

The Stalwarts were no more fortunate in their choice of a candidate to oppose La Follette's bid for renomination. In State Senator John M. Whitehead the League picked a man of rectitude, experience, and ability whose strong stand against La Follette's primary legislation endeared him to conservative politicians.[36] But Pfister was disastrously

---

[33] Barton, *La Follette's Winning of Wisconsin,* 183.
[34] Lovejoy, *Direct Primary in Wisconsin,* 68.
[35] *Ibid.,* 184–188.
[36] Keyes to W. H. Stennett, January 8, 1902, in the Keyes Letterbooks.

Progressives and Stalwarts 63

wrong in his assurances that the Germans of Milwaukee and the lakeshore counties would support Whitehead despite his well-known prohibitionist leanings and unbending demeanor. By the time the publishers of the German-language papers *Germania* and *Herald* made this clear to Spooner, Quarles, Taylor, and Payne in Washington, it was impossible to rectify the error. Going over the head of Pfister, the Washington leaders and others tried to induce a moderate state senator and manufacturer, Fred A. Dennett, to enter the race, but he declined to do so, partly because Whitehead would not withdraw and partly because the Eleventh Story League's blunders had made the prospects unattractive for any anti-La Follette candidate.[37]

La Follette and his friends took no chances. The governor had so strained himself during the 1901 sessions as to bring on illness. But after some months of convalescence, he was ready for action and in the spring of 1902 began to sow what Emanuel Philipp called "the pernicious seeds of political and social discord" in the state. He took to the stump and recited the voting records of legislators on the primary election and railroad tax bills, an extraordinary step. Meanwhile, a *Voter's Handbook* was sent to almost every voter in the state. This 144-page document told of the recent legislative session, included roll calls on important measures, and reiterated the story of the Eleventh Story League.[38]

If it had been difficult to assess blame for the remarkable conflict among Republicans before, now it was virtually impossible. From the La Follette perspective, the activities of the Eleventh Story League required strong countermeasures. From the stalwart view, though, the

[37] Keyes to John Spooner, January 12, 1902; Keyes to John Gaveney, January 14, 1902, in the Keyes Letterbooks; Joseph Quarles to Keyes, April 21, 1902; F. A. Dennett to Keyes, April 25, 1902; John Gaveney to Keyes, April 26, 1902, in the Keyes Papers; Keyes to Gaveney, May 1, 1902; Keyes to Dennett, May 27, 1902; Keyes to Taylor, May 27, 1902, in the Keyes Letterbooks.
[38] Barton, *La Follette's Winning of Wisconsin*, 192.

League's efforts had been occasioned in the first instance by La Follette's treacherous treatment of fellow Republicans and by his dangerous abuse of executive power. Thus, even as La Follette was winning the battle of the caucuses in 1902, the stalwart prejudices were being reinforced.

Party conventions had been held in Milwaukee since 1884, but La Follette succeeded in switching the 1902 convention to the University of Wisconsin gymnasium in Madison, away from the corrupting influence of the Eleventh Story League. There La Follette was renominated by a vote of 790–266, and the rest of the ticket and the platform were compounded to his prescription.[39]

One way of gauging the extent of the Republican schism as of 1902 is by studying the relationship between the La Follette forces and Senator Spooner. As Belle La Follette noted, Spooner "had a strong hold on Wisconsin quite independently of the old political machine with which he cooperated as inconspicuously as possible."[40] As one of a small group of Republicans who dominated the United States Senate, a celebrated orator and constitutionalist, deferred to by Presidents, Spooner lent honor to his state. Pride in Spooner cut across factional lines; ideology meant less, and party and state loyalty more. In short, "ordinary politics" survived.

Spooner had retracted his announced decision to retire and was available for re-election in 1903. La Follette recognized Spooner's strength by disclaiming opposition to him in the *Voter's Handbook*. The stalwarts, proud of Spooner and aware that his candidacy was their strongest card, warned direly that La Follette would dump the senator.[41] But many of the caucuses that chose La Follette dele-

---

[39] *Ibid.*, 206.
[40] Belle and Fola La Follette, *La Follette*, 1: 127. Spooner's strength among La Follette supporters is indicated in H. A. Taylor to Elisha Keyes, April 19, 1901; Robert S. Cowie to Keyes, August 8, 1901; John Hicks to Keyes, August 17, 1901, in the Keyes Papers; and Keyes to H. A. Taylor, October 6, 1901, in the Keyes Letterbooks.
[41] Barton, *La Follette's Winning of Wisconsin*, 190.

Progressives and Stalwarts

gates unconditionally endorsed Spooner's re-election,[42] and at the convention La Follette accepted the nomination with conciliatory words. The convention endorsed Spooner on the condition that he accept platform principles. In the campaign that followed, Spooner spoke for La Follette and the whole Republican ticket.[43] Though La Follette was embarrassingly noncommittal as to Spooner, yet most Republicans elected to the legislature were committed to Spooner, and early in the 1903 session the Republican legislature re-elected him without a fight. Spooner journeyed to Madison to accept the election, and later wrote of the reception he received there: "The performance out at Madison was one in the highest degree delightful to me. The vote was unanimous, and the ovation which was given me was beyond description."[44]

Even so, sweet harmony was far from all-pervasive among Republicans. After the Democrats nominated Mayor Rose of Milwaukee to oppose La Follette, the governor campaigned widely in the state, lambasting Rose as a reactionary tool of special interests. At the end of one of his meetings, a local politician asked La Follette whether he unconditionally favored the re-election of Senator Spooner. La Follette had avoided the question theretofore, but now he replied after some moments of silence:[45]

> I will answer you in this way, sir. I am for the success and for the principles of the republican party as laid down, and the day and the hour that Senator Spooner raises his voice for the principles of the republican party, as laid down in the state platform, I will raise my voice for his re-election to the United States senate, because I then can do so in conformity with the platform of my party.

---

[42] Fowler, *Spooner*, 296; Belle and Fola La Follette, *La Follette*, 1: 150.
[43] Lovejoy, *Direct Primary in Wisconsin*, 71.
[44] Spooner to R. R. Frazier, March 25, 1903, in the Spooner Papers, cited in Fowler, *Spooner*, 298.
[45] Barton, *La Follette's Winning of Wisconsin*, 222.

Political observers felt that La Follette's statement might cost him twenty to thirty thousand Republican votes, and perhaps the election. But the Eleventh Story League's heavy-handed campaign had given La Follette a measure of leeway for retaliation. Moderates might deplore the state of things within the party, yet blame the stalwarts, not La Follette.[46] Even so, La Follette's statement did reflect an escalation of the conflict within the Republican party and would cost some Republican votes.

The momentum of events, beginning with the legislative clashes of 1901, had carried Wisconsin politics well beyond conventional bounds in any case, quite apart from La Follette's statement on Spooner. Many stalwarts had long since determined to bolt quietly to the Democrats on the governorship.[47] To La Follette, much more than to his more conventional Republican opponents, division along progressive-versus-stalwart lines, irrespective of party, seemed both logical and desirable. He was quite willing to trade the votes of stalwart Republicans for those of progressive Democrats. His appeal to Democrats became more blatant in 1904, but it was already a significant political factor in 1902. The Democratic party had much the same division as the Republican, but it lacked a progressive leader comparable to La Follette. La Follette was able to make an appeal to Democrats quite similar to his appeal to Republicans. John Whitehead's statement of the case, supported by other sources, was illuminating: "It is . . . current opinion . . . that he made common cause with the Democrats, giving them the city of Madison and he taking the county, and it has been a fact that the leading Democratic managers in Madison, such as Aylward and O'Connor, have cooperated with La Follette in many devious ways. These young Democratic leaders were University men, as was La Follette, and

---

[46] See, for example, John Hicks to Elisha Keyes, August 17, 1901, and Hicks to Keyes, April 24, 1901, in the Keyes Letterbooks. Hicks, the publisher of the *Oshkosh Northwestern,* had long been close to Sawyer in Republican politics.

[47] Elisha Keyes to W. H. Stennett, July 20, 1902, in the Keyes Letterbooks.

they had a kind of freemasonry among them which held them together, whether they were Democrats or Republicans."[48] William Jennings Bryan urged Wisconsin Democrats to support La Follette against Rose. Many progressive Democratic leaders refused to endorse the party platform or support the ticket, and of course the Republicans gave this fact wide publicity. In the general election, La Follette defeated Rose, 193,413 to 145,818.

It was estimated that about 30,000 of La Follette's votes came from Democrats.[49] To a lesser extent, the governor owed his re-election to the votes of Social Democrats. The party had been building strength in Milwaukee under the powerful revisionist leadership of Victor Berger since the late nineties. Because the Social Democrats made common cause with trade unionism, and because of the Old Country attachments of many German workers, it was possible for the union leaders of Milwaukee to be Social Democrats. Those of German birth or parentage constituted a majority of Milwaukee's population at this time. If Victor Berger stressed party unity and regarded La Follette as a "half-baked reformer," he still had to acknowledge that La Follette had won the "mistaken sympathy of the working man." Thus, in 1902, the Social Democratic candidate for governor, Emil Seidel, ran over 1,200 votes behind his ticket in Milwaukee County and polled only 10,824 votes there to La Follette's 26,754.[50]

[48] Whitehead to Ralph Gabriel, April 22, 1914, in the Whitehead Papers. Keyes judged that La Follette controlled Dane County in 1902 only through the help of Democrats. Keyes to John Spooner, June 26, 1902, in the Keyes Letterbooks.
[49] Barton, *La Follette's Winning of Wisconsin,* 213, 230.
[50] Marvin Wachman, *History of the Social Democratic Party of Milwaukee, 1897–1910* (Urbana, 1945), 11, 45; E. E. Witte, "Labor in Wisconsin History," *Wisconsin Magazine of History,* 35: 83–86, 137–142 (Winter, 1951). Witte makes the point that Milwaukee's labor leaders were "trade unionists first and Socialists second." The link betweeen unionists and socialists is well described and explained in Thomas W. Gavett, *Development of the Labor Movement in Milwaukee* (Milwaukee, 1965), 91–105; see also Frederick I. Olson, "The Socialist Party and the Unions in Milwaukee," *Wisconsin Magazine of History* 44: 110–116 (Winter, 1960–1961).

The Republican unanimity in re-electing Spooner early in 1903 did not reflect the state of things generally in that legislative session. La Follette renewed his appeal for the primary election and ad valorem taxation of the railroads and added certain other recommendations, chief of which was for a strong railroad commission. The stalwart element was in control of the state senate, however, and after a series of meetings in Washington, Representative J. W. Babcock, whose flirtation with La Follette had been brief, was deputized to come to Madison to provide leadership. Senators Spooner and Quarles agreed to help out in the next election campaign.[51] Meanwhile, a vast lobby, exceeding the legislators in number, set to work. Much attention was focused on the railroad commission bill, as La Follette put forth 178 pages of elaborate statistics to show a pattern of discriminatory rates in Wisconsin and his opponents hurled their own figures back at him.

The advantage was on the side of "the interests" in this skirmish. To be sure, La Follette was fortified by a Tax Commission report that on a conservative ad valorem basis the railroads should have paid $2,788,530 in 1901 instead of the $1,600,379 that they actually did pay, and in the face of this the stalwarts thought it best to let the ad valorem railroad tax bill pass. But they blocked the direct primary bill until La Follette agreed to a referendum in the 1904 elections, and their main aim—the defeat of the railroad commission bill—was achieved. Along the way, they also blocked anti-lobby, anti-rebate, grain-inspection, and two-cent railroad-fare bills, as well as legislation to regulate telephone companies.[53]

The railroad men sincerely believed that La Follette had made unfair rate comparisons in his arguments for the railroad commission.[54] But the conflict could no longer

[51] Barton, *La Follette's Winning of Wisconsin*, 238–239.
[52] Raymond Vincent Phelan, *The Financial History of Wisconsin*, Bulletin of the University of Wisconsin no. 193, Economic and Political Science Series (Madison, 1908), 386.
[53] Barton, *La Follette's Winning of Wisconsin*, 256–260.
[54] Maxwell, *Rise of the Progressives*, 52, 38.

be viewed by participants in terms of honest differences of opinion among men of basically common views and interests; factional and ideological conflict dominated participants on both sides. From La Follette's standpoint, the results of the 1903 session were not overly discouraging. He had achieved one major reform; the way was open for a second, the direct primary; and he noted with pleasure that the defeat of other measures, especially the railroad commission bill, provided issues for the next campaign.[55]

In 1903 Jerre Murphy quit Wisconsin for Montana, "to fight the copper dragons," and La Follette took a new private secretary: another fighting Irishman, "Colonel" John J. Hannan, a tall, stout man of ready wit and keen political instinct. Hannan reputedly liked a fight even more than La Follette did,[56] and if so, he had signed on at the right time. The flames of intraparty warfare that had flickered for a decade now flared into a conflagration. The two factions had battled to a draw in 1902, when Spooner won back his Senate seat and La Follette the governorship. Now both stalwarts and progressives recognized that a fight to the death was inevitable: "Each group was determined to annihilate the other and neither was scrupulous about the methods used."[57] Under the circumstances, the 1903 legislative session was not followed by the usual slump in political activity. Instead, both sides set immediately to work on the 1904 campaign.

La Follette's main task was to ready his lists. Barton noted this: "In the course of his campaigning Governor La Follette had obtained the most complete list of voters in the state, perhaps, that any politician ever had. There was first an emergency list of live and influential adherents who could be relied upon to jump a train or open their purses at a single flash when needed, a splendid militant force of some 1500 or more; then a list of 10,000 unquestioned supporters, and finally a large list of 100,000 or more voters to whom

[55] Barton, *La Follette's Winning of Wisconsin*, 262.
[56] *Ibid.*, 323, 325.
[57] Fowler, *Spooner*, 300–301.

reasonable appeal for aid could be made." The latter noted residence, nationality, party, age and factional ties, or sympathies.[58] The job at hand was to revise and enlarge the list based on the smallest political unit, the school district, not only for the distribution of literature, but for political organization as well. One man in each district was deputized to propagandize and get out the vote. Here, indeed, was a party within a party, and perhaps more thoroughly organized than the regular Republican party had ever been. Over a million pieces of literature were sent from La Follette headquarters in 1904 on the basis of the updated lists.[59]

As the campaign developed that spring, the traditional kind of legwork had to be done. For this, La Follette used state employees and paid workers liberally, thus countering, to some extent, the federal officeholders, railroad employees, and others working for the stalwarts.[60]

The immediate prize was control of the party's state convention, meeting in May, 1904. At the same time, both sides were looking ahead to the nomination of candidates for the legislature. In this connection, La Follette inaugurated his famous "roll call" device. Convinced that the voters must be informed about men as well as measures, La Follette would go into a stalwart legislator's district to speak, describe the major issues recently acted on by the legislature, and then read the roll-call records of the local legislators on these bills. Such action by a governor was unheard of, and to voters, even progressive-minded ones, it came as a shock. Belle La Follette recalled the usual reaction:[61]

> Before he spoke, his friends would often urge him to omit the roll call, saying people knew the

---

[58] Barton, *La Follette's Winning of Wisconsin*, 416.
[59] *Ibid.*, 417; Belle and Fola La Follette, *La Follette*, 1: 183.
[60] Keyes to Marvin Hughitt, April 12, 1904, in the Keyes Letterbooks; William W. Culver to Herbert W. Chynoweth, April 20, 1904; E. E. Browne to John K. Parish, April 23, 1904; Gerhard M. Dahl to H. W. Chynoweth, April 24, 1904; Roy S. Smelker to H. W. Chynoweth, April 25, 1904; R. E. Smith to Chynoweth, May 11, 1904, in the La Follette Papers.
[61] Belle and Fola La Follette, *La Follette*, 1: 172.

stalwart candidate had voted wrong in the last legislature and didn't intend to vote for him, but that he was personally well-liked, and publicly humiliating him by reading his record could only create sympathy; it would hurt the cause more than it would help. Bob always answered he could make no exceptions; he must hew to the line regardless of the candidate's personal popularity. I have sat on the platform many times and felt the audience "freeze" as he began to read the ayes and nays disclosing the record of senators and assemblymen to their constituents.

La Follette's message was a simple one. In the most general terms, "the fight is between the railroads and the people." A little more elaborately, the issues were fourfold: the railroads should pay at least an additional million dollars a year in taxes; they should be made to pay hundreds of thousands of dollars in back taxes; a railroad commission should be established capable of equalizing Wisconsin freight rates with those in neighboring states; and the primary election should be put on the books.[62]

Charles Pfister had been discredited by the 1902 fiasco and generally repudiated as stalwart leader.[63] Joseph Babcock continued to direct the stalwart campaign. He had plenty of assistance. About five thousand federal employees, picked through the years on the basis of political acceptability among other things, could be counted on. The railroads and other business corporations and most of the newspapers were also in the stalwart camp, as were the two senators and most of the state's congressmen. Emanuel Philipp took an active part, and the Chicago and North Western and the Chicago, Milwaukee and St. Paul railroads together contributed over fifty thousand dollars prior to June 8, 1904. In all, an estimated half million dollars were spent against La Follette in 1904, and the Hill interests of Minnesota

[62] [John Hannan?] to Frank Tucker, April 15, 1904; La Follette to Ole Harvey, April 21, 1904; La Follette to "Dear Sir," April 24, 1904, in the La Follette Papers.
[63] Maxwell, *Philipp*, 37.

were said to have sent in sixty men to work against La Follette.[64] Wisconsin railroads contributed men, too, some of whom showed "more zeal than discretion," in Elisha keyes's view.[65]

But the stalwarts continued to be handicapped by lack of leadership. "Especially was it lacking in available candidates for public favor to pit against the aggressive governor," Barton observed. Babcock, determined to avoid the blundering rawness of Pfister's 1902 campaign, induced two well-respected men, Judge Emil Baensch and Samuel A. Cook, to offer their names, with the understanding that their forces would be pooled against La Follette at the convention. Baensch was a German-American editor of high ability and integrity; Cook was a Civil War veteran-lumberman-politician. Both had earlier been friendly to La Follette, but they now urged his defeat in order to restore party harmony. Neither was a spirited or exciting political leader.[66] Even so, the stalwarts were aroused and basically united as never before in preparation for the showdown.

The suspicions of the La Follette men, acute in any case, were further stimulated as the stalwarts produced contesting delegations from a number of counties in the weeks preceding the convention, which was scheduled for the university gymnasium on May 18. The stalwarts were indeed preparing for a possible bolt; they rented the Madison opera house several weeks before the convention met. But while ready for that expedient as a last resort, they hoped to gain control of the convention. This, too, the La Follette men understood. What they did not fully appreciate in the heat of battle was that the stalwarts were not simply bent on theft, that at least some among them honestly believed in the justice of their delegate claims.

[64] *Ibid.*, 40; Barton, *La Follette's Winning of Wisconsin*, 286, 417.
[65] Keyes to Marvin Hughitt, April 24, 1904, in the Keyes Letterbooks.
[66] Barton, *La Follette's Winning of Wisconsin*, 295; Emil Baensch to John N. Miller, April 18, 1904, in the La Follette Papers.

In the stalwart view, La Follette did just what he accused the stalwarts of doing. As Keyes described it to "Hod" Taylor a week before the convention, La Follette was "putting forth superhuman efforts to save it to himself by the most absurd claims ever presented. Their game is where they get beat to get up a bolt, and then they intend to have the Central Committee recognize the bolters." If La Follette tried to carry this through, Keyes foresaw, "the convention will be smashed into smithereens, and two conventions will follow. It can not be prevented. . . ." Four days later, after the last of the caucuses, Keyes felt that the stalwarts had a legitimate majority but was apprehensive due to the contests La Follette had instituted. On the eve of the convention, he wired Taylor: "Running close. Bob intends to steal convention through medium Central Committee. St. Croix stolen."[67] Stalwarts also accused La Follette of improperly using the votes of Democrats and Social Democrats to control Republican caucuses. They knew, too, that many caucus decisions had been very close and uncertain, sometimes necessitating second meetings and giving rise to legitimate contests. The stalwarts, prepared for chicanery in the State Central Committee, controlled 16–6 by La Follette, were not satisfied when that body met the day before the convention and decided the contests in a way that would give 59½ votes to the administration and 43½ to the opposition. They felt that they had a real case to present to the convention on some of these contests, and a good chance legitimately to control the convention. Thus, when the stalwarts gathered at the opera house on the eve of the convention, an extraordinary proceeding in itself, there was a large measure of sincerity in their demand that the rights of delegates be respected the following day.[68]

Rumors flew about possible violence, and every train

---

[67] Keyes to H. A. Taylor, May 11, 1904; Keyes to John Gaveney, May 15, 1904; Keyes to H. A. Taylor, May 17, 1904, in the Keyes Letterbooks.
[68] J. M. Olin to M. Jeffries, May 31, 1904, in the James Olin Papers, quoted in Fowler, *Spooner*, 302–303; Barton, *La Follette's Winning of Wisconsin*, 346.

discharged crowds of politicians into Madison. The convention was scheduled to begin at noon on May 18. At eleven, the anti-LaFollette delegates and many of their sympathizers gathered at the opera house, arrayed themselves four abreast with two American flags in front, and began the march of almost a mile to the gymnasium. Their arrival had been anticipated, and when they reached the gymnasium they encountered unusual physical arrangements and procedures. The convention hall had been so transformed that Barton found it "not unlike a penal institution," policed by a small regiment of burly guards, including football players past and present, the famed wrestler Evan "Strangler" Lewis, and some who had previously seen jail from the perspective of inmates. The delegates were diverted towards a small side entrance, to which they had to proceed single file through a barbed-wire passage, supervised at either end by a dozen or more husky attendants. Inside, a strong wire fence eight feet high, also heavily guarded, separated delegates from observers.[69]

Barton described the entrance of the stalwarts: "Tickets countersigned by the state central committee were required of both spectators and delegates and as each side charged the other with having printed counterfeit tickets over night everyone admitted was 'manhandled,' as the stawarts declared, by these guards, much to the resentment of many dignified party warhorses of the past whose entrance upon other conventions they recalled had been marked with pomp and circumstance, with deference and salvos from the admiring crowds. What a pitiful and humiliating contrast this! But swallowing their pride they fell out of ranks and—some with smiles, others with flushed faces and sharp words of censure—filed singly into the building."[70] To some, these arrangements seemed to prove the contention that La Follette was a dictator who would stop at nothing in his lust for power.[71]

[69] Barton, *La Follette's Winning of Wisconsin*, 348–349.
[70] *Ibid.*, 349–350.
[71] Lovejoy, *Direct Primary in Wisconsin*, 86.

The first test of strength was on the temporary chairman's ruling that all delegates seated by the State Central Committee were entitled to vote on all questions except their own right to a seat in the convention. The La Follette people carried this, 574 5/6 to 485 1/6. Following completion of the organization of the convention, the disputed La Follette delegates being seated, the Baensch forces stalked out. The manager of Cook's delegates, E. R. Hicks, influential Oshkosh Republican and former state attorney general in the period 1899–1903, pleaded for unity, condemned the bolt, and kept his 129 2/3 votes in the convention, which in due course nominated La Follette.

The stalwarts, contesting the legitimacy of the gymnasium convention, convened the following morning at the opera house, this time not as a caucus but as the "legitimate" Republican party convention. Meanwhile, Baensch had withdrawn, leaving the stalwart field open for Cook, whose forces had already caucused and decided to go over to the bolters.[72]

The gathering was a dramatic affair. Among the assembled were the two United States Senators, two former governors, Upham and Scofield, Representative Babcock, and other luminaries. Cook was chosen Republican nominee for governor. Then came the dramatic moments when Quarles and Spooner, the latter notorious for his dislike of political controversy, each rose and unequivocally cast his lot with the bolting stalwarts.[73]

"The convention was a great success," Keyes exulted. "It fairly represented the Republican party, and stood out in most favorable contrast with the game wardens carnival in the armory. The lobbies of the Opera House convention were filled with the best men in Wisconsin, all representative

---

[72] Belle and Fola La Follette, *La Follette*, 1: 176–177; Barton, *La Follette's Winning of Wisconsin*, 360; Lovejoy, *Direct Primary in Wisconsin*, 87; Plumb, *Badger Politics*, 133.
[73] Fowler, *Spooner*, 305; Plumb, *Badger Politics*, 133.

business men, men who have so long fought the battles of the Republican party."[74]

Each convention sent four delegates to the Republican national convention. There, through the influence of such national figures as Payne, Spooner, and Babcock, the stalwart claimants were seated with little difficulty. This was not sufficient for stalwart purposes, however, for the Wisconsin secretary of state was a La Follette man and he would place the La Follette ticket in the Republican column on the ballot unless otherwise ordered by the Wisconsin Supreme Court. Though both sides proposed to persist in any event, the symbol of party regularity was vital to each. Finally, on October 6, by a three-to-one vote, the court ruled in favor of the La Follette convention and ticket, not basing its judgment on the merits of the credentials dispute, but holding that under the law the party's state central committee, which had already ruled in La Follette's favor, was the deciding agency.[75] At this point Cook, who had never been a diehard stalwart, withdrew. The irreconcilable Scofield took Cook's place, but it was clear that the gambit had failed and many stalwarts switched their support to the conservative Democrat, ex-governor George W. Peck, in the general election.

While La Follette's side won the legal contest for political legitimacy, clearly the stalwarts still considered themselves the true Republicans. Theirs were the familiar names and faces of the past; theirs were the spokesmen for Republicanism nationally; and it was they who were in tune with the national organization and all its traditions. The La Follette group by contrast was comprised of new young men, some with strange, radical ideas, who seemed to imbibe from their leader a complete disrespect for the niceties of politics, especially loyalty to party. The La Follette crowd seemed little more than pirates who had by foul means captured the party ship, casting the owners adrift.

[74] Keyes to H. A. Taylor, May 20, 1904, in the Keyes Letterbooks.
[75] Barton, *La Follette's Winning of Wisconsin*, 405–406.

And the fact that these pirates continued to sail under the old flag was but one more piece of chicane, which might fool some, but could not fool the original proprietors, who remained determined to regain what was rightfully theirs and redeem their state and party.

Spooner and Quarles, true to their word, spoke strongly against La Follette. Reconciled to the fact that the party label had been usurped, most stalwarts were ready to ignore it and vote Democratic. For his own part, La Follette had no reluctance about appealing to Democrats. This he could now do more effectively than ever, for he himself was prepared to endorse those Democratic legislative candidates whose positions on the issues were more satisfactory than their Republican opponents. Despite stalwart mutterings that he was a menace to man and beast, La Follette tore furiously about the state in a red automobile, accompanied by a second car for emergencies. Concerned about the composition of the next legislature, he concentrated his efforts on the questionable legislative districts, thus doing excellent service for Democrats and earning the gratitude and the votes of men who were being described by La Follette partisans as "fair minded Democrats." The most prominent object of La Follette's ire among Republican candidates was Representative Babcock, whose Democratic opponent received the governor's undisguised support.[76]

As the decade-long La Follette wave rose to a crest, the power and prestige of the Old Guard ebbed further. In October, death came to Henry C. Payne, national committeeman for sixteen years and lately Postmaster General and adviser to President Theodore Roosevelt. Roosevelt, of course, remained vibrantly alive, especially to his own chances for re-election. Seeing the drift of things in Wisconsin, he swung to La Follette despite the actions of the party

---

[76] La Follette, *Autobiography,* 145; Belle and Fola La Follette, *La Follette,* 184; Plumb, *Badger Politics,* 136; "Report of the Republican Congressional Campaign Committee of the Anti-Babcock Republicans of the Third District," September 16, 1904, in the O. G. Munson Papers.

that summer. Speakers going into Wisconsin were instructed to couple the names of Roosevelt and La Follette; Babcock, chairman of the Republican congressional campaign committee, was instructed to give no aid to the stalwart state committee, since its members were the bolters.[77]

Politics was taking a strange turn. To many, it seemed that just as La Follette's activities as a party wrecker had reached their peak, Roosevelt's strategy lent him respectability. Favorable national publicity in a major eastern journal, *McClure's,* greatly augmented this respectability. Lincoln Steffens' article, "Wisconsin: A State Where the People Have Restored Representative Government—The Story of Governor La Follette," came on the newsstands in the last week of September and sold out by October 2.[78] To some who had been doubtful, this must have seemed an impartial judgment; to others, it perhaps suggested that La Follette was really like Spooner after all, that he was winning glory for the state. To the extent that this was so, La Follette benefited from a booster psychology reminiscent of nineteenth-century politics.

With respect to issues, too, La Follette reverted to nineteenth-century orthodoxies in the last days of the campaign. "Keenly appreciating its value as a political stroke on the eve of election," Barton wrote, "the administration on October 31 issued a statement that all state taxes of the coming year would be remitted. This was one of its practical replies to the stalwart charges of extravagance in state affairs. Attention was also called to the fact that the taxes of the previous year likewise had been remitted. . . ."[79] Here was the old economy appeal, as useful to La Follette as it had been to Jefferson and Jackson. It was a fortuitous refund by the federal government on a Civil War debt that permitted the two-year moratorium on property-tax collection, but there seemed no need to stress that point.[80]

[77] Fowler, *Spooner,* 312.
[78] Belle and Fola La Follette, *La Follette,* 1: 185.
[79] Barton, *La Follette's Winning of Wisconsin,* 437.
[80] William Raney, *Wisconsin: A Story of Progress* (New York, 1940), 294.

La Follette's victory in 1904 was a momentous climax not just to his campaign of that year but to his whole ten-year crusade. By winning control of the legislature along with the governorship, the way was paved for enactment in 1905 of the railroad commission bill, an anti-lobby measure, a civil service law, and other substantial reforms. It was possible, too, to continue to build up and support the various administrative and regulatory agencies like the Tax Commission and the Dairy Commission, which by their expert and honest work were to win fame for the "Wisconsin Idea."[81] Adoption of the primary opened the prospect for future political successes, based in part on appeal to Democrats and Social Democrats.

Yet La Follette's victory was not entirely unalloyed. Though he again won votes away from the Social Democratic candidate,[82] and many more from Democrats, stalwart defection was such that La Follette ran forty to fifty thousand votes behind the rest of the state ticket and about a hundred thousand behind the national ticket. Though the primary carried by a vote of 130,699 to 80,192, the total vote on the referendum was less than half that cast in the governor's race. Disquieting too was the vote in predominantly German counties. While La Follette and the primary ran strongly in the newer, poorer, and predominantly Scandinavian counties, the German counties voted against the primary, and against La Follette in the general election, just as they had in the caucuses. The Germans still inclined towards the Democratic party, and the more so because they were farmers: industrious, relatively prosperous, and politically conservative. They were especially leery of devices such as the primary, arguing that this was a blow to their personal liberty, specifically the constitutional right to assemble. This was a strong argument with the Germans, "who always tended to guard their personal liberties more jealously than their political liberties."[83] Recollections of

[81] See Maxwell, *Rise of the Progressives,* 74–104, for the best account of this.
[82] Wachman, *Social Democratic Party of Milwaukee,* 55–56.
[83] Lovejoy, *Direct Primary in Wisconsin,* 94, 61

the Bennett Law and constant agitation of the temperance issue doubtless kept this traditional feeling strong.[84]

Perhaps as significant as the extent of stalwart defection was the pervasive bitterness towards La Follette. To be sure, many of the La Follette people harbored the same animosity towards the stalwarts. But that was part of the problem, and, from the stalwart standpoint, part of the reason for their hatred of La Follette. Not only had he vilified them; he had also brought this disturbing new spirit into politics and into everyday life, disrupting party, state, communities, even families. That the percentage of the people who voted for governor in 1904 was higher than in any other election from 1900 to 1914 was perhaps no source of alarm in itself. But accompanying this upsurge of voter interest was animosity, suspicion, and strife. "Houses were divided against one another; father was set against son, brother against brother, and even sister against sister," Barton recalled. In this year of decision, "in many places practically every question with reference to men and politics was considered, if not settled, in the light of its connection with La Folletteism. . . . If a man stopped at a postoffice to mail a letter he was suspected of conspiring with the stalwart postmaster." Codes were used for political communication and wires were tapped. "In the intensity of the passions aroused," Barton concluded, "in desperate, relentless, dramatic warfare no other campaign in the state's history approximates this one."[85] La Follette of course blamed the stalwarts for these conditions, but to stalwarts the simple if not wholly relevant fact remained that no such conditions had prevailed before La Follette's time.

To those already inclined to skepticism about La Follette and his impact on state affairs, the events of 1904 provided plenty of fuel for heated feelings. An exponent of democracy, he had built and commanded a political machine

---

[84] The liquor issue was a factor in the campaign against Babcock in 1904. T. M. Hare to Rev. C. E. Butters, February 4, 1904, in the Munson Papers.
[85] Barton, *La Follette's Winning of Wisconsin*, 286, 421, 423–426.

of unprecedented strength; an adherent of honest and efficient government, he had used state employees like any old-time boss; a Republican, he had vilified many of his fellows while wooing Democrats and Socialists; a professed defender of Wisconsin and its people, he had brought unprecedented rancor into the tribal tents.

There was no minimizing the extent of the stalwart defeat in 1904. The results had discredited the old leaders—Babcock, the Spooners, Quarles, Pfister, and the rest of the Old Guard.[86] The outcome, on which stalwarts had staked so much, was shattering. Defeated, demoralized, their leaders dead or discredited, the stalwarts would require some time to recover. Yet in Emanuel Philipp they had in training a leader who would later show great capacity as a candidate and an organizer. And in their own rancor towards La Follette and "La Folletteism," they had motive enough for remaining relatively united and determined in their opposition.

Considering the justifiable fame achieved by Wisconsin's progressive movement, it would be presumptuous to criticize La Follette's polarizing techniques. Strong opposition was perhaps a precondition for success, though it contributed also to eventual defeat; it may well be that only so much could have been accomplished, and that La Follette came very close to that limit. But the inescapable fact is that the intense opposition aroused by La Follette was an important factor in the later decline of his movement. The group called the stalwarts probably never constituted a majority of Republicans after 1900, but they were always significant enough to give encouragement to those within the progressive ranks who contemplated defection. They kept alive the conservative ideology through the progressive years and, in the crucial period 1912–1914, were able to use this ideology in exploiting openings left by the progressives. Finally, it was the stalwarts who or-

[86] Maxwell, *Philipp*, 42.

ganized and led the successful counterrevolution of 1914.

Working ceaselessly towards political control, La Follette had brought to bear immense skill, force, dedication, and personal magnetism in accomplishing the political victory of 1904 and the resultant reforms in legislation and administration. Much of his success rested on conventional tactics in a conventional setting: ticket balancing, nationality appeals, patronage, and the like. But he had also resorted to an ever-growing measure of unorthodoxy. Given to moralistic rhetoric and firmly committed to a strategy of simplification and attack, he had shattered parties and caused a polarization of forces along factional and ideological lines to a degree unprecedented in the state's history. The early county fair campaigns, the attacks on party and corporate leaders, the roll call, the organization of a faction, and the institutional representation of this new kind of politics, the primary, were all part of a bi-factional politics that was and is unusual in American political life. In the combination of old and new, of conventional and unconventional, is to be found part of the explanation for La Follette's success. Inevitably, here too were sown the seeds of the movement's ultimate decline. And the creation of an aroused and relatively unified stalwart opposition was but one factor contributing to that decline. There were other sources of weakness as well—some of which became evident within months of La Follette's election victory of November, 1904.

III

Factionalism, 1906-1916

BY 1905, Wisconsin was well on its way to leadership in the progressive movement. Already notable legislative and political victories had been won. Governor La Follette had emerged as a national figure and was soon to become Senator La Follette, the tenacious, pioneering, uncompromising progressive leader. Even in Wisconsin, however, progressives had their tribulations. Beginning with the primary election of 1906, in fact, they sustained a series of discouragements that did not end until the spectacular progressive resurgence of 1910. Soon thereafter, even as progressivism was advancing further on the legislative front, the progressives found themselves in a yet more turbulent sea of troubles, with the result that control of the governorship and the legislature was lost to conservative Republicans in 1914 and not regained in 1916.

The decline of Wisconsin progressivism in the period from 1906 to 1916 sprang from a variety of causes and occurred in a variety of ways. To place partial blame on factionalism is valid but not very informative. More to the point is the question of why Wisconsin progressivism was so susceptible to factionalism and schism. The 1906 campaign, in which factionalism proved decisive and the erosion of progressive fortunes first became evident, revealed a number of major underlying political limitations to Wisconsin's progressive movement, each contributing in greater or lesser degree to the occurrence and seriousness of the schism. These limitations, with some others, continued to inform the process of factional erosion through the succeeding decade.

The victory of 1904 brought the progressives great opportunity for legislative achievement, and this they did not waste, enacting an excellent railroad commission law and other reforms in 1905. But control of the legislature brought another responsibility too, one that was welcome but was nevertheless a source of embarrassment and danger: to elect a United States senator. Among the influential supporters of La Follette, more than one man aspired to the honor. The politically ambitious might be defeated, but at a price. They might be placated, but only in part, and again at a price. To no one's surprise, Isaac Stephenson, who had defected to La Follette when Joseph Quarles was given the Senate seat in 1899, and whose *Milwaukee Free Press* had proved of great value, now wanted to replace Quarles. To everyone's surprise, so too did William D. Connor.

Connor, a soft-spoken yet forceful lumberman from Marshfield, forty years old in 1904, had enlisted very late in La Follette's cause. Following one of the governor's speeches in December, 1903, he had come to La Follette's hotel room, introduced himself, and said that he had suffered for years at the hands of the railroads, favored better regulation of them, and wanted to help La Follette. At the famous gymnasium convention in May, H. W. Chynoweth, a leader of the Madison bar, former University Regent, and one of La Follette's "inner circle," told the governor that Connor's friends were urging Connor's selection as chairman of the Republican State Central Committee, on the grounds of Connor's wealth and in order to show by the election of a businessman that the reformers were not hostile to business. Connor was duly elected, and was also chosen as one of four delegates to the national convention.[1] At an early meeting of the new State Central Committee, Connor was reported to have said in a jocular way

---

[1] Barton, *La Follette's Winning of Wisconsin*, 331–332.

that the only one who could be elected senator was W. D. Connor. Even so, La Follette was taken by surprise when in November, 1904, John Hannan and a few others came to St. Louis where he was attending the World's Fair and, in a state of some agitation, said that Connor was actively laying plans for the senatorship. They feared that a fight between Connor and Stephenson would wreck chances for reform legislation and might do lasting damage to the progressive movement.[2]

La Follette was supporting Stephenson and continued to do so despite the news of Connor's activities. A second disquieting report reached him at St. Louis, however, and this must have shaken his conviction somewhat. It was to the effect that legislators would not elect Stephenson and might re-elect Quarles unless La Follette himself offered to take the post.[3]

On La Follette's return home, Connor sought an interview with him. According to Barton, when La Follette would not commit himself to Connor's support, the latter said, "Are you aware that the man who can control twelve votes cannot only control the senatorship but can defeat your legislation?" A stormy scene followed and Connor left in anger.[4]

Finally La Follette decided to take the senatorship himself, though he did not intend actually to assume the office until 1906, after his legislative program in Wisconsin had been enacted, and claimed that he accepted the Senate position solely in order to compromise the differences between Connor and Stephenson.[5] If this was the motive, and apparently it was, the effort failed. Connor immediately broke with La Follette and, in so doing, drew substantial strength away from the progressive coalition. Stephenson moved more warily, but his resentment was nevertheless evident in 1905 and 1906.

---
[2] *Idem.*
[3] Strange, "Autobiography," 27.
[4] Barton, *La Follette's Winning of Wisconsin*, 332–333.
[5] Belle and Fola La Follette, *La Follette*, 1: 130–131.

Connor's declaration of war came in December, 1905. La Follette had called the legislature into special session to act on a bill to permit a "second-choice" vote in primary elections, such votes to be counted when the recipient of the first choice vote was eliminated. The purpose of the bill was to overcome the danger of a stalwart being nominated because of division among progressive votes. Connor, however, wielded his full influence against the bill and was generally credited with causing its defeat.[6] Meanwhile, he planned to abandon La Follette and pursue his political fortunes independently in the 1906 primaries. At first he set his sights on the governorship. But unforeseen developments caused him to shift his strategy.

When La Follette finally took his seat in the United States Senate, the lieutenant governor, James O. Davidson, succeeded him as governor. A handsome man with a full black mustache and ruddy complexion, Davidson's appearance and especially his heavily accented speech suggested his Scandinavian origin. Born in Sogn, Norway, in 1854, he had migrated with his family in 1872. In Madison, poor and ignorant of the English language, he secured work on a Dane County farm, then learned the trade of tailoring, became clerk in a general store, and finally opened a store of his own at Soldier's Grove, in Crawford County. Though later the butt of jokes and stories that turned on his naïveté and gullibility, the genial young man made many friends, particularly among his fellow Norwegians, and rose in business and politics. He was first elected to various local offices and then, in 1892, to the legislature. As assemblyman through 1898, Davidson earned a reputation as a pioneer reformer in the anti-railroad-pass fight and by introducing bills to tax telegraph, telephone, sleeping-car, and other public service corporations. He represented the La Follette and Norwegian progressives on the state ticket in 1898,

[6] Keyes to John C. Spooner, December 16, 1905, in the Keyes Letterbooks; La Follette to Isaac Stephenson, June 23, 1906, in the La Follette Papers; Herman Ekern to Nicolai Grevstad, December 17, 1905, in the Herman L. Ekern Papers.

1900, 1902, and 1904, first as candidate for state treasurer, then for lieutenant governor. In winning these offices, he proved his continuing "availability." As of January, 1906, Davidson was a logical candidate for his party's nomination for governor.[7]

But despite all the factors in Davidson's favor, La Follette and a group of friends decided in the summer of 1905 to bring out Irvine Lenroot instead. Born in Superior in 1869, young Lenroot attended a business college, then studied law while serving as a stenographer in a law office and as a court reporter. Admitted to the bar in 1897, he soon moved into politics. Belle La Follette remembered him as "a ready debater with a special gift in drafting legislation." Lenroot had strongly influenced legislation from 1901 through 1905; he had early won La Follette's confidence and affection; he had been valuable in the inner councils of the movement.[8]

La Follette, his young law partner, Alfred T. Rogers, and such other staunch young progressive leaders as Herman L. Ekern of Trempealeau County and James A. Stone of Sauk County, both attorneys, agreed that Davidson was too easy-going and too uneducated for the office of governor. La Follette explained that Davidson was no fighter, no leader of men, nor even equal to the complications of legislation. Progressivism must either move vigorously forward or fall victim to apathy and then defeat at the hands of the ever-vigilant stalwarts. Davidson would simply hold the line; he would not push forward. Lenroot, said La Follette, was by contrast a fighter, a young lawyer, vigorous and experienced in legislation and politics.[9] Rogers echoed this theme in a campaign letter. Special interests "will first attempt to elect men who are unaggressive or unable to carry forward the progressive work. The discouraged and

---

[7] *Wisconsin State Journal*, February 17, 1920; interviews with Craig Ralston, January 20, 1953; with Herman Ekern, May 6, 1953; and with O. A. Stolen, January 4, 1955.
[8] Belle and Fola La Follette, *La Follette*, 1: 156.
[9] *Milwaukee Free Press*, July 21, 1906.

apathetic public sentiment which will surely follow readily lends itself to the election of public officials who are subservient tools of special interests."[10] La Follette and Stone played the same tune in their intraparty correspondence.[11]

La Follette's task in displacing Davidson, difficult in any case, was made almost impossible by W. D. Connor. Connor, shrewd and adaptable, realized that Davidson had pre-empted the anti-La Follette field. Perhaps disappointed at the blow to his own gubernatorial ambitions, but seeing some long-range advantages in any successful anti-La Follette candidacy, he now joined forces with Davidson as candidate for lieutenant governor. In all parts of the state, Connor organized Davidson-Connor clubs. On the surface, both men appealed for progressive votes, calling themselves true progressives. Undercover, however, Connor bargained effectively with the die-hard anti-La Follette stalwarts and, as it turned out, secured their support.[12]

The role of Isaac Stephenson in assisting the Davidson rebellion was less evident than that of Connor, but no less important. The old lumber baron was very disgruntled at the way he had been treated in 1905. First, he had been passed over for the Senate. Later, he had not been consulted in the decision to bring out Lenroot against Davidson. Was this his reward for founding and sustaining the *Milwaukee Free Press?* Stephenson was not in a position to break openly with La Follette in 1906, for he still hoped to get the next Senate vacancy. But he did go so far as to

---

[10] Printed letter by A. T. Rogers, n.d., in the Ekern Papers.
[11] La Follette to John J. Blaine, May 30, 1906, in the La Follette Papers; Stone to Otto Schuster, January 29, 1906, in the James A. Stone Papers.
[12] Keyes to John C. Spooner, December 16, 1905; Keyes to H. C. Adams, December 16, 1905; Keyes to Henry Casson, February 17, 1906; Keyes to H. A. Taylor, May 29, 1906, in the Keyes Letterbooks; David Atwood to James O. Davidson, January 24, 1906; W. A. Jones to Davidson, March 9, 1906; D. C. Owen to Davidson, May 5, 1906, in the Davidson Papers; Robert M. La Follette to Perry Wilder, June 25, 1906; W. H. Dick to La Follette, June 18, 1906; Edward E. Browne to La Follette, July 16, 1906, in the La Follette Papers; W. D. Connor to John G. Gregory, May 25, September 10, 1906, in the John G. Gregory Papers; Fowler, *Spooner*, 324.

impose a policy of neutrality on the *Free Press,* despite the pro-Lenroot feelings of the editor.[13] Moreover, he provided no financial support for the Lenroot campaign, a policy encouraged by Davidson's flattering personal and political attentions, which he increasingly reciprocated.[14]

The money problem was always a difficult one for La Follette, and when Stephenson closed his purse for the 1906 fight it became acute. Despite La Follette's legendary reliance on volunteers, most of his people were paid. Edwin J. Gross, the young Milwaukee lawyer who had been put in charge of Lenroot's campaign, recalled with fondness a Negro barber named Sam Banks, "one of the few men who worked for our cause without asking or receiving any pay."[15] Money was needed not only to pay workers but for office rental, the expense of publishing and distributing campaign literature, billboards, and the like. Gross found himself in short supply, while the opposition seemed to have plenty. As a result, La Follette had to take to the Chautauqua circuit from July through November of 1906 to raise money, with only a few weeks taken out for campaigning in Wisconsin. Late in June, he wrote an old friend: "They are nearly wild at thought of my leaving the state. But the only way a dollar can be raised for Lenroot's campaign is for me to go out on the lecture platform and earn it. We are in hard times for money."[16]

But money was by no means La Follette's only problem. James O. Davidson was more than a figurehead for disgruntled politicians; he was a political power in his own right. Otherwise Connor and the stalwarts would certainly have gone their own way, instead of subordinating their ambitions to his candidacy. The factor that made

[13] H. C. Myrick to La Follette, July 11, 1906, in the La Follette Papers.
[14] J. A. Van Cleve to James O. Davidson, February 5, 1906; J. H. Stout to Davidson, March 16, 1906; F. H. Magdeburg to Davidson, March 27, 1906, in the Davidson Papers; Davidson to Elmer Grimmer, May 26, 1906, in the Davidson Letterbooks.
[15] Gross, "A Political Grab Bag."
[16] Belle and Fola La Follette, *La Follette,* 1: 211.

Davidson an independent political force in the state was simple: he was the chief representative of the Norwegian-Americans in Wisconsin politics. The Scandinavian element, especially the Norwegians, had been vital to La Follette since 1894. They remained so.[17] In the midst of the 1906 primary fight against Davidson, Alfred T. Rogers warned La Follette: "It has always been your mainstay to line up the solid Scandinavian elements and it's like having a broken arm to fight without them. . . ."[18]

The La Follette men had hoped that Lenroot's Swedish ancestry would work in his favor among all Scandinavians in the state, but extraneous events made a shambles of that strategy. The task of separating Davidson and his Norwegian support would have been difficult at any time; in 1906 it was impossible. Norway and Sweden, united since 1814, divided in 1905. The two countries had been on the verge of war, and feelings among Americans of Norwegian and Swedish descent reflected homeland hostilities. A Wisconsin agent for the influential Chicago paper *Skandinaven,* described by Professor Rasmus B. Anderson as a "Swede hater," found ready outlet for his feelings as he toured Norwegian settlements in the course of his business. In every home he said, according to Anderson, "You cannot support the Swede Lenroot against the splendid Norwegian Davidson." He urged those who agreed with him to write *Skandinaven.* Since Davidson's Norwegians numbered 155,122 in 1900, against 48,812 of Lenroot's Swedish, the governor had quite an advantage on the nationality question.[19] Despite prodigious efforts by Lenroot supporters of Norwegian descent to win the favor of *Skandinaven* and to woo the Norwegian voter, Davidson retained the loyalty of the paper and of his countrymen.[20]

[17] See Jorgen Weibull, "The Wisconsin Progressives, 1900–1914," *Mid-America* 47: 191–221 (July, 1965), for a demonstration of the point by means of voting and population statistics.
[18] A. T. Rogers to La Follette, January 11, 1906, in the La Follette Papers.
[19] Rasmus B. Anderson, *Life Story,* 623; *Twelfth Census, 1900,* 1: cxcvi.
[20] F. A. Walby to La Follette, November 14, 1905; Henry Johnson to La Follette, November 20, 1905; August Lehnhoff to La Follette, November 13,

Davidson's success in winning Norwegian votes did not demonstrate that the Norwegians of Wisconsin were not true progressives. On the contrary, stalwart candidates of Norwegian descent almost invariably failed to win nomination and elections. Davidson understood this very well, and made a great point of his progressive ties throughout the 1906 campaign and after. The Norwegians, after all, had a strong tradition of liberty and self government. They were predisposed to sympathize with La Follette's campaign against "machines," "bosses," "trusts," and "interests." They were largely farmers, mainly from the hilly and relatively less fertile western part of the state, and their progressive traditions were reinforced by economic circumstances.

Within the general context of progressivism, however, strong national pride motivated Norwegian-American voters. Davidson, in seeking the nomination for treasurer in 1898, very frankly appraised the nationality question in a letter to another Norwegian progressive: "While I do not believe in making nationality a point, that question does and will enter in the making up of the state ticket, and if our people are given the usual representation I shall be proud of being their choice. I became a candidate for the office of state treasurer because it seemed to me that our people ought to hold the high position they have attained."[21]

The events of 1906 demonstrated that while Norwegians remained firmly "progressive," they were not so devoted

---

1905, in the La Follette Papers; Herman Ekern to Nicolai Grevstad, December 17, 1906; Lenroot to Herman Ekern, March 17, 1906; Ekern to La Follette, February 17, 1906, in the Ekern Papers; Henry Pitusa to James O. Davidson, June 26, 1905; P. Oscar Thompson to Davidson, August 30, 1905; Ed. Emerson to Davidson, October 29, 1905; James Thompson to Davidson, December 1, 1905; C. L. Nelson to Davidson, December 21, 1905, in the Davidson Papers; James A. Stone to Irvine Lenroot, May 22, 1906, in the Stone Papers. The daily edition of *Skandinaven* had a circulation of 18,640 and the biweekly 49,628. How much of this was in Wisconsin is uncertain. N. W. Ayers' and Sons, *American Newspaper Annual* (Chicago, 1907), 162.

[21] James O. Davidson to Andrew Dahl, March 29, 1898, in the Davidson Letterbooks.

either to the person or the viewpoint of La Follette as to desert a progressive leader who was also a Norwegian.

The defection of Davidson, Connor, and Stephenson from the La Follette ranks was a serious blow to Wisconsin progressivism. But the underlying roots of these rebellions, the factors that made them politically possible, were in the long run even more disturbing. So long as these underlying weaknesses were present, there would surely be similar rebellions till there remained little against which to rebel. The actions of these three men apparently had diverse roots. Yet in one respect they were similar: their defection was the result of divided loyalty. Even when they were part of the La Follette coalition, Davidson, Connor, and Stephenson were loyal to their own ambitions as well. And their divided loyalty was rendered dangerous to La Follette only because of a second factor that these men had in common: independent strength. Probably few of La Follette's partisans were completely selfless, but how many were strong enough to oppose their leader and survive politically in 1905? Even Stephenson, a millionaire with statewide political and business connections, had to move cautiously. But with his assets, he had some bargaining power. He had not only the inclination to strike out on his own, but also the ability to do so. The same was true of Connor and Davidson. A significant weakness in Wisconsin progressivism was the degree to which it depended upon independent men such as these. The remarkable political abilities of La Follette, together with certain other factors, such as the unique role of the University of Wisconsin, favorably influenced the character of progressive legislation in the state and obscured this point. Actually, however, even at its height, Progressivism depended to a high degree on extraneous sources of strength, on the money and effort of men whose motives were primarily personal, and on voters who were interested in nationality recognition.

A second major element of weakness in the progressive political situation, a weakness that also became apparent in 1905 and 1906, was La Follette's rather special view of the progressive movement with respect to purposes and methods. This view was neither understood nor shared by most of his followers. When he acted on it, as perhaps he had to, one consequence was to cause dissatisfaction and ultimately schism among his followers. Progressives had favored railroad regulation, equitable taxation, favorable treatment for dairy farmers, and greater popular control in government, and had loyally followed La Follette toward these goals. But by the end of La Follette's third administration, after the early goals had been reached, many of his followers wondered whether there was need for a continuation of the reform movement at the same fast pace, marked as it was by intensely bitter factionalism and party strife.

La Follette parted company with the doubters at this point. His answer was distinctly in the affirmative. It was well stated in a letter that he wrote to a young political lieutenant early in 1906, with the Davidson question in mind: "We have accomplished much in Wisconsin toward the restoration of representative government. That is just what we have accomplished.... No backward step must be taken. The ground we have gained must be held."[22]

Not content with achieving any particular reform or group of reforms, La Follette had come to focus his efforts and thought on the fundamental idea of keeping the predatory "interests" out of public office. To achieve this purpose it seemed necessary that the one weapon the people possessed—their numbers—be fully utilized. Complacency was the menace to be feared above all. The role of the progressive leader was to keep people vigilant, mobilized, to raise ever-new issues, to dramatize the existence of the fundamental conflict between the people and the interests. He would simplify issues, to make them readily comprehensible; he would publicize them by speeches and articles; and above all, he would personalize them, for most people think in personal terms.

[22] La Follette to Otto Bosshard, January 6, 1906, in the La Follette Papers.

Issues, for La Follette, were weapons; they were means more than ends. His handling of one of the early progressive measures, the railroad commission bill, illustrated this. The idea of a strong commission had been popularized during the nineties, and La Follette and his friends heartily backed it. Yet La Follette persuaded A. R. Hall, veteran crusader for railroad reform, not to raise the issue in 1900 or 1901, preferring not to scatter his fire too widely, as A. O. Barton put it.[23] In the 1903 legislative session the La Follette men did raise the commission issue, but as a political tool. "The regulation bill did not pass at that session, nor did we expect it to pass," La Follette later wrote. But the main purpose was accomplished: stalwart rejection of it "stirred the people of the state as they had never been stirred before."[24] A similar tactic was unsuccessfully attempted by Andrew Dahl, one of La Follette's "inner circle," in connection with a bill to tax street railways. Dahl hoped to block the bill in order to blame stalwarts for its defeat during the 1906 campaign, when a new issue would be badly needed.[25]

La Follette always contended that he was concerned with principle, not personalities. Yet his recitation of the voting record of candidates in their own districts, his crusading manner of campaigning, his rhetorical bitterness and irony, his interference in contests for office high and low, his undisguised factionalism, all combined to make the political strife of his time intensely personal. For a time the free-swinging brawl was novel, exciting, even invigorating. But despite the best rhetorical efforts of La Follette and his chief opponents, neither progressive nor stalwart Republicans had horns or cloven hoofs. By 1906 many men on both sides were weary of the constant turmoil, and looked to the day of renewed peace in the Grand Old Party. James O. Davidson was such a man; Isaac Stephenson was another.

[23] Barton, *La Follette's Winning of Wisconsin,* 178.
[24] La Follette, *Autobiography,* 70.
[25] George B. Hudnall to John J. Esch, August 6, 1912, in the John J. Esch Papers.

And they represented thousands of nameless voters and leaders of lesser prominence. Stephenson reflected a widely shared view when he wrote: "In Wisconsin the old railroad-corporation crowd, the inner ring which controlled party affairs to the exclusion of all others, had been fairly routed and some good laws were placed on the statute books. There the task ended for me."[26]

James O. Davidson was the rallying symbol for progressive dissidents during these years. Though a leading progressive, he saw no need for perpetuating the bitter factionalism of Republican politics. He regarded division among Republicans as undesirable, not as a useful and necessary adjunct to reform. Furthermore, he believed in 1905 that after the previous years of turmoil and change, the time had come for consolidation of gains and "a business administration." A naturally friendly man, Davidson prided himself on the amicable relations that he had always maintained with persons of all factions. Under the "business administration" that he planned, there seemed no reason why these relations should not be continued, he wrote a stalwart early in 1906.[27] Later that year he wrote optimistically to his ally Connor: "If I may judge of the situation, a very good proportion at least of the people, are willing to have a rest from the turbulence that has been with us in the past, but none are willing to sacrifice a single principle that we have contended for."[28]

Most stalwarts appreciated the differences between La Follette and Davidson. They would have supported any formidable opponent of La Follette in 1906, but they were especially pleased over Davidson's candidacy, for they saw in the good-natured Norwegian a man of peace. Old Elisha Keyes wrote confidently to Senator Spooner that Davidson was "a peaceable man, . . . not belligerent or aggressive. He

[26] Isaac Stephenson, *Recollections of a Long Life* (Chicago, 1915), 289.
[27] James O. Davidson to John Gaveney, January 19, 1906, in the Davidson Letterbooks.
[28] James O. Davidson to W. D. Connor, June 22, 1906, in the Davidson Letterbooks.

is the kind of man the party needs in this state. ...."[29] Henry Casson, former Wisconsin secretary of state and sergeant-at-arms of the House of Representatives, was equally confident of Davidson's intention to bring peace. Casson had known Davidson for thirty years.[30] A number of other stalwarts wrote with the same confidence directly to Davidson.[31]

Probably a majority of the progressives took the less subtle approach espoused by Davidson. Former governor William D. Hoard, for example, sided with him. Hoard wrote bitterly in 1911, "Never in all the fifty-three years of my experience in Wisconsin politics have I seen developed so malign and selfish a spirit as La Follette has infused his present day followers with."[32] An equally prominent progressive, Nils Haugen, the man La Follette enlisted as candidate for governor in 1894 when he launched his reform campaign, and later the guiding spirit behind vital tax reforms, came to share some of Hoard's views. In his later years he regarded La Follette as surly, contentious, and vituperative.[33] The man who ran in tandem with Lenroot in 1906 as candidate for lieutenant-governor, John Strange, later observed: "Bob La Follette's biggest weakness has been, and is, his hostility toward his opponents and critics." Many progressives supported Davidson on grounds of political custom, i.e., his right to the office that La Follette's resignation had given him.[35] In short, many of the progres-

[29] Keyes to John C. Spooner, January 10, 1906, in the Keyes Letterbooks.
[30] Henry Casson to Keyes, February 5, 1906, in the Keyes Papers.
[31] E. E. Sherwood to James O. Davidson, December 4, 1905; A. H. Strange to Davidson, December 21, 1905; Walter J. Benedict to Davidson, January 3, 1906; O. W. Arnquist to Davidson, May 9, 1906; A. H. Reid to Davidson, May 17, 1906, in the Davidson Papers.
[32] William D. Hoard to Lucien Hanks, February 1, 1911, in the Lucien Hanks Papers.
[33] Nils P. Haugen, *Political and Pioneer Reminiscences* (Madison, 1930), 113–114.
[34] Strange, "Autobiography," 26.
[35] *Milwaukee Free Press*, July 24, 1906; *Oshkosh Northwestern*, August 25, 1906; George Cooper to James O. Davidson, May 12, 1906, in the Davidson Papers; Plumb, *Badger Politics*, 138.

sives who followed Davidson in 1906 did so because they were not prepared to accept party, community, and even family discord as a permanent way of life.

Davidson's candidacy brought to light other phases of progressive ideology that did not accord with the thinking of La Follette and his "inner circle." State Senator James McGillivray, for example, took sharp exception to La Follette's idea that a lawyer was needed for the governorship. Foreshadowing an argument that became increasingly embarrassing to progressives in later years, McGillivray said that the state needed a businessman to effect economies, not a theorist.[36] More pithily, a correspondent to the *Milwaukee Free Press* wrote: "It is said the Governor of Wisconsin should be a lawyer. Buckle up your coat when they tell you a lawyer will make the best governor. Your pocketbook is in danger."[37]

Yet another serious limitation to progressivism was the incongruity between the democratic ideology to which the La Follette forces had committed themselves and the realities of practical politics. That they were committed there can be no doubt. La Follette and his allies had fought stoutly against "bosses" and "machines." From 1897, major attention had been focused on the primary, which La Follette finally put across over strong stalwart opposition. ". . . It is an essential part of the progressive belief that there shall be no boss system," La Follette later wrote. "No one to give and no one required to take orders. . . ."[38] The campaign against bossism had some obvious advantages, of course. Votes were won with the popular Jeffersonian theme; in party primaries, progressive Republicans might get help from "fair-minded" Democrats.[39] But there were some grave disadvantages too. If the progressives steered faithfully on their anti-boss, direct-primary course, they would be wrecked

[36] *Milwaukee Free Press,* July 25, 1906.
[37] Thomas J. Ford to the editor, *Milwaukee Free Press,* August 26, 1906.
[38] La Follette, *Autobiography,* 127.
[39] Interview with Craig Ralston, January 11, 1953. Mr. Ralston had been political reporter for the *Milwaukee Journal.*

on the rocks of disunity. Consensus on candidates and programs would not occur automatically. But if the progressives tried to achieve unity through caususes, conventions, or the dictation of La Follette, they might be beached by the strong currents of democracy. Aggravating the situation for progressives was the fact that the law recognized neither factions nor the means for achieving factional unity. Organizational efforts would have to be extralegal and therefore doubly difficult and suspect. In practice, the progressives vacillated between both unsatisfactory approaches, and were hurt by each.

Davidson took full advantage of this weakness in the 1906 campaign, charging that La Follette contradicted the spirit of democracy and of the primary and was engaging in the same kind of boss-rule that he had once campaigned against.[40] A host of prominent progressives broke with La Follette and backed Davidson on the basis of this argument. The well-respected attorney Robert M. Bashford attacked La Follette for bossism and violation of the spirit of the primary, and announced his support for Davidson.[41] Many lesser lights echoed the view. "I feel that I have just as good a right to dictate who should be Governor, as Bob La Follette or any other man," a Davidson supporter wrote. "And I find nearly every one feels about the same way. He taught us how to do up the bosses and we did it, and he need not now expect that he can act as our boss."[42]

Lenroot suffered from certain other disadvantages. His alleged prohibitionism was offensive to some Germans; a vote that he had cast in 1905 on a minor bill was taken to be anti-labor; and, as his campaign manager later acknowledged, he was rather "stiff" as a campaigner.[43]

Davidson's pre-emption of the democracy issue, combined

---

[40] *Milwaukee Sentinel*, August 2, August 25, 1906.
[41] *Ibid.*, August 29, 1906.
[42] J. D. Stuart to Davidson, November 14, 1905, in the Davidson Papers.
[43] Padraic Kennedy, "Lenroot, La Follette and the Campaign of 1906," *Wisconsin Magazine of History*, 42: 163–174 (Spring, 1959); Gross, "A Political Grab Bag."

with his other advantages, and Lenroot's various disadvantages, led to the first major defeat of the La Follette faction since it took power in 1901. Davidson trounced Lenroot by a vote of 109,593 to 61,178, carrying all but three of Wisconsin's seventy-one counties.[44] Connor won the nomination for lieutenant-governor at the same time.

The primary election results confirmed the importance of three major political limitations in the Wisconsin progressive movement. First, the progressives had depended strongly on men and groups whose loyalties were divided and who were powers in their own right, independent of La Follette. Wealth and nationality appeal chiefly underlay their independence as of 1906. Second, the progressives were deeply divided ideologically. The faction included a large number of Republicans who did not share La Follette's belief that constant factional warfare was desirable, but instead wanted peace in the party after certain reforms had been won. The relatively favorable economic circumstances of the state probably contributed to this ideological division. Finally, the progressives were seriously embarrassed by their commitment to an anti-boss ideology, which made it difficult and costly for them to achieve organization and unity. In the years that followed the election of Davidson as governor, these same factors continued to work against the La Follette men. For a time, many astute politicians foresaw an end to La Follette's senatorial career and to the progressive movement in the state in the election of 1910.

In 1907, the progressives' debt to Isaac Stephenson at last fell due. Senator Spooner resigned two years before the expiration of his term and moved to New York City, where he practiced law for the remainder of his life. A united progressive bloc in the legislature at last had the power to reward "Uncle Ike" for his services. The wisdom of placating the old gentleman was not lost on La Follette and his chief assistants in the legislature, especially assembly

---

[44] *Wisconsin Blue Book, 1907,* 389. The three he failed to carry were strongly Swedish in composition.

speaker Herman Ekern. Unfortunately for them, instead of patching up old wounds, the event served only to reopen them.

La Follette expressed a preference for Stephenson early in the legislative session, but he did not or could not prevent Lenroot and two other progressives from entering the contest. Seven weeks later, the legislature was still deadlocked and La Follette wired Ekern, "Stephenson must win. Fight hard."[45] Stephenson did win, but he emerged an embittered victor. The crusty old lumberman later recalled:[46]

> The La Follette influence . . . appeared to be very ineffective at this time, for it brought about no appreciable change in the situation. To what extent it was exercised others may surmise for themselves. Senator La Follette himself said that he could do no more than he had, because the men generally recognized as his followers or supporters were his friends. A sudden delicacy of feeling, I suppose, forbade any zealous attempt to influence the action or mold convictions of these men whom the outer world had erroneously regarded as parts of a well organized political machine.

The editor of Stephenson's newspaper, the organ of the progressives to that time, confided to Elisha Keyes that he was bitter over the treatment La Follette had accorded his employer. He saw little hope for progressive harmony in the future.[47]

Prior to the 1907 fight, it had been generally understood that if Stephenson were given the short term in the United States Senate, he would not seek re-election in 1908, leaving the field open to deserving and ambitious younger men. But Stephenson, piqued at the manner of his election and further antagonized by later snubs, came to feel himself absolved from any obligation to retire. Instead, in

---

[45] La Follette to Ekern, May 15, 1907, in the Ekern Papers.
[46] Stephenson, *Recollections*, 101.
[47] H. P. Myrick to Keyes, May 21, 1907, in the Keyes Papers.

June, 1908, the seventy-nine-year-old senator announced his candidacy for re-election.

By this time, Stephenson was hopelessly lost to the progressives. In any case, it would have been impossible for La Follette to deliver further progressive support to him. The legislature would make the final choice, but first would come preferential primaries. The problem for La Follette was to unify progressive votes behind a single, strong progressive in opposition to Stephenson. But how could such unity be secured without dictation? La Follette was so wary of the boss-rule charge and the danger of another major schism that he refused to commit himself publicly. The result was that two progressives, State Senator William Hatton, chief author of the railroad commission act, and Francis E. McGovern, the vigorous young Milwaukee district attorney, divided progressive support. Important La Follette men met in Madison early in the summer and decided to give Hatton quiet backing, but feared to go further.[48] Thousands awaited word from La Follette, but it never came. Nor was his law partner, A. T. Rogers, forthright on the subject, even in private conversation.[49] La Follette, Lenroot, Ekern, James Stone, and others of the "inner circle" distrusted McGovern but lacked the organization and the ideology to oppose him successfully. There was no legal mechanism by which they could formally choose Hatton as their candidate; even informal organization against McGovern would open the door once again to the boss-rule charge. With strong support in the Milwaukee area, McGovern was in a good position to duplicate Davidson's successful revolt, if provoked. Perhaps caution was the wiser course in 1908. But the result was that McGovern and Hatton divided over 78,000 votes and Stephenson won with 59,839.[50]

[48] R. Ainsworth to Ekern, July 23, 1906, in the Ekern Papers.
[49] W. J. McElroy to Ekern, July 25, 1908; W. W. Powell to W. H. Dick, July 31, 1908; W. H. Dick to Ekern, August 14, 1908, in the Ekern Papers.
[50] *Report of the Senate Members of the Joint Senatorial Primary Investigation Committee* (Madison, 1911), 6.

Such experiences led a number of sincere and thoughtful progressives to acknowledge the weaknesses of the primary system and to seek some modification of it. State Senator A. W. Sanborn and Herman Ekern favored a progressive organization within the primary system in 1908.[51] The plan received support from other progressives from time to time, but was long delayed. Opposition came from such men as McGovern, who had stronger support outside the ranks of the leadership than within it. Equally important, though, was the continuing fear of the boss-rule charge.[52] In 1909 La Follette himself gave some support to the idea of an organization, but as the 1910 election campaign developed he squashed plans for an organization or even a factional meeting that might resemble a convention.[53] Finally, after division had contributed to the defeat of the progressives in the gubernatorial contest of 1914, an organization was formed. Even then, however, it was unable to mobilize complete progressive support.[54]

The embarrassments associated with the direct democracy commitment, together with the other elements of weakness exhibited earlier, produced further difficulty for La Follette following the 1908 primaries. The La Follette men did not dare contest the popular Davidson's renomination in 1908. Even so, they sustained another defeat at his hands at the Republican platform convention that met

[51] Ekern to A. W. Sanborn, October 27, 1908, in the Ekern Papers; A. W. Sanborn to James Stone, October 8, 1909; Stone to Sanborn, October 13, 1909, in the Stone Papers.
[52] A. W. Sanborn to Ekern, October 24, 1908; Minutes of the Progressive Organization Meeting in Madison, June 3, 1909, in the Ekern Papers; James Stone to Edward F. and Julius T. Dithmar, June 4, 1909; Stone to Sanborn, October 13, 1909; Sanborn to Stone, October 16, 1909, in the Stone Papers; Theodore Kronshage to Tom Morris, May 21, 1910, in the La Follette Papers.
[53] John Hannan to James Stone, October 8, 1909; Charles Crownhart to A. W. Sanborn, May 26, 1910, in the La Follette Papers.
[54] By 1920, such prominent progressives as former State Senator A. W. Sanborn, Legislative Reference Librarian Charles R. McCarthy, and Professor John R. Commons felt that the primary system had done much harm. See Sanborn to McCarthy, August 5, 1920, and McCarthy to Sanborn, August 10, 1920, in the Charles R. McCarthy Papers.

in Madison shortly after the primaries. Senator La Follette had battled William Howard Taft for the Republican presidential nomination. At the national convention, Wisconsin had backed its own draft platform to the last. The La Follette forces now asked the state platform convention to endorse their proposals rather than the more conservative platform of the national party. In this they were opposed by the governor. Davidson had walked a tightrope up to this time, hoping to patch up relations with La Follette as much as possible without surrendering outright to him. The sharply drawn issue of the platform convention forced him to take a stand, however, and, showing surprising vigor and ability, spoke and worked forthrightly for the national Republican platform and against La Follette's.[55] Davidson and his forces won again. The convention rejected the second-choice primary and a tariff plank more liberal than the one in the national platform by votes of 70–51 and 79–43. Then it chose Stephenson's campaign manager chairman of the State Central Committee and adjourned.[56] "The La Follette crowd was cleaned out, horse, foot and dragoon, with Edmonds as Chairman and the platform just as the conservatives wanted it," Elisha Keyes exulted.[57]

In the general election, La Follette and Davidson again crossed swords. During the primaries young Herman Ekern met defeat in his bid for renomination to the assembly. Charging corruption, Ekern entered the general election as an independent, and La Follette came into rural and heavily Norwegian Trempealeau County to stump for his loyal and able protégé. Davidson, standing on the principle of party regularity and the sanctity of the primary, toured the smaller Trempealeau towns for Albert Twesme. In this highly publicized clash of titans, Davidson again won.[58]

These events served as appetizer for stalwarts, who

---

[55] Keyes to John Gaveney, September 23, 1908, in the Keyes Letterbooks.
[56] *Milwaukee Free Press,* September 24, 1908.
[57] Keyes to John Gaveney, September 23, 1908, in the Keyes Letterbooks.
[58] *Milwaukee Journal,* October 28, 30, 31, 1908.

sharpened their knives in anticipation of the main course that was to come, in the election of 1910. La Follette's first term in the United States Senate was coming to a close and the new legislature could deny him a second term. Stalwarts determined to see that the right legislative candidates were chosen in the Republican primaries and that La Follette was defeated in the preferential primary. To this task they brought not only zeal but also a campaign fund exceeding $114,000, contributed by such men as Philipp, Stephenson, Connor, and Pfister and presumably by certain corporations as well. President Taft, hopelessly at odds with La Follette, took a hand in their effort, too, and Vice President Sherman addressed the "Taft Republican" convention that kicked off the campaign in June, 1910.

The La Follette progressives greeted the 1910 election as a showdown like that of 1904. They were determined to arrest the erosion in their fortunes and turn back the stalwart threat; more than that, they were spurred to extraordinary effort by the possibility of a big victory that might begin a new era of power and a fresh wave of reform. Early in 1910, Charles Crownhart directed a successful effort to revise and enlarge poll lists in preparation for the all-out campaign that would follow.

The La Follette men had good grounds for optimism. As in 1904, it seemed possible to present the voters with a clear and simple choice between the champions of the people on the one hand and "the interests" on the other. Immensely advantageous to the progressives was the fact that La Follette was himself the main issue. Opinion about "Fighting Bob" had long since been formed, largely to his advantage. After 1906, the image of La Follette as champion of the people was strengthened as a result of national events. Lonely and ridiculed when he came to the Senate in 1906, La Follette's fortunes rose with the national tide of progressive sentiment in the years that followed. President Theodore Roosevelt, at once following and leading public opinion, lent his vast talent and prestige to popularizing the progressive cause. By 1909, La Follette was no longer politically isolated in the Senate, but stood forth as the recognized leader of the "Insurgent" Republicans. The fact that these Insurgents warred with a Republican President, William Howard Taft, did them no harm with the public, for it was they who championed the popular side of the major issues, notably the Payne-Aldrich tariff, the Ballinger-Pinchot conservation controversy, and the despotic rule of "Uncle Joe" Cannon in the House. By the middle of 1910, Taft's reputation was thoroughly tarnished.

Illness kept La Follette off the stump in 1910, but thirteen of his Insurgent colleagues, including Gifford Pinchot, Senators Borah, Bristow, Clapp, and Cummins, and Congressman George Norris, came into the state to deliver 108 addresses in his behalf. Living costs had risen steadily in the decade and were the subject of much public discussion. The Insurgent visitors and Wisconsin progressives capitalized on this, linking rising costs to recent legislation, especially the Payne-Aldrich tariff. Such issues were easily related, in turn, to Wisconsin's own earlier struggles against "the interests" and "bosses."

The popularity of progressivism in 1910, in Wisconsin and the nation, was incontestable. The stalwarts, to win in such circumstances, had to muddy the waters. This they tried to do, but with little success. They presented themselves as Taft Republicans and claimed that Taft, Roosevelt's chosen successor, was a "true," "sane" progressive. Taft's maladroit handling of the issues, his endorsement of the Payne-Aldrich tariff as the best tariff bill the Republican party had ever passed, and his friendly association with men like Nelson Aldrich made this strategy tenuous. For a time, there was some hope that Roosevelt would say something to bolster the Taft Republicans. The Rough Rider destroyed that prospect in August as he toured the West delivering a series of pro-Insurgent speeches, culminating in the Osawatomie speech in which he outlined the New Nationalism and even attacked the judiciary. The only other person who might have given the Wisconsin stalwarts effective camouflage was Governor Davidson. If he could be induced to head a stalwart slate, either for governor or senator, there would still be a chance to claim that true progressivism lay on the anti-La Follette side. But Davidson stayed entirely out of the contest for two reasons. First, W. D. Connor, unpopular with many and by 1910 at odds with Davidson, had secured a position of leadership for himself among the conservatives by winning and bringing national Republican support to bear. Davidson would not run under Connor's management. Second, the temperance question had become prominent, and the brewing and distilling interests, representing not only themselves but also the German press and electorate, would not tolerate Davidson. The stalwarts found themselves headed by Samuel A. Cook for senator and Edward T. Fairchild, a candidate of the Milwaukee stalwarts, for governor.

Nineteen ten proved a good year for progressives generally, whether Democratic or Insurgent Republican. Perhaps the most notable progressive victory came in Wisconsin. La Follette led the way, defeating Cook by 144,056 to 41,342. Francis E. McGovern, progressive candidate for governor, won the Republican nomination by 82,265 to 55,933 for Fairchild and 40,879 for an independent anti-liquor progressive. The legislative ticket reflected the progressive tide and was entirely safe for La Follette. The Democratic party was torn by dissension in 1910 and presented no challenge to the progressive Republicans, who swept into office in November.[59]

As of 1910, then, the La Follette forces seemed to have survived the breaks with Connor, Davidson, and Stephenson, and emerged stronger than ever. But appearances were deceiving: the victory of 1910 itself brought closer the day of another and still more dramatic schism within progressive ranks. The election of Francis E. McGovern as

[59] For elaboration on the preceding eight paragraphs, see Herbert F. Margulies, "Issues and Politics of Wisconsin Progressivism, 1906–1920" (doctoral dissertation, University of Wisconsin, 1955), 144–152; Adolph Gerd Korman, "Wisconsin's German-American Press during the Progressive Movement, 1909–1912" (master's thesis, University of Wisconsin, 1953), 38–40.

governor of Wisconsin elevated to power a man who was already on a collision course with Senator Robert M. La Follette. The crash came on June 18, 1912, before the assembled delegates to the Republican national convention in Chicago.

At that convention, Senator La Follette was a candidate for the presidential nomination. McGovern was head of the Wisconsin delegation. Early in the proceedings, McGovern's name was placed in nomination for temporary chairman of the convention by a fellow Milwaukeean. Delegates from other states seconded the nomination. Then occurred what was surely one of the more startling events in the party history. La Follette's campaign manager, Walter Houser, strode to the front of the platform and shouted to the delegates: "This nomination is not with Senator La Follette's consent. We make no deals with Roosevelt. We make no trades with Taft."[60]

Explanation for this extraordinary event must begin with the fact that by mid-June, 1912, La Follette had become hypersensitive to signs of betrayal. As the candidate of progressive Republicans since 1911 he had enjoyed the avowed support of prominent progressives throughout the nation and believed that he had the tacit support of Theodore Roosevelt. One by one, though, his supporters had grown cool. Then Roosevelt declared his own candidacy and progressive Republicans stampeded to him. La Follette, wounded by each overt defection and sly hint that he should withdraw, came to see himself as the victim of a well-planned betrayal, masterminded by Roosevelt.[61]

Evidences of covert collaboration between McGovern and Roosevelt in the spring of 1912 alerted La Follette to the possibility of betrayal within his own delegation. Unyielding in his determination, fired by his hatred of Roosevelt and all those who played him false in favor of the Rough Rider, La Follette reached the point where he was

[60] *Wisconsin State Journal,* June 20, 1912.
[61] La Follette, *Autobiography,* 204–321.

willing publicly to repudiate McGovern's candidacy for temporary chairman.

For Wisconsin progressives, the events at the national convention opened a huge rift which never completely closed and was to prove a significant source of weakness in later contests in the state. During the factional battles of 1914 and 1916, McGovern's course at the 1912 Republican convention was the chief subject of progressive dispute. The dramatic break was constantly revivified in the public imagination. For this reason, and because the hostility between McGovern and La Follette and their followers first came to public attention as a result of the 1912 convention events, it was generally assumed that this was the sole cause of the rift. Neither La Follette nor his biographers dispelled the impression.[62] Nevertheless, it was not so.

Had the La Follette-McGovern schism resulted only from differences between the two men over Roosevelt and 1912 presidential strategy, it might have been settled without too much damage after tempers had cooled. In fact, the convention events were in large part the result of a deep-rooted and long-standing division. La Follette intimated as much when he wrote on June 18, the day of Houser's dramatic repudiation of McGovern's candidacy, "I have been suspicious of that bunch for a long time."[63] La Follette's suspicion, which was not without cause, contributed to the public break with McGovern at the convention, as did McGovern's years of political independence.

Mutual fear and hostility between the La Follette and McGovern men fed on itself over a period of years. Each side regarded its own actions as defensive, but to the wary "ally" they seemed aggressive, selfish, and deceitful. As McGovern gradually grew in political strength, the day of the inevitable showdown came closer. The 1912 presidential race provided a peculiarly apt cauldron for the blending of fear, suspicion, and misunderstanding. The break

[62] *Idem.*, Belle and Fola La Follette, *La Follette.*
[63] La Follette to Walter L. Owen, June 18, 1912, in the Ekern Papers.

in 1912 came as a surprise, but few informed Wisconsin politicians would have been startled by a division in progressive ranks in 1914, even had the events of 1912 never occurred. McGovern headed a clearly defined group within the progressive faction. This group was not formed on the basis of agreement with McGovern's position at Chicago; it was in existence long before then. In all likelihood, even if La Follette had never sought the presidential nomination, he and McGovern would have clashed in 1914 in a contest for the leadership of the progressives in the state.

Francis E. McGovern began as a farm boy of Irish parentage. At the University of Wisconsin he distinguished himself as a debater, orator, and scholar. Following his graduation in 1890 he taught school and studied law. Admitted to the bar in 1897, he had become assistant district attorney of Milwaukee County by 1900. In this capacity, he won a statewide reputation by prosecuting corrupt aldermen and city officials. The young reformer was elected district attorney in 1904. McGovern was slight of stature and by 1910, when he was elected governor at the age of forty-four, his dark hair was thinning at the top. But his large, piercing eyes gave some suggestion of the strong, vigorous, stern, and very able man that he was.[64]

McGovern was leader of a powerful Milwaukee Republican reform faction that had been growing since the mid-nineties. The reformers were already well organized as the Republican Club of Milwaukee County and engaged in their local contest when they became unofficially united with La Follette's statewide progressive movement.[65] As the local battle continued into the twentieth century, they retained their identity. Unity was a necessity in the battle for control of the Republican organization and in the party struggle against Mayor Rose and his Democrats, as well as

[64] *Milwaukee Journal,* May 17, 1946; interviews with Craig Ralston, January 20, 1953; with Charles Rosa, January 15, 1954; and with O. A. Stolen, January 4, 1955.
[65] Barton, *La Follette's Winning of Wisconsin,* 116–132.

against the rising Social Democratic party. Control of the district attorneyship from 1905 through 1909 provided a patronage base.

Similar local groupings of reformers existed throughout the state, but none had the political power of the Milwaukeeans. In 1900 the city of Milwaukee had 285,315 inhabitants, and the county population was 330,017 in a total state population of 2,069,042.[66] Milwaukee was the only large city in the state, and it continued to grow at a rapid rate. While the state population rose by 12.8 per cent to a total of 2,333,860 in the decade 1900 to 1910, the city's population increased by 31 per cent, to 373,857, and the county, which included industrial as well as suburban developments, rose to a population of 433,187.[67] When the Milwaukeeans, headed by McGovern and his astute law partner Theodore Kronshage, joined forces with La Follette, they did so as equals, not as subordinates. Progressives from other parts of the state were not in the same position. Only the Milwaukeeans were strong enough to differ with the statewide leadership; only they might pose a threat to that leadership. As a result, a spirit of guarded suspicion and hostility gradually developed between the Milwaukeeans and those progressive leaders who identified themselves most closely with La Follette. Each side needed the other, so antagonisms were kept in check. But to each, the power of the uncertain ally almost invariably assumed the aspect of a threat. This dangerous situation was clearly discernible by 1905. The events of that year and those that followed not only evidenced the state of things, but contributed to the animosities that finally resulted in open schism.

Many progressives throughout the state were afraid, in 1905, that La Follette's attempt to sidetrack James O. Davidson and secure the gubernatorial nomination for Irvine Lenroot would divide progressive strength in local con-

---

[66] *Wisconsin Blue Book, 1901*, 492; *Thirteenth Census of the United States, 1910*, 3: 1096.
[67] *Thirteenth Census, 1910*, 3: 1075, 1048, 1096, 1090.

tests. But only the Milwaukeeans felt free to show their fears openly. They feared that Davidson men, resentful of La Follette's interference, would oppose McGovern in his bid for renomination as district attorney. Lenroot, in turn, regarded the "McGovern crowd" with apprehension as the primary contest approached. He considered the Milwaukee reformers selfish, sensitive, and uncertain allies. Lenroot indicated his attitude when writing to La Follette early in January that "if the McGovern crowd try to make any trouble he would find that he isn't as big a man as he thinks when it gets down to a question between you and him." Lenroot was confident of McGovern's support only because McGovern could not afford to desert La Follette's camp at that time. Nevertheless, Lenroot wanted the help of John Hannan, La Follette's secretary, in establishing personal contact with key men in the city.[68] As the campaign developed, McGovern told Lenroot frankly that he planned to stay entirely out of the statewide fight. Under the circumstances, Lenroot was reluctant to be drawn into the county contest, and in mid-June refused to send a telegram to Milwaukee backing McGovern, though he did propose to help him later in his Milwaukee speeches.[69] For his part, McGovern remained aloof throughout and, according to Lenroot's manager, the Milwaukeean Edwin J. Gross, "what little support he gave was given to the opposition." "Old Bob never forgot that conduct," Gross later recalled.[70]

Milwaukee was not without reformers who gave their first loyalty to La Follette. Two young lawyers, Gross and William J. McElroy, headed a small La Follette contingent. But these men, though co-workers with McGovern and his friends in the local reform movement, were isolated dissidents. Like the La Follette leaders throughout the state, the Milwaukee La Follette men treated with McGovern as with a mercenary, not as a trusted friend. But, like the other

[68] Lenroot to La Follette, January 5, 1906, in the La Follette Papers.
[69] Lenroot to Edwin J. Gross, June 16, 1906, in the Gross Papers.
[70] Edwin J. Gross, "A Political Grab Bag."

La Follette leaders, they could not ignore the usefulness of the McGovern men and the inadvisability of antagonizing them. As McGovern launched an independent candidacy for district attorney in the 1906 general election, McElroy urged La Follette to come into Milwaukee and speak for him. "You know my opinion of their treatment of you," McElroy began, "but I presume it won't improve, nevertheless it seems to me that [it] is in the line of duty for us to follow and I pledged them my support some time ago."[71] Reluctant to see the stalwarts sweep the field, La Follette came to Milwaukee to make a number of speeches for McGovern.

Though McGovern won through the help of La Follette, feeling between the two wings of the progressive Republican faction did not improve. Herman Ekern, Charles Crownhart, and others close to La Follette began to engineer a presidential boom for the senator early in 1907. McElroy and Gross were enthusiastic about the idea. But they found that the men in the district attorney's office, while of course not opposing the idea in principle, were in favor of a "gum-shoe" campaign rather than an open canvass.[72] Late in July, 1907, Gross reported that the McGovern group was "very quiet and clammy."[73]

During the spring of 1908, Ekern appraised the Milwaukee situation from the pro-La Follette point of view in a frank letter to his close friend Lenroot. He wanted Lenroot to help persuade Gross to withdraw from the race for district attorney in favor of one of McGovern's

---

[71] McElroy to La Follette, October 17, 1906, in the La Follette Papers. For the statewide progressive cause, the Milwaukee district attorney contest was second in importance only to the gubernatorial battle, at least in the opinion of the veteran stalwart Elisha Keyes. Keyes to M. C. Douglas, August 24, 1906, in the Keyes Letterbooks. Once Lenroot had been defeated in the primary by Davidson, La Follette was in no position to press the contest in the general election, for Davidson clearly retained an unsullied reputation as a progressive. In Milwaukee, however, the chances of an independent candidacy were excellent, for the incumbent's record was highly vulnerable.
[72] McElroy to Ekern, July 1, 1907, in the Ekern Papers.
[73] Gross to Ekern, July 20, 1907, in the Ekern Papers.

lieutenants, Jim Backus. "Backus had been the only one connected with the district attorney's office who has shown a disposition to do active, unselfish work for our cause," Ekern wrote. "Through his affiliation, he is in very close touch with a very desirable element with whom we must reckon. I think it would benefit us in the future to put him under obligations in this matter as well as to have him in the district attorney's office."[74] To this suggestion Lenroot promptly replied, "So far as I am concerned, I feel very kindly toward Backus, but if McGovern and Cochems are going to be his spokesmen, and advisers, I do not feel that I have the slightest interest in it either from a personal or a public standpoint."[75] La Follette's two trusted lieutenants, each a speaker of the assembly in the two previous sessions, disagreed on specific strategy. But they were united in fearing that trouble would be forthcoming from their Milwaukee "friends."

The wariness, suspicion, and animosity of each ally towards the other increased during the 1908 senatorial contest. When the Senate vacancy opened in 1907, many progressives had balked at La Follette's choice of Stephenson and had given their support to men whom they considered better qualified. Of Stephenson's progressive rivals, only one remained in the race to the end. Irvine Lenroot and Representative Henry A. Cooper both bowed out in the interests of harmony. But William Hatton earned the respect of independent-minded men by contesting Stephenson to the last. Immediately after the election of Stephenson, Hatton announced himself as a candidate for the 1908 senatorial nomination.

William Hatton was not of the progressive "inner circle." Better known as a cautious and successful lumberman than as a politician, he had little speaking ability or personal magnetism. But the quiet, studious little New Londoner had won general respect as the chief framer of the

[74] Ekern to Irvine Lenroot, April 28, 1908, in the La Follette Papers.
[75] Lenroot to Ekern, May 1, 1908, in the La Follette Papers.

1905 Railroad Commission Act, and the events of 1907 had put him in a strong position to secure progressive support for a campaign in 1908 regardless of Stephenson's actions. When Stephenson decided to run for re-election, the challenge to progressive control was great and the need for unity extreme. Hatton would probably have won the primary race against Stephenson and Samuel A. Cook, the stalwart's choice, but for the candidacy of another progressive. When Francis E. McGovern announced himself, the division of progressive votes was ensured.

In marked contrast to Hatton, McGovern displayed considerable speaking ability and a forceful personality. La Follette-Hatton men found that McGovern attracted considerable support among the younger, more enthusiastic, and pronouncedly radical elements in the state.[76] A powerful and dangerous figure in progressive politics prior to the campaign, McGovern took on more ominous proportions as the result of his statewide canvass.

Despite the preference of La Follette's lieutenants for Hatton, their side dared not openly endorse him. In the final reckoning, while Stephenson won with 59,839 votes, McGovern outdistanced Hatton by 42,631 to 35,621.[77]

The 1908 primary not only demonstrated once again the hostility between McGovern and La Follette elements, but also intensified the ill-feeling, by confirming the La Follette men in their conviction that McGovern always put his own advancement ahead of the progressive cause. But distrust continued to mingle generously with fear, for each side was still forced to respect the power of the other.

James A. Stone of Reedsburg was one of La Follette's most devoted and trusted lieutenants. Stone's reaction to the primary results was amazement and apprehension at the strength demonstrated by McGovern. He feared that McGovern would join Governor Davidson, William D. Con-

---

[76] F. M. Jackson to Ekern, July 18, 1908; Ekern to La Follette, July 24, 1908, in the Ekern Papers.
[77] *Report of the Primary Investigation Committee*, 7.

Factionalism, 1906-1916

nor, and Stephenson as the head of a faction that would challenge La Follette for progressive leadership in 1910.[78] When the 1909 legislature authorized an investigation of the recent senatorial primary, in which Stephenson had spent over a hundred thousand dollars, Stone gave his political correspondence to the joint investigating committee. He explained to La Follette that "I was particularly anxious that the McGovern correspondence with me should be in that record, where Frank McGovern would have in the most public manner declared himself committed to you and your policies in future campaigns...."[79]

The shadow of future schism moved closer in 1909 and 1910. McGovern made it clear that he wanted to run for governor. Most La Follette leaders favored State Senator Tom Morris of La Crosse. Hoping to avoid a contest between the two, Stone and A. W. Sanborn of Ashland attempted to promote a progressive conference or poll to choose between McGovern and Morris. Morris agreed to the idea, but McGovern balked and refused to delay announcing his candidacy.[80] The decision only increased the La Follette men's resentment against McGovern for what seemed to be extreme selfishness and obstinacy.[81] Once again, however, they had to swallow their bitter dose in silence. La Follette was up for renomination and re-election; all else had to be subordinated. Campaign manager Charles Crownhart cautioned Lenroot that La Follette would need McGovern's help in Milwaukee, and told Sanborn that conciliation was the order of the day.[82] According to Theodore Kronshage, La Follette himself intervened to per-

---

[78] James A. Stone to La Follette, September 7, 1908, in the Stone Papers.
[79] Stone to La Follette, April 9, 1909, in the Stone Papers.
[80] Stone to McGovern, January 15, 1910; McGovern to Stone, January 18, 1910; Stone to Morris, January 22, 1910, in the Stone Papers.
[81] George Beedle to Ekern, July 17, July 22, 1909, in the Ekern Papers; Tom Morris to Stone, January 21, 1910; Stone to Morris, January 22, 1910; A. W. Sanborn to Stone, January 29, 1910, in the Stone Papers.
[82] Charles Crownhart to Lenroot, May 27, 1910; Crownhart to Sanborn, May 26, 1910, in the La Follette Papers.

suade Morris to bow out in favor of McGovern.[83] Most of his followers fell in line behind McGovern. Only the outspoken Racine progressive, Walter Goodland, who was supporting his neighbor William M. Lewis for governor, felt free to express feelings and opinions that others held in check. He editorialized in his paper: "Those who are close to La Follette know that he does not have the highest opinion of the qualities of Mr. McGovern. He believes, as thousands of other Wisconsin voters believe, that McGovern is self-centered, selfish and cares nothing for anything or anybody that stands in the way of his own personal ambitions. . . ."[84]

As La Follette returned to the Senate and McGovern took office in Madison, conservative political seers predicted a showdown between the two in 1914. Colonel William J. Anderson, a journalist who had served as private secretary to the conservative governors Upham and Scofield in the nineties, reported to President William Howard Taft that he thought it "quite unlikely that La Follette and the new governor will work together harmoniously for a year. McGovern is nearly as vain and ambitious as La Follette, though he is far from being as selfish; and I think they are sure to clash when a successor to Sen. Stephenson is to be chosen, if not before. La Follette will champion Lenroot's cause, and McGovern thinks he is entitled to succeed Stephenson. . . ."[85] Elisha Keyes, the old stalwart, agreed that a clash between the La Follette-Lenroot forces and the McGovern men was inevitable.[86]

There was substance to conservative hopes; it was well known that McGovern was ambitious for the senatorial post and that La Follette wanted his protégé Lenroot as his junior senator. Indeed, Tom Morris had secured progressive support against McGovern in 1909 on the basis of the

[83] *Milwaukee Sentinel,* August 27, 1914.
[84] *Racine Times,* August 23, 1910.
[85] William J. Anderson to William Howard Taft, January 27, 1911, in the William J. Anderson Papers.
[86] Keyes to David C. Owen, November 19, 1910, in the Keyes Letterbooks.

fear that once elected, the governor would set his sail for the 1914 senatorial nomination.[87]

The new governor was not only aggressive and ambitious, but also very able, and in the prime of life. He saw his personal advancement as coincidental with the best interests of the progressive movement. Re-election as governor was no problem for him, but after that, what? The hostile La Follette men blocked his way to a national career. Though he was the leader of a powerful faction, McGovern knew he was not yet a match for La Follette in an open contest. He therefore set about strengthening his position in the Republican party, and in so doing augmented the suspicions and fears of the already hostile La Follette leaders.

Even before his election as governor, McGovern had used his position on the ticket to fullest advantage. He not only assured himself of a friendly chairman of the Republican state central committee (recognized prerogative of the candidate for governor), but also saw to it that all of the officers, members of the executive committee, and top employees were McGovern men, with but one exception. Once in office, he wielded the axe of patronage to the fullest advantage. O. G. Munson, astute secretary of the outgoing governor, Davidson, observed late in January, 1911: ". . . It is evident that the new executive has the building of a good vigorous machine in mind."[88] A La Crosse politician reported from Madison that "Governor McGovern, as we anticipated months ago when he sidetracked Tom Morris, is building up a little machine all his own. All the appointments he has made thus far have been made without consulting any of the leaders in this part of the state, and a fine new insurrection is well under way. . . . You may look for an explosion most any time and a brand new alignment."[89]

---
[87] Morris to Stone, January 21, 1910, in the Stone Papers. Ekern voiced this fear in conversation with the legislative reference library head, Charles McCarthy. McCarthy to George E. Scott, August 4, 1914, in the McCarthy Papers.
[88] O. G. Munson to Davidson, January 21, 1911, in the Davidson Papers.
[89] C. A. Worth to John J. Esch, January 23, 1911, in the Esch Papers.

In ignoring the western part of the state, McGovern was slighting the area of La Follette's greatest strength. Any patronage in that section would only strengthen confirmed La Follette men like Morris, Ekern, Houser, and other leaders who dominated the Mississippi River counties. McGovern prefered to concentrate on the populous eastern area, where he already had considerable strength. Late in 1911, McGovern and his secretary Harry Curran Wilbur began to give serious attention to candidacies for the next legislature.[90] Wilbur continued his intense efforts in that direction early in 1912. McGovern and Wilbur were not simply concerned to secure a legislature favorable to progressive legislation; they were interested in advancing men who would back McGovern. Early in February, 1912, Wilbur wrote Edward E. Browne, soon to become congressman from the Eighth District, "Rumor has reached me that Spencer Marsh may seek reelection. While Marsh is a Progressive, for some reason he is unfriendly. . . ." Wilbur intimated that Browne would receive McGovern's support if he would block Marsh's path and put control of the district into friendlier hands.[91] At the same time, Wilbur worked with McGovern's ambitious young spokesman in the assembly, Thomas J. Mahon, to prepare a list that would include the name of at least one man in every precinct in the state. But he shied away from correspondence on the subject, indicating mysteriously that he preferred talking to letter writing, "in more ways than one."[92] Clearly, Wilbur was seeking to build an organization in McGovern's personal interest. So far as the La Follette progressives were concerned, no new lists were necessary. They had just completed the most thorough political canvass in their history, and possessed voluminous and up-to-date lists.[93]

[90] McGovern to Tom [Mahon], December 20, 1911; McGovern to J. C. Gilbertson, December 29, 1911; McGovern to R. E. Smith, December 29, 1911, in the Francis E. McGovern Papers, Wilbur Correspondence.

[91] Harry Curran Wilbur to E. E. Browne, February 5, 1912, in the McGovern Papers, Wilbur Correspondence.

[92] Wilbur to Mahon, February 15, 1912, in the McGovern Papers, Wilbur Correspondence.

[93] See the La Follette Papers and the Ekern Papers for 1910.

McGovern and Wilbur were also interested in the make-up of the next Republican platform convention, which would select the party officers. As the Republican legislative candidates, with the nominees on the state ticket, were the delegates to the platform convention, it was in McGovern's interest to encourage the candidacies of his friends for the assembly and senate. In Milwaukee, the Social Democrats had gained control in 1910, and elements of the Republicans and Democrats then moved to unite on a single ticket to oppose the socialists in 1912. But McGovern and Wilbur did all in their power to block the fusion effort. They feared that it would weaken the Republican party in Milwaukee, where McGovern had his greatest strength, and prevent the selection of a solid pro-McGovern legislative ticket.[94]

McGovern and his friends gave strong support to La Follette's pre-convention presidential campaign.[95] But McGovern did not share the optimism of La Follette partisans.[96] Even more important, he disagreed with them in his assessment of Theodore Roosevelt. While La Follette men saw the Rough Rider as a "flash-progressive," and hence more dangerous to the movement than the conservative President Taft, McGovern felt friendly to Roosevelt, shared many of his New Nationalism views, and regarded him as much preferable to Taft as a presidential candidate. From his point of view, it was entirely logical that Roosevelt and La Follette delegates should unite to control the choice for temporary chairman of the convention.[97] Ambitious for the opportunity to address the convention,[98] McGovern was willing to see the Roosevelt and La Follette delegates unite behind him.

[94] Wilbur to Clem Host, April 8, 25, 1912, in the McGovern Papers, Wilbur Correspondence.
[95] Wilbur to Host, March 23, 1912, in the McGovern Papers, Wilbur Correspondence; letterhead on Mahon to Ekern, November 17, 1911, in the Ekern Papers.
[96] McGovern to Ocha Potter, March 9, 1912, in the McGovern Papers.
[97] McGovern to William Mauthe, June 5, 1912, in the McGovern Papers.
[98] McGovern to J. J. and P. H. McGovern, June 12, 1912, in the McGovern Papers.

Had McGovern been a trusted lieutenant of La Follette's in the past, the senator would certainly have dealt frankly with him well before the convention and thus prevented the schism that occurred. But La Follette and his friends, distrustful and fearful, were not disposed to treat him as one of their own. Thus, when the steering committee of the Wisconsin delegation met in Theodore Kronshage's office just a week before the convention, no voice was raised against McGovern's candidacy for temporary chairman; the delegates agreed unanimously to support him if the La Follette delegates from North Dakota would agree.[99] Instead of dealing openly with the governor, La Follette's representatives attempted to block his candidacy by undercover methods. According to McGovern, shortly after the steering committee meeting, Alfred T. Rogers and James A. Stone wired North Dakota's La Follette leader asking him to reject the McGovern candidacy. But the telegram arrived too late.[100] Only after this strategem failed did La Follette bring direct pressure on McGovern to withdraw.[101]

McGovern was convinced of the honesty and wisdom of his course, had his heart set on addressing the convention, was committed to the Roosevelt men, and was temperamentally averse to a public retreat. Rogers, Andrew Dahl, and Houser condemned his candidacy in the press; La Follette told delegates by telephone from Washington that he opposed anything that might be interpreted as signifying an agreement with Roosevelt; and Houser and Hannan personally secured the delegates' rejection of McGovern's candidacy by a vote of fifteen to eleven on the morning of

---

[99] Minutes of the secretary of the Wisconsin delegation to the Republican national convention of 1912, in the Stone Papers.

[100] Statement by Francis E. McGovern in the *Milwaukee Free Press*, August 18, 1914. McGovern wrote that he was told of the telegram by North Dakota delegates at the convention. As the North Dakota delegates supported McGovern on the floor of the convention, against the wishes of La Follette, and did not deny McGovern's published statement, McGovern's account appears to be true.

[101] *La Follette's Magazine*, 4: 44 (October 26, 1912); Belle and Fola La Follette, *La Follette*, 1: 436.

the convention. Yet McGovern and Henry Cochems remained adamantly determined not to back down.[102]

During the weeks that followed the dramatic Chicago convention, La Follette's men charged treachery. Rogers provided the keynote when he told the *Milwaukee Journal* that McGovern had sold out to Roosevelt for the promise of the vice-presidential nomination.[103] McGovern stoutly defended himself. In elaborate statements to the press, he argued that unity with Roosevelt on the temporary chairmanship would have prevented Taft's conservative forces from seating their disputed delegates and gaining control of the convention, that his candidacy had been in the interests of La Follette.[104] Eventually, faced by strong conservative opposition at home, La Follette and McGovern put a temporary end to their wrangling. The governor won renomination without opposition and received the support of La Follette during the hotly contested campaign. But La Follette made clear that McGovern would be dealt with at the proper time.

The warfare among progressives resumed in full fury at the outset of the 1913 legislative session, when McGovern accused insurance commissioner Herman Ekern of illegal political activity and tried to oust him from office. A hostile factional atmosphere continued through the session, and limited its productivity. In 1914 the division among progressives wrought its inevitable results in the primaries and general elections. When La Follette men failed to defeat McGovern in his bid for a senatorial nomination, they threw their support to a Democrat, Paul Husting, and helped secure his election. Most calamitous, the rejuvenated stalwarts (led now by Emanuel Philipp) capitalized fully on progressive division and won the party's nomination for governor for Philipp. In November, Philipp was elected governor.

[102] *Milwaukee Journal,* June 13, 1912; minutes of the secretary of the Wisconsin delegation . . . 1912, in the Stone Papers.
[103] *Milwaukee Journal,* June 19, 1912.
[104] *Milwaukee Free Press,* June 25, 27, 1912.

The failure of the progressives to unite on a single candidate for governor was due in large part to the Mc-Govern-La Follette split, and the consequent impossibility of finding a candidate who was acceptable to both sides. State Senator A. W. Sanborn was acceptable to McGovern, but La Follette apparently vetoed the idea. William Hatton, who did run, was also closely associated with the McGovern administration. Though he secured the support of many strong La Follette men, La Follette and the "inner circle" put forward the candidacy of a man who had no taint of McGovernism about him, Andrew Dahl. And though the conservative campaign, based on the questions of high taxes and "extravagance," was more formidable than anything that had been seen in two decades, the La Follette and McGovern forces directed much of their fire against one another. La Follette himself exploded the political bombshell of the primary campaign with a long editorial that in effect agreed with conservative charges and denounced the extravagance of the McGovern administration.[105]

Two years later the rival progressives returned to their factional quarrel with unabated vigor. Walter Goodland, a La Follette man, engineered a conference designed to nominate a single slate of primary candidates. But McGovern denounced the idea and persisted in his gubernatorial ambitions. Goodland's convention, dominated by La Follette partisans, chose William Hatton as candidate for the nomination; but McGovern, though friendly to Hatton, stayed in the race to the last. Emanuel Philipp had little difficulty securing renomination against his divided opposition. He was duly re-elected that year and again in 1918. Meanwhile, McGovern, no longer in public office, saw his hold on Milwaukee Republicanism gradually weaken. With it went much of his importance in state politics. But the damage had already been done.[106]

The rebellion of McGovern was like those of Connor,

---

[105] *La Follette's Magazine*, 6:30 (July 25, 1914).
[106] See Chapter 5 *infra* for further detail on the 1916 events.

Stephenson, and Davidson in many ways. All were ambitious. More important, each had a base of independent power and felt able to treat with La Follette as with an ally or, if need be, an enemy. For Connor and Stephenson, money and business connections were the source of independence. Davidson relied on an ethnic group as the nucleus of his power. McGovern was the prime beneficiary of a third source of power—regional support.

Virtually all of the major politicians of Wisconsin relied to some extent on local or regional backing in support of their statewide ambition. But considering the influence La Follette had gained among leaders and voters in the state, most politicians dependent mainly on regional support could not stand up against him. Men like Walter Houser and Herman Ekern, from rural Buffalo and Trempealeau counties, could exert statewide influence only as La Follette's lieutenants. Milwaukee County was the one locale populous enough to provide a sufficient base for a factional leader within the progressive coalition.

Localism and regionalism continued to qualify ideological commitments, as in pre-La Follette days and despite the impact of La Folletteism. This fact constituted a significant limitation for the progressive movement in the state. Within the context of that limitation, the presence of but one major commercial and industrial city in a largely rural state was especially dangerous.

IV

Accomplishment and Disaster, 1911-1914

THE LONG PERIOD of progressive domination in Wisconsin, marked by the personality of Robert M. La Follette and an imposing array of reform legislation, was brought to an abrupt halt in 1914. The election as governor of Emanuel Philipp, the refrigerator-car magnate and veteran anti-progressive leader, signaled the end of the era. Philipp was described by La Follette as late as 1913 as "an out and out corporation man."[1] Along with Philipp, an anti-progressive majority assumed control of the legislature. At the same time, the electorate decisively rejected ten constitutional amendments supported by the progressives, including proposals for initiative, referendum, and a modified recall. The break between La Follette and McGovern was a major factor behind the conservative victory. It was not the only factor, however.[2]

It was quite true that Philipp's nomination resulted in part from division among progressive Republicans. But this

---

[1] La Follette, *Autobiography*, 229.

[2] Fola La Follette writes: "The split in the progressive Republican forces had enabled the Stalwarts to nominate Philipp for governor, although the official returns showed that out of 125,000 Republican votes he had received only a third. All the other state officers were renominated over their reactionary opponents. . . ." Robert Maxwell joins in placing Philipp's victory solely in the context of progressive division. Belle and Fola La Follette, *La Follette*, 1: 506; Maxwell, *Rise of the Progressives*, 192–193. Of course, Miss La Follette's attention is centered on the national events with which Senator La Follette was preoccupied. Her statements bearing on the Wisconsin situation are therefore of a relatively casual, background nature.

division did not explain the results in the Democratic party primary, in which the rabidly anti-progressive John C. Karel won the nomination for governor against the more liberal John A. Aylward. Nor could progressive Republican division explain the repudiation of the constitutional amendments, or the election of an anti-progressive legislature, or the very poor showing of John J. Blaine, La Follette's independent candidate for governor in the general elections.

Nor was it true that a majority of the votes cast in the Republican gubernatorial primary were somehow "progressive," as some have contended. One of the five candidates who divided the "progressive" vote, Henry Roethe, had been a progressive of the most dubious sort. A small-town editor who polled over twelve thousand votes, Roethe was the first of the candidates, including Philipp himself, to raise the conservative cry against taxes, extravagance, and commissions. In June of 1914 he addressed the same anti-tax, anti-spending convention that nominated Philipp. A state senator who served with him on the finance committee considered Roethe "a dyed in the wool Stalwart," and the Wisconsin Society of Equity, a progressive farmers organization, omitted his name from a list of acceptable candidates.[3]

Andrew Dahl, William Hatton, Merlin Hull, and Bruce Utman had stronger claims than Roethe to the progressive label. With the exception of the little-known Utman, however, these claims were based more on their records prior to 1914 than on their statements during the 1914 primary campaign, when all of them acquiesced in many of the conservative complaints raised most persuasively by Philipp. Distinctively progressive issues were available, but of all the candidates only Utman, a political outsider who polled the fewest votes, campaigned largely on these issues. The campaign appeals of the so-called progressives was, in fact,

---

[3] *Wisconsin State Journal*, June 23, 1914; Henry Huber to H. E. G. Keup, September 24, 1915, in the Henry Huber Letterbooks; *Janesville Gazette*, August 22, 1914.

the most striking testimony to the strength of conservative sentiment in 1914. The election of Philipp was not merely the result of progressive Republican division. On the contrary, it reflected the hard truth that a majority of Wisconsin voters had become disillusioned with progressivism.

Several other noteworthy and interrelated new factors were involved in the conservative victory of 1914. Increasingly after 1910, and most disastrously in 1914, the La Follette element was hurt by the defection of a group on whom they had come to rely—the "fair minded" Democrats. With that defection, the makeup of the Republican party became more evident. And lo, that party's family portrait revealed many more stalwart faces than had theretofore been noticed. The true state of things was described by the astute journalist-politician William J. Anderson in a letter to the secretary of President Taft:[4]

> ... Were it not for the utter demoralization of the democratic organization in this state during the past eight years, La Follette would have at the most but a bare majority of his party with him. He has succeeded through his primary election measure in seducing the democrats away from their own primary. To illustrate:
>
> In the state primary for the nomination of officers last Sept. the vote of the various republican candidates aggregated 190,967 while the democratic total vote was only 48,280. But in the regular election two months later, when in the nature of the case the vote should have been heavier, the total republican vote was 161,619 while the democrats cast 110,442 votes.

Anderson went on to note that the Democrats were repairing their organization. He estimated that among Republicans the anti-La Follette force constituted 40 per cent.

La Follette had never commanded the votes of all the progressive Democrats, either in conventions, primaries,

---

[4] William J. Anderson to Charles D. Hilles, October 28, 1911, enclosed in Anderson to John Whitehead, October 28, 1911, in the Whitehead Papers.

or general elections. Even during obviously Republican years, some progressive Democrats stayed within their own party. Thus, the progressive Democrat John A. Aylward had twice run for governor though chances for victory were almost nil in order to win control of his party from what he called "the old railroad crowd."[5] Presumably, many who voted for him in the primaries and general elections were progressive Democrats who shared his goal. Nevertheless, so long as Republican control on the state and national level was secure, La Follette had been able to count on the votes of many "fair-minded" Democrats—at least in the primaries.

But in 1910 Democratic fortunes revived dramatically in the nation. The party won control of the House of Representatives, made substantial gains in the Senate, and captured a number of key statehouses. With the Democratic gubernatorial victories of 1910, the party had obtained "able leaders of national stature" to replace its traditional loser, William Jennings Bryan.[6] The result, largely at the expense of standpat Republicans, was clearly an expression of progressive sentiment. As the break between Taft and Roosevelt, and between the standpat and progressive Republicans, became even more severe in 1911 and 1912, Democratic prospects for winning the presidency grew brighter. Wisconsin's Democratic leaders of every ideological hue viewed the prospects for state office and federal patronage optimistically, and gave full attention to control of the party and its nominations on the state level. Progressive Democrats, delighted that their party might soon serve as the chief vehicle for progressivism, were in turn alarmed at the strength of the conservatives in their own ranks. Democratic factional activity was warm early in 1912, and most of the progressives, led by Aylward, supported a pro-

[5] John A. Aylward to Senator Paul Husting, March 22, 1915, in the Michael Olbrich Papers.
[6] George E. Mowry, *Theodore Roosevelt and the Progressive Movement* (Madison, 1946), 156.

Wilson slate against a pro-Clark group led by Representative Charles H. Weisse of Sheboygan.[7] Wilson's victory in the presidential election of 1912 meant that the progressive Democrats of Wisconsin could have progressivism and office too. For the ensuing eight years at least, they were lost to La Follette.

Just as the defection of progressive Democrats from La Follette to their own party was becoming evident, the old stalwart Republican element, augmented by many Davidson and Stephenson followers, regrouped for a counterattack.

Following La Follette's momentous victory in 1904, the stalwarts had been not only demoralized but leaderless. They continued to work covert mischief against the La Follette faction, but did not emerge again as an independent force until 1910. Their timing was poor, for progressive sentiment nationally was at its height, and circumstances contrived to put leadership in the hands of W. D. Connor, an unsuitable choice. They had at least reformed their ranks, however, and with the failure of the 1910 campaign they were rid of Connor.

Meanwhile, Emanuel Philipp had been readying himself for leadership. He had become the state's conservative leader "because of his ability to present cogently the views of the business man, because of his fluency in stating the conservative position, and because of his character and forthrightness which were recognized by even his most bitter opponents."[8] Philipp wrote a series of articles and a book presenting the conservative position. He was active in organizing for Taft in 1908 and 1910, became quite friendly with the President, and by 1911 was generally regarded as Taft's spokesman in the state.[9]

Philipp had worked his way up in the employ of the Chicago and North Western Railroad Company and then the

---

[7] Printed notice, January 5, 1912; Ernest G. Fiedler to John A. Aylward, March 1, 1912; Charles Weisse to Ward Clemons, March 3, 1912; all in the John A. Aylward Papers.
[8] Maxwell, *Philipp*, 58.
[9] *Ibid.*, 69.

Schlitz Brewing Company. As a direct result of these associations, he had established his own refrigerator-car company, a substantial enterprise but one which depended on the favor of railroads and brewers. Though vulnerable to attack from progressives and pro-temperance stalwarts, Philipp had secured the support of William J. Anderson and the well-respected pro-temperance conservative John M. Whitehead.[10] In 1911, he came forth as the accepted leader of the Taft forces in Wisconsin, and remained to give capable leadership to his faction on the state level after Taft's defeat.

The symbolic role played by President Taft in the revival and reunification of Wisconsin's conservative Republicans was considerable. The stalwart reputation had been tarnished by the actions of Old Guard leaders such as Sawyer, Payne, and Pfister, and by the aggressive campaigns of La Follette. But when La Follette clashed with Taft, from 1908 on, the stalwarts gained a chance to redeem themselves, to become associated with the noble cause of William Howard Taft, chosen and annointed by Theodore Roosevelt, President of the United States, champion of the people, and leader of the Republican party.[11]

The stalwart revival was aided by many of the factors that had first worked to undermine the progressives in the period 1905 through 1909. The problem of the primary remained unsolved, despite enactment of a law allowing a second-choice vote. Progressive failure to unite in 1914 was due in part to lack of a formal mechanism for achieving unity. The ethnic question was not so obvious a source of embarrassment as it had been earlier, largely because the stalwarts had abandoned James O. Davidson without replacing him with an equally popular Norwegian. But the German-Americans remained quite nationality-conscious, and when some of them allied with La Follette, it was on their

[10] William J. Anderson to Charles D. Hilles, October 28, 1911, in Anderson to John M. Whitehead, October 28, 1911, in the Whitehead Papers.
[11] For a firsthand comment on the revived enthusiasm Taft's cause evoked from conservatives, see W. D. Hoard to B. J. Castle, February 9, 1912, in the Castle Papers.

terms, not his.[12] The need for and scarcity of campaign funds remained a problem for the progressive Republicans. With the rise of McGovern, division along geographical lines had become an important source of trouble. Opposition to La Follette because he created discord within the party, an important issue in 1906 and 1908, was less prominent, but only because newer complaints occupied the minds of disgruntled voters, both stalwart and progressive.

The defection of the Democrats, the persistence of the stalwarts, and the revival in the spirit and leadership of that element, combined with the older sources of trouble to provide a really formidable challenge to the progressive Republicans. This challenge might have been met, however, had the stalwarts not been able to pre-empt a portion of the progressives' ideological appeal and thus win the backing of many who had previously voted progressive. Paradoxically, this opening was created for the stalwarts by the progressives themselves when they legislated beyond the limits of majority sentiment in the 1911 and 1913 sessions.

The cost-of-living question, which had aroused voter discontent and promoted progressive revival in 1910, gave impetus to several economic reforms. The newly created Board of Public Affairs advanced many grandiose schemes for co-operatives of several sorts.[13] The *Milwaukee Free Press* remarked ruefully, "The unrest, the dissatisfaction of the times, the eagerness of so large a portion of the people for all sorts of subversive or at least dubious experiments and panaceas in government are largely assignable to the constantly mounting cost of the necessities of life."[14] For some of the most influential progressives, however, the cost-of-living complaint was but a convenient excuse for reforms which they deemed desirable for other and more fundamental reasons. The spirit of optimism and the desire for change permeated the American intellectual community during the

[12] Korman, "Political Loyalties, Immigrant Traditions and Reform," 161–171.
[13] *Milwaukee Free Press*, October 30, 1912.
[14] *Ibid.*, June 14, 1912.

Accomplishment and Disaster, 1911–1914

progressive years and informed the La Follette movement in Wisconsin.

Madison's State Street was a much-used thoroughfare during the progressive era, for it connected the University of Wisconsin with the state Capitol. Traffic moved in both directions. John R. Commons, Balthasar Meyer, Richard T. Ely, Charles R. Van Hise, and many other scholars gave advice and sometimes administrative service to the state. La Follette and many of his lieutenants, in turn, as devoted alumni of the University of Wisconsin, tried to use their power to help their alma mater and to make fullest use of the services of faculty and students in the business of government. The relationship became known as the Wisconsin Idea.

The thinking of Professor Richard T. Ely was both influential and representative. Ely studied economics in Germany under Karl Knies, from whom he drew the institutional approach, rejecting Adam Smith's mechanistic view of the economic system as an unchanging entity governed by immutable laws. Ely and the new institutionalists, organized into the American Economic Association in 1885, suggested that changing historical circumstances rendered obsolete all *a priori* systems. Specifically, they rejected the Smithian idea that government interference in the economy is invariably a bad thing, or that labor unions unduly interfere with the law of supply and demand.[15]

The intellectual leaders of the progressivism that developed under Governor Francis E. McGovern in 1911 took new views on many issues. Unlike their purely Jeffersonian colleagues, men like Charles McCarthy, McGovern, President Van Hise, John R. Commons, and Ely, among others, were not wedded to direct democracy, small government, or free competition. Their view on the subject of trusts perhaps reflected much of their thought. These men all flirted with Roosevelt's New Nationalism in 1912, as opposed to

[15] See especially Richard T. Ely, *Ground Under Our Feet* (New York, 1938).

the more traditional reform views of Woodrow Wilson and Louis Brandeis. As McCarthy expressed it, "The policy of bursting combinations is a mistaken one." Even if effective, he argued, trust-busting would deny to society economies of scale. Governmental price fixing on monopoly-produced articles was McCarthy's solution.[16]

Probably the best statement of the new progressivism was contained in McCarthy's book *The Wisconsin Idea*. The dynamic chief of the Legislative Reference Library began by outlining the situation that had aroused Henry George: the simultaneous advance of progress and poverty. This process, McCarthy felt, sprang inevitably from industrialism. It would surely bring the liquidation of the middle class, in a classical Marxian sense, except for one factor, the growth of intelligence. Salvation would be achieved if the power of the State, guided by intelligence and reason, mobilized against the sinister forces of concentrated capital and industry. McCarthy pointed to Germany as the prime example of what could be done through the union of intelligence and state power. Wisconsin was his Exhibit B.

The key to McCarthy's system was the nonpartisan commission of experts. "Why should not the state be the Efficiency Expert?" he asked. Already, McCarthy found that the state was harnessing the best brains to the service of the people through regulatory commissions. He looked forward to even wider state service directed toward generating still greater intelligence and efficiency.[17]

These ideas accorded with those of Governor Francis E. McGovern, who always maintained a close and friendly collaboration with McCarthy.[18] McGovern was acutely aware of the new industrial and urban problems.[19] The meteoric

[16] Charles McCarthy to Ekern, November 7, 1911, in the Ekern Papers. Van Hise's views were presented in his book *Concentration and Control* (New York, 1912); McGovern's Marketing Commission bill was constructed in conformity with this outlook.
[17] Charles R. McCarthy, *The Wisconsin Idea* (New York, 1912), 1–20.
[18] McGovern to John M. Nelson, February 28, 1912, in the McGovern Papers.
[19] Agricultural output in Wisconsin jumped from an annual rate of $115,000,000 in 1900 to $200,000,000 in 1910; industrial output in the state

Accomplishment and Disaster, 1911–1914

rise of the Social Democrats in Milwaukee, culminating in Emil Seidel's election as mayor in 1910, doubtless demonstrated to McGovern the political relevance of these problems. He was eager to find new solutions, and sought ideas from a wide range of sources, including the newly formed Saturday Lunch Club, where he met with men like Charles R. Van Hise and Edward A. Ross, and the annual governors' conference, where he was impressed by his scholarly colleague from New Jersey, Woodrow Wilson.[20] McGovern did not shy away from McCarthy's notion of a positive, service state, and in this respect he differed somewhat from La Follette. While La Follette was chiefly concerned for the preservation of democracy, and saw economic issues as means towards that end, McGovern subordinated political to economic reform. "Perfection in political machinery is indeed important and vital," he told the 1911 legislature, "principally because by making the government more representative, it paves the way for laws, social adjustments and civil institutions which are calculated to secure and maintain desirable conditions in the daily life and occupations of men."[21]

Members of the 1911 legislature were themselves influenced by the new ideas abroad in the land. An unprecedented number of legislators, fifty-three, constituting 43 per cent of the whole, had some college training. By contrast, in the conservative 1915 legislature, only thirty-one members, or 27 per cent, had comparable college backgrounds.[22] Charles McCarthy was especially influential with the legislators. Two veteran progressives recalled as late as 1954 the eagerness with which assemblymen and senators

---

rose from $360,000,000 to $600,000,000. *Wisconsin Blue Book, 1913*, 48, 109; *The Thirteenth Census, 1910*, 5: 486, 548; 9: 1322.

[20] Ekern to Charles J. Bushnell, March 12, 1912, in the Ekern Papers; Leslie R. Fort to McCarthy, January 6, 1911, in the McCarthy Papers.

[21] *State of Wisconsin Assembly Journal, Fiftieth Session*, 27, January 6, 1911.

[22] Howard J. McMurray, "Some Influences of the University of Wisconsin on the State Government of Wisconsin" (doctoral dissertation, University of Wisconsin, 1940), 34.

responded to McCarthy's enthusiasm over reforms in New Zealand or Australia, Germany or Denmark.[23]

"You have greater opportunity than any Governor in the state's history to do big things," Alfred T. Rogers wired Frank McGovern as the vigorous Milwaukeean took office. McGovern was more than ready. The seed had been sown in other years, he told the new legislature; this was the time for the harvest.[24] The 1911 legislature, enthusiastic, optimistic, and buoyed up by the progressive landslide of 1910,[25] enacted an unprecedented number of important reform proposals in both the political and economic spheres. Some of the political reforms were already well exploited and revitalized by La Follette and his cohorts in their campaigns for the direct primary and against the rule of corrupt bosses. The second-choice vote in the primary was finally adopted. So too were proposals for constitutional amendments on the initiative, referendum, recall of nonjudicial officials, and liberalization of amendment procedure. Home rule for cities was advanced by several laws. The question of woman suffrage was referred to the people. Moving in the other direction in the political sphere, the office of insurance commissioner was made appointive instead of elective.

Probably more significant than the political reforms were the economic. The legislature passed a workmen's compensation law, established an Industrial Commission, regulated hours for women and children, and created an Industrial Education Board. It enacted a state income tax, provided liberal aid to highway construction, and created a Highway Commission. It passed a comprehensive law for conservation of water power and another setting up a forest reserve and a forest commission. Wisconsin entered the insurance business with the creation of a state insurance

---

[23] Interviews with Charles Rosa, January 15, 1954, and with William Kirsch, January 18, 1954.

[24] Alfred T. Rogers to McGovern, January 2, 1911, in the McGovern Papers; *La Follette's Magazine*, 3: 2 (January 14, 1911).

[25] John E. McConnell to Esch, February 20, 1911, in the Esch Papers.

fund to back state-granted life insurance and annuity policies. Rural problems were attacked by laws authorizing the formation of co-operatives, and permitting counties to loan money for the purpose of improving farm lands or to borrow money to establish schools of agriculture and domestic economy. As part of the same program, the legislature made civic centers of public school buildings.

Among the most important new governmental agencies was the multi-purpose Board of Public Affairs, which was created to modernize the state's financial practices. In addition, it was authorized to investigate a wide range of subjects and make recommendations to the governor and legislature. Soon after its creation, the board launched studies of the public school systems, community credit and co-operative marketing problems, city planning ideas, the problem of settling unoccupied farm lands, and the subject of prison labor.[26]

McCarthy took the view that the philosophy and progressive reforms of 1911 were extensions of the original movement, not additions to it. He traced the idea of regulatory commissions, the use of experts, and the idea of the positive state to the La Follette administration. (Events were to show that McCarthy and his colleagues were overly optimistic. But significantly, the reaction that quickly developed against reform and reformers was infused with ideas and attitudes that had previously served the progressives.)

McCarthy was partly correct in associating La Follette with the new reforms. Although the senator differed from McCarthy and McGovern on the subject of trusts and in placing democracy before economic questions, he did share many of their views. In fact, it was La Follette who first proposed creation of the Board of Public Affairs, the darling

---

[26] The legislation of the first McGovern administration is well presented in Maxwell, *Rise of the Progressives*, 153–173. A concise summary is contained in Harry C. Wilbur to Medill McCormick, December 4, 1912, in the McGovern Papers, Wilbur Correspondence. A convenient summary of labor legislation may be found in Gavett, *Labor Movement in Milwaukee*, 107–111.

of both McCarthy and McGovern.[27] Though he was devoted to Jeffersonian democracy and the yeoman farmer, La Follette was no enemy to a strong state, labor legislation, or the use of reason and "science" in the process of government.

Yet La Follette was himself unrepresentative of many of his fellow progressives, as James O. Davidson had amply demonstrated when he won the governorship against La Follette's opposition in 1906. To many who supported the progressive movement in the early days, the new welfare measures, increased state regulation, the proliferation of appointive officials and commissions, and rising state expenditures had little appeal. The renewed conservative drive begun in 1912 would have been unsuccessful and insignificant but for the fact that it appealed so strongly to the voting backbone of progressivism.

The focus of conservative attention in 1912 was the new state income tax law. The Wisconsin Manufacturers Association, in which Democratic politician Harry Bolens was prominent, had lobbied against the bill in 1911.[28] After the bill's adoption, the association linked forces with other conservatives in urging repeal.[29] The issue proved an excellent catalyst for the unification of several important strands of discontent. The new law involved forty appointive officials, responsible to the tax commission, as well as confusing forms to be filled out by the taxpayer. Inevitably, the question of inefficient, undemocratic bureaucracy was raised. The tax also suggested the question of state expenses, and served as a springboard for attacks on the growth of commissions and the rising cost of government.

Tax assessments were to be made in July, 1912, on the basis of information provided by the taxpayer during the winter. But as early as February, 1912, speeches were being made in conservative Rock County attacking the in-

[27] McCarthy to George E. Scott, August 4, 1914, in the McCarthy Papers.
[28] Otto Falk to Harry Bolens, June 2, 1911, in the Harry Bolens Papers.
[29] Wisconsin Manufacturers Association to Theodore Kronshage, September 15, 1912, in the Theodore Kronshage Papers.

come tax and the University of Wisconsin, the latter largely because of increased appropriations. These speeches were widely reported and the same lines of attack were followed elsewhere. In March, the anti-tax disgruntlement increased as the people began to grapple with the tax forms.[30] Following a statewide tour in April, Irvine Lenroot reported "very general opposition to the income tax law." He felt that it should have started "in a less comprehensive way."[31] In June, Attorney General Levi Bancroft, himself a onetime progressive, condemned the administration and the income tax, arguing that the tax drove capital from the state, encouraged perjury, and humiliated and degraded citizens.[32]

The Democrats swung into action in July. Judge John C. Karel, a former University of Wisconsin football star from Milwaukee who made friendship his hobby and was active in fraternal, church, and civic circles,[33] launched his gubernatorial candidacy with the charge that the state income tax was "obnoxious and inquisitorial" and that "extravagance has run riot in the administration of state affairs."[34] His liberal opponent, A. J. Schmitz, defended the tax but condemned extravagance. The party's primary platform called only for amendment of the tax law, not repeal, but deplored unnecessary commissions and appointive officers as subversive of popular and economical government.[35] The entire conservative attack intensified during the election campaign of 1912. Karel, who won his party's nomination, led the way, calling the income tax the "most pernicious law that was ever put on the statute books of Wisconsin."[36] The law served the interests of political self

---

[30] Edward E. Browne to McGovern, March 28, 1912, in the McGovern Papers.
[31] Lenroot to Edwin J. Gross, April 29, 1912, in the Gross Papers.
[32] *Milwaukee Free Press*, June 17, 1912.
[33] L. Albert Karel, *The Story of a Friendly Man* (n.p., [1939?]).
[34] *Milwaukee Sentinel*, July 4, 1912.
[35] *Janesville Gazette*, July 12, 1912.
[36] *Racine Times*, November 5, 1912.

seekers, he charged; and stalwart Republican papers like the *Janesville Gazette* and the *Fond du Lac Reporter* agreed.[37] Harry Bolens, Democratic candidate for lieutenant governor, concentrated on the popular outcry against state expenses. He pointed out that in 1901 La Follette had viewed with alarm the recent increase in state expenses.[38]

A Milwaukee lawyer concisely brought together the strands of another popular theme when he wrote: "The people are tired of this paternalistic, Progressive probing into their private and personal affairs; they are tired of being governed by the university clique; they are tired of theorists, socialists and sociologists. They want to return to a safe and sane government by the people."[39]

Though progressive defection did not reach dangerous proportions until 1914, there was much evidence as early as 1912 that skepticism about some features of the progressive movement was not confined to the Old Guard. Merlin Hull, a progressive editor from rural Jackson County, had inveighed against increased spending at the university as early as 1908.[40] The progressives, in their 1912 campaign, showed a hearty respect for the growing popularity of the economy appeal.

Reforms directed at improving the conditions of laboring men proliferated in 1911. Yet farmers, the voting backbone of Wisconsin progressivism, were reserved on the whole subject of labor legislation. They balked at such legislation because they feared the cost to taxpayers, and, as employers, feared regulation of hours, wages, and safety conditions. It proved impossible to pass workmen's compensation and child labor laws until farmer employers were exempted from the provisions.[41]

Some progressives could not swallow one of the progressives' key ideas, that in the interests of scientific effi-

[37] *Janesville Gazette*, October 10, 16, 1912.
[38] *Milwaukee Sentinel*, October 26, 1912.
[39] *Janesville Gazette*, October 1, 1912.
[40] Curti and Carstensen, *The University of Wisconsin*, 2: 179.
[41] Schmidt, "Labor Legislation in Wisconsin," 89, 119, 147.

Accomplishment and Disaster, 1911–1914 139

ciency and the short ballot, many offices should be appointive rather than elective. George Cooper, a staunch pro-La Follette editor, and Merlin Hull were among the opponents of the bill to make the office of insurance commissioner appointive. Cooper wrote to Herman Ekern, the insurance commissioner, who was actively backing the bill: "If the logic for a change of the office to an appointive one is carried to a conclusion, it will eventually do away with all state elective offices except that of governor."[42] But McCarthy, in *The Wisconsin Idea,* espoused the very thing that Cooper could not even contemplate seriously: conversion of the offices of secretary of state, treasurer and attorney general to appointive positions.[43]

However consistent the ideas of efficiency and democracy may have appeared to McCarthy and McGovern, less sophisticated men saw contradictions. A progressive county judge from Waukesha wrote Herman Ekern, "I am very much disappointed in you after learning that you campaigned the state, recommending the primary law and the nomination of public officers directly by the people. . . , and then bringing about such legislation as to make your office an appointive office and extending your term, within a very short term after the people were kind enough to elect you."[44]

With the defection of Isaac Stephenson, the *Milwaukee Free Press* was lost by the La Follette faction. *La Follette's Magazine* had been launched in 1909 to fill the gap. In early 1911, in preparation for his presidential campaign, La Follette engineered the purchase of Madison's *Wisconsin State Journal* by a young muckraker from the staff of *Collier's,* Richard Lloyd Jones. Loans of $60,000 from the Chicago philanthropist Charles R. Crane and of $25,000 from such Wisconsin progressives as William H. Hatton, John M. Nelson, A. W. Sanborn, Herman Ekern, and

---
[42] George Cooper to Ekern, May 26, 1911, in the Ekern Papers.
[43] McCarthy, *The Wisconsin Idea,* 90.
[44] David W. Agnew to Ekern, October 14, 1912, in the Ekern Papers.

others made the deal possible.[45] The acquisition was timely, not so much for La Follette's abortive presidential effort as for publicizing the progressive position on state issues. During the 1912 campaign, the *State Journal* and other progressively inclined papers, together with progressive officeholders, recognized the potency of their opponents' arguments by taking up defensive positions instead of advancing new reform proposals. Tax Commissioner Haugen, though cool towards La Follette by this time, joined McGovern, State Chairman George E. Scott, and such papers as the *State Journal* and the *Superior Telegram* in stoutly defending the income tax. They argued that it was lower than the old property tax, but had the advantage that it would be collected. Haugen denied that the tax cost a great deal to administer or required a large staff. McGovern charged that the opposition came from tax-dodgers and predatory interests bent on undoing all the progressive accomplishments in the state.[46]

The progressives were equally sensitive to the extravagance issue. Secretary of State James Frear released several statements during October, claiming that the department was being efficiently and economically run, and that the state tax for the coming year would be over a million dollars less than in 1912.[47] Assistant Treasurer Henry Johnson, candidate for state treasurer, brought figures from his office to refute Harry Bolens' charge that the taxpayers were paying five million dollars annually for the salaries of state employees.[48] La Follette and the Republican state

---

[45] Norman Weissman, "A History of the Wisconsin State Journal" (master's thesis, University of Wisconsin, 1951), 72; notation dated July 29, 1911, in the A. O. Barton Papers; A. W. Sanborn to Ekern, November 6, 1911; Ekern to William Hatton, January 8, 1912, in the Ekern Papers; John M. Nelson to McGovern, May 27, 1912, in the McGovern Papers.

[46] *Racine Times,* October 23, 1912; *Wisconsin State Journal,* October 1, 19, 1912; *Green Bay Semi-Weekly Gazette,* October 30, November 2, 1912; *Superior Telegram,* October 24, 1912.

[47] *Wisconsin State Journal,* October 2, 1912; *Green Bay Semi-Weekly Gazette,* October 30, 1912.

[48] *Wisconsin State Journal,* October 13, 1912.

Accomplishment and Disaster, 1911–1914 141

central committee pounded on the same argument. La Follette denied that state expenses had risen from three to thirteen million dollars annually in the previous decade, pointed out that some of the "disbursements" were merely transfers from one fund to another, and showed that over three million dollars were turned over by the state government to local governments and associations. According to La Follette's calculations, state expenditures for 1912 amounted to roughly 7.3 million dollars.[49] The state central committee backed him up in charging the Democrats with exaggeration on the extravagance issue.[50] The *Wisconsin State Journal* contended that the Industrial Commission amply justified its expenses by the money it saved by eliminating costly litigation.[51]

The ticklish question of experts in government was frankly faced by La Follette, who argued that experts and commissions were necessary in readjusting to new conditions. The method, he claimed, had been used successfully, had not brought ruin to business, and had purified democracy.[52]

The progressives retained one key weapon: they were able to raise the old cry against vested interests and ravenous corporations. La Follette, McGovern, and other progressives argued that the cost of commissions was far less than the price unprotected consumers and workers would have to pay the predatory pack.[53] The hue and cry against "the interests" had not yet abated on the national level. The progressive tide swept Wilson into the Democratic presidential nomination, Roosevelt into a third-party effort, and inundated Taft in the election. The tariff and the high cost of living remained in the public eye.[54] Not the advisa-

---

[49] *Green Bay Semi-Weekly Gazette,* October 26, 1912.
[50] *Wisconsin State Journal,* October 5, 1912.
[51] *Ibid.,* October 18, 1912.
[52] *Ibid.,* October 22, 1912.
[53] *Ibid.,* October 5, 18, 19, 1912; *La Crosse Tribune,* October 11, 21, 1912.
[54] *Janesville Gazette,* July 11, October 21, 1912; *La Follette's Magazine,* 10: 5 (May, 1918).

bility but rather the method of dealing with monopoly emerged as the leading issue in the presidential race. Reinforced by this national trend, Wisconsin's traditional wariness towards large corporations constituted a substantial obstacle to the conservative drive.

Even so, the election results revealed that progressivism in its new phase was in real jeopardy. While the progressives had won in a landslide in 1910, the 1912 results were quite close and the outcome of the gubernatorial race remained in doubt for some days. Finally, McGovern was declared the winner; he received 179,317 votes to 167,296 for Karel.[55] The rest of the Republican ticket did somewhat better, winning by from 21,000 to 24,000 votes.[56] Despite Mrs. La Follette's oratory, woman suffrage was turned down, 227,024 to 135,545.[57] The Democrats showed unwonted strength and unity, and this too boded ill for the future of the progressive Republicans. The warring factions—one concerned for Wilson, the other for Karel—had been forced to make common cause behind the straight party ticket.

Again in 1913 and 1914 the tax issue spearheaded the conservative campaign. This time, however, the issue emerged in a virtually unbeatable form. An inordinately heavy tax levy, resulting from the precarious condition of the state's finances, was announced late in October, 1913. A remission of $1,900,000 in 1912 had put the state in a vulnerable position. When the 1912 legislature appropriated roughly $25,000,000 for the next biennium, and corporation and inheritance taxes failed to meet expectation, the state was forced to seek new funds.

Several factors combined to raise state spending. The automobile age came suddenly, and highway construction was not cheap. The 1911 legislature bound the state government to pay one-third of the cost of all highway construction undertaken by county and local units. Although

[55] *Wisconsin Blue Book, 1913*, 260.
[56] *Ibid.*, 261–264.
[57] *Wisconsin Blue Book, 1942*, 215.

Accomplishment and Disaster, 1911–1914   143

$350,000 was set aside for the purpose, applications for aid totaled $800,000. The 1913 legislature appropriated the extra $450,000 (and an additional $1,200,000) as an annual appropriation.[58] New buildings for the university, normal schools, and charitable and penal institutions added to the appropriation load.[59] The University of Wisconsin appropriation for 1913–1914 exceeded $2,000,000, which was $900,000 more than in 1910–1911. The appropriations for 1900–1901 had been under $300,000.[60] Another important factor in boosting state expenses was the new budget system, which made appropriations more systematic and definite, but by producing omnibus appropriations bills late in the session curtailed the governor's power to veto extraneous items.[61] County and local expenses and taxes rose along with those of the state, chiefly as a result of extensive road building, but the leaders of the state government absorbed most of the blame.

Here at last was the key the conservatives needed. With it, they opened the door to voter attention and displayed a full and attractive stock of ideological goods. Anti-extravagance, anti-bureaucracy, anti-intellectualism, and anti-radicalism were all aggressively marketed. The first murmurs of discontent were heard the day after Governor McGovern signed the record appropriations. The announcement at the end of October, 1913, that an extraordinary general-purpose tax levy of $1,500,000 would be necessary occasioned further protest.[62] By the end of January, 1914, McGovern's chances for election to the United States Senate seemed dim to a *Janesville Gazette* political reporter. "McGovern has got to answer for this high tax proposition," he

---

[58] Wisconsin Highway Commission, Bulletin No. 3, *The State Highway Aid Law* (Madison, 1913), 7, 52.
[59] Circular to county clerks from the Department of State, October 27, 1913; John S. Donald to A. R. Kempter, November 10, 1913, both in the Donald Papers.
[60] Curti and Carstensen, *University of Wisconsin*, 2: 606.
[61] *Milwaukee Free Press*, August 8, 1914.
[62] *Janesville Gazette*, October 28, 30, November 1, 1913; *Wausau Record-Herald*, October 28, 29, 1913.

observed, "and there is the whole trouble in a nut shell. Taxes, taxes, taxes." Friends of the governor ruefully agreed. There always have been such complaints at taxpaying time, one of them observed to McGovern's secretary, Harry Wilbur, but "it seems that the people quite generally are of the opinion that the last legislature was too extravagant." A pro-La Follette assemblyman from rural Polk County wrote a La Follette lieutenant: "I greatly fear it will be hard to defend the ever increasing taxes with the ever increasing number and size of commissions. . . . We must depend on the natural progressive spirit of our strong rural countys and here taxes is felt the worst."[63]

Amid a general flurry of protest generated by conservative newspapers and by Ellis B. Usher, whose weekly column was carried by such papers as the *Janesville Gazette,* the *Wausau Record-Herald,* the *Beloit Free Press,* and the *Oshkosh Northwestern,* the anti-tax campaign began to take form in February. Two conventions, ostensibly representing farmers and businessmen from three southern counties, laid the groundwork for the formation of the Home Rule and Taxpayers League.[64] Charles Pierce of Janesville and T. C. Richmond of Madison, conservative lawyers who had long been politically active, took the lead in the new organization. Richmond had been an ardent progressive in the early days.[65] Behind the scenes was Emanuel Philipp.[66] Conservative organization moved a step further when the Home Rule League met in Madison in May and resolved in favor of a pre-primary convention to organize the anti-administration campaign.[67]

---

[63] *Janesville Gazette,* January 31, 1914; George Thompson to Harry Wilbur, February 27, 1914, in the McGovern Papers, Wilbur Correspondence; Axel [Johnson] to Charles Rosa, January 2, 1914, in the Charles D. Rosa Papers.
[64] *Janesville Gazette,* February 13, 16, 28, 1914.
[65] Barton, *La Follette's Winning of Wisconsin,* 247.
[66] Harry Wilbur to D. B. Worthington, February 25, 1914; Wilbur to Percy Ap Roberts, March 12, 1914, in the McGovern Papers, Wilbur Correspondence; *Milwaukee Journal,* November 21, 1914.
[67] *Milwaukee Journal,* November 21, 1914.

Though the Home Rule and Taxpayers League was ostensibly nonpartisan, and included conservative Democrats in its leadership, the new organization was soon turned to the advantage of Emanuel Philipp. The league decided to back Philipp for governor,[68] and was instrumental in bringing about a Republican pre-primary convention on June 22 in Madison.[69] Charles Pierce represented the league at the convention and delivered an address denouncing the extravagance of the previous fourteen years and the meddling of the University of Wisconsin in politics. Within three hours of convening, the delegates had adopted a platform, nominated Emanuel Philipp for governor at the head of a complete slate of conservative Republican candidates, and adjourned.[70]

Conservative argument, like progressive, centered on two main areas, economic and political. The economic argument involved personal gain or loss for the voter; the political argument turned on the question of democracy. In earlier days, the progressives had had much the better of the ideological warfare over both these issues. In the economic sphere, the conservatives had warned that progressive measures would drive industry from the state. But the years were prosperous ones and industry had actually expanded. In the political sphere, the conservatives charged La Follette with "boss rule." This argument had served the purposes of anti-La Follette progressives like James O. Davidson, but it could hardly benefit stalwart candidates, for La Follette had effectively countercharged that his enemies opposed and continued to oppose the primary while supporting the discredited convention system, the symbol of boss rule.

[68] *Janesville Gazette,* May 25, 1922. The story, an obituary of Charles Pierce, reports that the decision to back Philipp was made in an office in the Janesville City Hall.
[69] Philipp was apparently chief mover in bringing about the convention, for he bore the expense of it, $562.82. Statements of expenses of Emanuel Philipp . . . November 3, 1914, in the Emanuel Philipp Papers.
[70] *Wisconsin State Journal,* June 23, 1914.

With the 1912 and 1914 campaigns, the conservatives mounted their assault from higher ground, and it was disastrous to the progressives because it utilized arguments that the progressives had used themselves in their successful appeals to the voters. The conservatives attacked on the question of equitable taxation, as the progressives had done in early days, when the taxation of railroads and other corporations had been a central issue. The conservatives now asked for economy in government, as the progressives had done when they attacked corruptionists for wasting and misusing state funds. The conservatives attacked commissions and theoreticians in the name of popular government, as the progressives had earlier attacked boss rule.

It has frequently been remarked that many men who had been known as progressives in the days of Theodore Roosevelt's presidency emerged as archfoes of Franklin Roosevelt. In Wisconsin, at least, where the break from progressivism could be traced as far back as 1912 and 1914, no real inconsistency was involved. For the progressivism of the McGovern administrations, with its pro-labor, welfare bias, its emphasis on experts, its expansion of taxation and spending, while quite similar to phases of the New Deal, was dissimilar in many respects to the seminal progressivism of 1890–1900. Small wonder that the tenuous progressive coalition of the early days began to break up when some of its disunities became evident to all.

The argument of the conservatives was neat and potent, a fusion of the two main issues into one. Government by commission, the alleged retreat from democracy, was blamed for "extravagance" and high taxes. But, though attacks on commissions, experts, and the university had priority logically, politically it was the "bread and butter" issue of extravagance and taxation that supported the entire ideological edifice.[71] The increase in state expenses since

---

[71] McCarthy to Charles R. Crane, March 7, 1914, in the McCarthy Papers; Oscar Schoengarth to Harry Wilbur, May 16, 1914; D. O. Mahoney to Wilbur, May 19, 1914; Guy A. Benson to Wilbur, May 23, 1914, in the McGovern Papers, Wilbur Correspondence.

1900 was the major theme of Emanuel Philipp's opening campaign address, which provided the material for his subsequent speeches. He said that expenses had risen from four million dollars in 1900 to thirteen in 1913. The Taxpayers League, which was active during the campaign, owed its very existence to the issue of extravagance. The conservative papers, led by the *Milwaukee Sentinel,* gave prime attention to that issue.[72]

Heralded by the extravagance issue, the question of democracy came forth in full panoply. T. C. Richmond of the Taxpayers League gave voters a preview of campaign argument in February. "A few years ago we had in Wisconsin something like a democracy," he wrote the *Madison Democrat.* "Now all that is changed. . . . The people are no longer trusted to manage their own affairs. . . . Real democracy is gone. Bureaucracy has taken its place. . . ."[73] Months later, the Taxpayers League issued a pre-primary statement to the voters in which it posed the issue as one of local self-government or rule by experts: "To put it briefly, do you want a democracy or a bureaucracy?" Emanuel Philipp stressed the same issue, but more elaborately. He listed the increases in appropriations and pointed out that the major ones occurred not in the regular departments but in the commissions and the University of Wisconsin. Taking off from this prosaic statistical springboard, the rotund businessman soared to the heights of oratory, history, and philosophy. "This is not a mere campaign for office," he assured his Waukesha auditors. "It is a fight for constitutional representative government, as opposed to the delegated powers which build up a dangerous bureaucracy." The history of human progress, he argued, had been a battle against usurped powers and burdensome taxation.[74]

The university emerged as the chief whipping boy of

---

[72] *Milwaukee Sentinel,* July 7, 10, 20, August 24, 1914; *Wausau Record-Herold,* August 14, 19, 1914; *Beloit Free Press,* August 20, 1914.
[73] *Janesville Gazette,* February 17, 1914.
[74] *Milwaukee Sentinel,* August 24, 1914, July 16, 1914.

the conservative campaign. The ground had been prepared for Philipp's attack by an intense and open campaign of criticism conducted since 1911 by State Superintendent of Instruction Charles P. Cary. In a series of open letters, Cary had criticized the university's entrance requirements and other forms of influence over state schools. It was Cary who contributed the phrase used by conservatives in the 1914 campaign, "Do we want a State University or a University State?" Now Philipp charged the university with causing increased spending and bureaucracy both directly and indirectly. Philipp said that the cost of the university had risen from $587,773 in 1910 to $2,389,959 in 1913, and that the budget for 1914 called for $2,863,320. While the University was getting more than its fair share, Philipp said, rural schools were being slighted. He argued also that the university was the spawning ground for commissioners, "experts," and socialists. He criticized academicians for mixing in politics and not devoting full time to teaching. As at least partial remedy for some of the evils he described, Philipp proposed that a single board be created to apportion money among the various state institutions of learning.[75] Linked with the university and the commissions in a bureaucratic conspiracy to control state government, in Philipp's view, was the Legislative Reference Library. Charles McCarthy's organization, he charged, had insidiously expanded its function beyond that of providing information and practically controlled the legislature. The antidote Philipp prescribed was simple and thorough: abolish it.[76]

The conservative Democrats found no difficulty in mastering the new issues. It was they, after all, who had led the way in 1912. The arguments about liberty, oppressive bureaucracy, and taxation were congenial to at least one

[75] Maurice M. Vance, *Charles Richard Van Hise: Scientist Progressive* (Madison, 1960), 122–125; *Milwaukee Sentinel,* July 16, 1914. Philipp ignored the fact that part of the 1913 and 1914 expenditures were covered by university income. In 1910, the comparable income had been spent directly by the university without passing through the hands of the state government.
[76] *Milwaukee Sentinel,* July 16, 1914.

phase of their Jeffersonian tradition. The group led by John C. Karel outnumbered the liberal Democratic faction at the party's pre-primary convention and secured the designation of a full conservative slate for the primary contests.[77]

After conferences with Joseph E. Davies, committeeman and liaison with President Wilson, the liberal Democrats put up a slate of their own, headed by John A. Aylward for governor and Paul Husting of Mayville for senator. Aylward's platform, however, was scarcely that of a rabid reformer. The Madison attorney denounced high taxes, promised to reduce commissions from forty-five to fifteen, cut the state payroll by a million dollars and the highway tax by another million, keep the university out of politics, and make the reference library the servant not the master of the people. He named a number of commissions that he would eliminate, including the Board of Public Affairs. Finally, he promised to reduce university appropriations and take the state out of the insurance business.[78]

The progressive Republicans themselves paid the most eloquent tribute to the strength of the anti-progressive arguments. Setting the pace, to the consternation of many, was Senator Robert M. La Follette. That La Follette should oppose the senatorial ambitions of Governor McGovern was not surprising, considering the mutual suspicion that existed between the two. But that he should condemn the work of McGovern's administration was astonishing. The administration was, after all, representative of "progressivism," as La Follette had himself recognized in 1912 when he urged his supporters to overlook factional differences and back McGovern against Karel. Nevertheless, on July 25, the cover of *La Follette's* carried the following signed editorial:[79]

> The appropriations for highways were much beyond the amount which can be wisely and economically expended.
> These appropriations doubtless carried with

[77] *Ibid.,* July 15, 1914.
[78] *Ibid.,* August 7, 1914.
[79] *La Follette's Magazine,* 6: 30 (July 25, 1914).

them others which are justly open to criticism. Such a course begets waste and looseness in administration. . . .

And upon whom should fall the responsibility of this wrong to a great cause and a great commonwealth?

The executive office is the clearing house on appropriation. There is focused detailed information on all legislation pending and passed, there the appropriations are listed, there the aggregates are known. And there is lodged the final power in one hand to insure the passage of an appropriation or to smite it with a veto, that makes an end to it. . . .

McGovern immediately replied to La Follette's attack by attempting to shift the blame for appropriations to the La Follette leader, Senator George Scott, who had presented the appropriations bills.[80] Scott in turn denied that he had been in contact with La Follette and put the blame on McGovern.[81]

La Follette's remarkable statement was the culmination of a stratagem that had been developing since March. Factional hostilities approached the boiling point as the 1914 primary approached. The La Follette leaders were determined to block McGovern's elevation to the Senate. Increasingly, they utilized the popular conservative arguments against McGovern, at once demonstrating the depth of factional hostility and the persuasiveness of the "extravagance" issue.

Pursuing the new strategy, La Follette's lieutenants gathered in Madison at the end of March, 1914, and decided to petition the governor to call a special session of the legislature to effect economies.[82] In June, Secretary of State John S. Donald, a La Follette man, urged Tom Morris,

---

[80] *Milwaukee Sentinel,* July 26, 1914.
[81] *La Follette's Magazine,* 6: 32 (August 8, 1914).
[82] Harry Wilbur to Hans M. Laursen, April 4, 1914, in the McGovern Papers, Wilbur Correspondence.

La Follette's chosen candidate against McGovern for the senate nomination, not to alienate stalwarts. Old differences no longer mattered, Donald wrote.[83] Even Richard Lloyd Jones, usually an uncompromising progressive, took conservative ground in backing Morris in his paper. His *Wisconsin State Journal* stated that Morris had sought to curb spending, had been involved in the movement for a special session, and was a protective tariff man.[84]

During the campaign for the Republican gubernatorial nomination, La Follette's choice, Andrew Dahl, made much of the fact that he was not implicated in recent extravagance, and pressed an attack on the administration very similar to Philipp's. Dahl first listed and praised the past achievements of the progressive movement. Getting to the issues of 1914, however, he attacked the extravagance of the previous administration, asked for reduced highway appropriations and greater local control, called for a cutback in university and normal school building programs, called the Legislative Reference Library a "bill factory," and advocated the abolition of the Board of Public Affairs. He made no mention of the initiative, referendum, or recall, nor of marketing or co-operatives, the more recent progressive issues.[85] Dahl began his speaking campaign in New Glarus on August 3 with an attack on the Board of Public Affairs as the cause of higher expenses. His position remained the same at the end of the month.[86]

To a greater or lesser degree, the other major progres-

---

[83] John S. Donald to William Bell, June 8, 1914, in the Donald Papers.

[84] *Wisconsin State Journal*, June 15, 1914.

[85] *Ibid.*, June 22, 1914. The implicit attack on Charles McCarthy was not surprising. McCarthy was never close to La Follette and his friends. He was, on the other hand, in close sympathy with McGovern and his measures. Moreover he had helped to draft Theodore Roosevelt's Progressive party platform in 1912, and La Follette and his friends retained considerable bitterness towards Roosevelt. By 1914 a number of La Follette leaders were hostile to McCarthy. See, for instance, Crownhart to McCarthy, June 27, 1914; George E. Scott to McCarthy, August 7, 1914, in the McCarthy Papers; Dahl to A. W. Sanborn, July 15, 1914, in the La Follette Papers.

[86] *Milwaukee Sentinel*, August 4, 24, 1914.

sive candidates for governor also acquiesced in the issue of extravagance. Merlin Hull claimed, and with some truth, to have been an early advocate of economy.[87] Even William Hatton, a member of the Board of Public Affairs, took cognizance of the issue, pledging efficiency and economy and stressing his success as a businessman.[88]

Despite some belated progressive efforts to draw a sharp line between themselves and Philipp, the dominant tone of the gubernatorial primary was conservative. It was perhaps fitting, therefore, that Emanuel Philipp won out. He polled 43,733 votes to 27,619 for Dahl and 23,275 for Hatton. Roethe drew 12,411 votes, Hull 10,841, and Utman 6,734.[89] Few voters used the recently enacted second-choice vote, despite the high hopes of the progressives.[90] Again, the Democrats had stayed in their own primaries, for party nominations were of value now and were hotly contested between conservatives and progressives. The conservative John Karel won the nomination for governor, though Paul Husting, a progressive, won the Democratic senatorial primary.

The victory of Philipp accentuated another major limitation in the political makeup of progressivism. Through the years, the progressives had received occasional help from Social Democrats, in elections and on legislation. For example, La Follette had gotten some socialist votes in the 1902 gubernatorial race; so did McGovern in his campaign for district attorney in 1906.[91] On the whole, however, the socialists had remained politically aloof. Until 1914, the absence of socialists from the progressive ranks had not proved a major handicap. The coalition that La Follette had gradually molded was broad enough even without them. But by 1914 the disadvantage had become serious. For one thing, the socialists had become quite numerous by then;

[87] *Ibid.*, August 11, 1914.
[88] *Milwaukee Free Press*, August 4, 1914.
[89] *Wisconsin Blue Book, 1915*, 234–235.
[90] *La Follette's Magazine*, 6: 32 (August 8, 1914).
[91] Wachman, *Social-Democratic Party of Milwaukee*, 45, 62.

Accomplishment and Disaster, 1911–1914 153

for another, the power of the conservative attack suggested the need for reinforcements. Finally, the fact that under McGovern the progressive movement had drifted to the left seemed to open the possibility for the more advanced progressives to win socialist votes. That possibility was not fulfilled, however, and the failure of the progressives to win substantial socialist help proved to be a significant limitation of the movement.

Under the leadership of the forceful immigrant intellectual, Victor Berger, a close symbiotic relationship had been established between the Social Democrats and the trade unionists of Milwaukee. Though industry and unionism were developing rapidly elsewhere in the state, Milwaukee remained the overwhelmingly pre-eminent center for industry, labor organization, and socialism. The unions and socialists continued to rely principally on German-Americans. In 1900, over 150,000 of the city's total population of 285,315 were of German stock.[92]

By 1899, the Federated Trades Council, representing seventy different unions, had been won over by the socialists. A few years later, the Wisconsin State Federation of Labor, centered in Milwaukee, was won.[93] The alliance was a happy one, and it solidified with the years. The socialists championed unionism in their press, supported labor legislation, and nominated union men for public office. The unions gave financial and voting support to the socialists.

As editor of the German-language *Wisconsin Vorwaerts* beginning in 1892, Berger took a gradualist approach, attempting always to adapt to the environment. The platform of the *Vorwaerts* in the mid-nineties emphasized immediate aims and soft-pedaled revolutionary goals. Corruption and mismanagement in Milwaukee government and reactionary business policies and practices opened the political door for the Social Democrats; and as they glimpsed the prospect

---
[92] *Ibid.*, 111.
[93] Gavett, *Labor Movement in Milwaukee*, 95, 96.

of success, they continued to moderate their demands in an effort to woo nonsocialist voters, abandoning, for example, the platform plank that condemned the granting of franchises to privately owned public utilities in favor of one demanding special guarantees from corporations applying for franchises.[94] At last "the patient wooing of the trade unions, the emphasis upon immediate reform in the administration of the city government, and the unexcelled political machine built up by the socialists bore fruit in 1910."[95] In that year, Berger won a seat in Congress, Emil Seidel was elected mayor, socialists carried the other city offices, and thirteen Social Democrats won seats in the state legislature.[96]

Though Victor Berger was willing to focus on immediate and popular goals, he remained a dedicated socialist theoretician. He saw the Social Democratic party as the vehicle for evolutionary progress towards socialism. So while he might moderate party demands, he would never compromise the party itself. During the 1890's he battled to break an earlier alliance with the Populists and to win the unions away from this fusionist approach. Having succeeded by 1899, he continued to oppose fusionist efforts. In fact, the more moderate the socialists grew, the more determined was Berger to distinguish that party from the Republicans and Democrats.[97] The State Federation of Labor and the Federated Trades Council of Milwaukee concurred fully in this strategy.[98]

More than Marxian theory underlay Berger's determi-

[94] Still, *Milwaukee*, 312.
[95] Gavett, *Labor Movement in Milwaukee*, 111.
[96] Wachman, *Social-Democratic Party of Milwaukee*, 72.
[97] *Ibid.*, 47–50, 61; Olson, "The Milwaukee Socialists," 133.
[98] Frederick Brockhausen, secretary-treasurer, Executive Board of the Wisconsin Federation of Labor, to the Executive Council of the A. F. of L., August 7, 1908; John Reichert, corresponding secretary of the Federated Trades Council of Milwaukee, to Samuel Gompers, August 22, 1908, in the A. F. of L. Papers, President's File, cited in Robert Griffith, "Irvine Lenroot and the Republican Primary of 1908," *Wisconsin Magazine of History*, 49: 16–28 (Autumn, 1965).

Accomplishment and Disaster, 1911–1914 155

nation to guard the identity of the Social Democratic party. Milwaukee had been a major center of late-nineteenth-century labor strife. During the eight-hour-day strikes of 1886, a serious riot erupted at the Bay View Steel Mills just outside the city limits. Governor Rusk had called out the militia which battled the rioters, killing two. A Union Labor Party sprang from this event and posed a serious political threat to the older parties.

The *Milwaukee Journal* editorialized that the political battle in Milwaukee was "one between American citizens of whatever extraction and the imported demagogues and agitators whose avowed purpose is the destruction of American institutions."[99] Significantly, the Union Labor party's candidate for mayor was countered by a fusion Republican-Democratic candidate.[100] As employers continued to be militantly anti-union, effectively using the injunction against strikes, there seemed to Berger and his associates ample reason to believe that labor could only depend on a party of its own, not on one which management controlled or influenced.

Though nonlabor reformers of Milwaukee had certain concerns in common with workingmen and Social Democrats, their movement was less concerned with purely labor questions. Certainly, it was completely different in personnel. In practice, the Republican reformers were as jealous of their identity and independence as were the Social Democrats. It was they who first rode the wave of reform into major office with McGovern's election as district attorney. Under these circumstances, the growing prospects for reform served only to intensify the rivalry between socialists and reform Republicans. From a political standpoint, the rise of the socialists constituted a threat to Old Guard Republicans and Democrats, but especially to progressives. After all, Berger's victory in 1910 was at the expense not of

[99] Still, *Milwaukee*, 294; E. E. Witte, "Labor in Wisconsin History," 86, 137.
[100] Still, *Milwaukee*, 284.

a conservative, but of McGovern's progressive ally Henry Cochems.

Following the election of 1910, with the Social Democrats now in control of Milwaukee and McGovern occupying the governor's office in Madison, rivalry between the socialists and the Republican reformers of Milwaukee intensified. McGovern, preoccupied with Republican factional politics, resisted anti-socialist coalition efforts. But some of his supporters, focusing on city politics, joined in the campaign to stop the socialists. "Nonpartisanship," a widespread reform device, was proposed in the 1911 legislative session in a covert attempt to undermine the socialists; but it was rejected, due partly to socialist votes. Republicans and Democrats of Milwaukee then formed a coalition against the socialists and, in the spring of 1912, recaptured the mayor's office and a majority on the city council. A nonpartisan bill was passed and, despite his opposition to it, was signed by Governor McGovern on May 6, 1912. Thereafter, in Wisconsin's municipal elections, party designations were removed from the primary ballots, and the two leading vote-getters, irrespective of party, would run against each other in the general election. This had the effect of reinforcing fusionism and promoting combinations of nonsocialists against socialists. But the socialist vote grew, nonetheless. This, in turn, brought the opposition to the socialists more into the open. In 1914, Gerhard Bading, the incumbent mayor of Milwaukee and a conventional "good government" man, posed the issue in rather drastic terms in his successful campaign for re-election. It was, he said, a choice between Americanism and Socialism.[101]

In sum, the socialists, as the result of their political and economic experience, had every reason to protect their identity and independence by remaining aloof from the factional politics and statewide competition of the major parties. This they did. Thus, in 1914, when the progressive Republicans had real need for reinforcements, and when the ad-

[101] Still, *Milwaukee*, 520–522.

Accomplishment and Disaster, 1911–1914

vanced progressivism of the McGovern administration seemed to merit help from the socialists, the Milwaukee Federated Trades Council, and the State Federation of Labor, no such aid was forthcoming.[102]

The Republican platform of 1914 was carefully tailored to voter sentiment. Patterned by shrewd political experts, the platform represented an attempt to recognize and placate all of the major elements of political strength in the state. It endorsed the past achievements of the progressives, and favored the general idea of regulation of business by the state. It did not include the anti-primary plank espoused by Philipp earlier. But it did support economy in education and road construction; the elimination of nonessential commissions; constitutional government; and greater local control over highway construction.[103]

In an effort to slow their headlong flight of the primary campaign into an orderly retreat,[104] progressives of various factions put an independent candidate into the field. Efforts to persuade La Follette to make the race for governor failed,[105] and the hopeless task fell to State Senator John J. Blaine of Boscobel. As an ardent Wilson backer in 1912, he was expected to win liberal Democratic support.[106] Blaine made a strong and forthright campaign. He tried to show that "The contest is between stalwarts and halfbreeds, just as it was in the beginning."[107] He also supported the amendments for initiative, referendum, and recall, which the La Follette men considered highly important.[108] La Follette,

---

[102] See the *Wisconsin Blue Book, 1915,* 222, 236–237, for primary and general election voting figures. The socialists evidently stayed in their own primaries and adhered to their own ticket in the general election.

[103] *Milwaukee Sentinel,* October 1, 1914.

[104] Ekern to La Follette, October 14, 1914, in the Ekern Papers; *Milwaukee Sentinel,* October 2, 6, 1914.

[105] Memo on conversation between Charles McCarthy and Richard Lloyd Jones, September 12, 1914, in the McCarthy Papers; Ekern to La Follette, September 24, 1914, in the Ekern Papers; *Milwaukee Sentinel,* October 5, 1914; Belle and Fola La Follette, *La Follette,* 1:506–530.

[106] *Milwaukee Sentinel,* October 6, 1914.

[107] *Ibid.,* October 15, 1914.

[108] Ekern to George A. Anderson, October 26, 1914; Ekern to C. B. Ballard,

after some delay in Washington, finally took the stump for Blaine and the amendments on October 29. Richard Lloyd Jones had been a prime mover in bringing Blaine into the field, and he now gave him cordial support in the *Wisconsin State Journal*.[109] Such pro-La Follette papers as the *La Crosse Tribune, Eau Claire Telegram,* and *Lancaster Teller* also backed him.[110] Nevertheless, Blaine's effort was simply token resistance. The candidates on the state ticket remained loyal to Philipp, as did many progressive Republicans, including Andrew Dahl and D. O. Mahoney, president of the Wisconsin Society of Equity.[111] Progressive Republican papers like the *Merrill Herald, Superior Telegram, Racine Times, Oshkosh Northwestern* and *Neenah News* supported the straight Republican ticket.[112] Nor did Blaine secure Democratic support. The national Democratic administration favored party harmony,[113] and senatorial candidate Paul Husting, leader of the liberal Democrats, was dependent on national financial help for his campaign.[114] In the end, Blaine polled only 32,940 votes, against 119,567 for Karel and 140,835 for Emanuel Philipp, the new governor. Oscar Ameringer, the Social Democrat, received 24,940 votes.[115]

The weakness of the Blaine candidacy evidenced another important, though rather intangible factor in the progressive decline. The widespread crusading zeal that ani-

---

October 26, 1914, in the Ekern Papers; *La Follette's Magazine,* 6: 42, 44 (October 17, 31, 1914). Judge Charles Rosa of Beloit, a strong La Follette man, conducted a campaign for the amendments.
[109] *Wisconsin State Journal,* October 7, 1914.
[110] *La Crosse Tribune,* October 3, 1914; *Milwaukee Journal,* October 9, 11, 1914.
[111] *Milwaukee Sentinel,* October 8, 1914; McCarthy to William Hard, October 8, 1914, in the McCarthy Papers.
[112] Reported in the *Milwaukee Journal,* October 6, 7, 8, 9, 10, 1914.
[113] Paul Husting to Burt Williams, October 1, 1914, in the Paul Husting Letterbooks.
[114] Husting to Joseph E. Davies, September 18, 1914, in the Husting Letterbooks.
[115] *Wisconsin Blue Book, 1915,* 222.

mated progressivism in the early days seemed to have dissipated to a considerable degree by 1914. The young men who had rallied to La Follette with such enthusiasm in the nineties had grown more cautious with the years. Charles McCarthy, as enthusiastic as ever, noticed that while many young progressives were backing Blaine, the older ones supported Philipp.[116] McCarthy's thoughtful friend William Hatton, looking back on the downward path, remarked on the same general factor. ". . . Many who had fought the good fight became more and more imbued with the desire to retain or gain public office," he wrote. "The spirit of sacrifice for principle's sake, which had been a marked characteristic of the movement in its earlier days, disappeared to no small extent. What also hurt was the fact that many men whose chief idea was to be on the winning side were attracted to the movement by its very success, and they, too, aided in weakening its morale. Selfishness largely displaced unselfishness. . . ."[117]

The decline of enthusiasm was caused by more than the process of aging. Diversion of attention to other concerns, public and private, also played a part. This had always been a problem for La Follette, of course. At the very height of the conflict between stalwart and progressive, there had been those on each side who were still influenced by such seemingly extraneous considerations as ethnic, sectional, state, and party loyalty. Considerations of this sort tended to weaken factional division based on political and economic interest and ideology. By 1914, another kind of consideration, equally extraneous, had become sufficiently prominent as to weaken factional devotion and contribute to the impression of apathy with respect to the issues of progressive politics. This new concern was religious; specifically, "the Catholic issue." The issue was to remain a diverting factor for years to come.

---

[116] McCarthy to William Hard, October 8, 1914, in the McCarthy Papers.
[117] *Milwaukee Journal*, November 24, 1914.

Sandwiched between the spectacular anti-Catholic movements of the American Protective Association and the Ku Klux Klan, and overshadowed by the "progressive movement" and World War I, a significant phase of anti-Catholicism covering the years 1914 through 1920 went largely unnoticed. Yet the religious issue was crucial in New York's gubernatorial election of 1914. The campaign against Martin Glynn, the Democratic candidate, was marked by the organization of a third party based exclusively on the Catholic issue.[118] The emergence of the religious question on the political surface, where all could see it, was not general. But anti-Catholic sentiment was a significant and at times a decisive factor in Wisconsin elections between 1914 and 1920.

In 1914 the ugly religious question was most prominent not in the stalwart-progressive contest but in the showdown between McGovern and La Follette. While Philipp was contesting for his party's gubernatorial nomination, McGovern was seeking nomination for senator against the hand-picked pro-La Follette candidate, Lieutenant Governor Tom Morris of La Crosse.[119] The conflict was not to be determined wholly on its merits, for Morris was a Catholic and that fact contributed heavily to his defeat.

The issue was of concern to some Scandinavians. Already sensitive to the danger, La Follette's astute cohort, Herman Ekern, was alarmed when he read in the influential *Skandinaven* the following letter: "Shall we, as Scandinavians and Protestant citizens of Wisconsin, bestow our confidence upon a Roman Catholic as our representative in Washington? . . . The history and record of the Catholic power is black, blood stained and rotten, and cannot bear the light of day, and remember that it never changes, of

---

[118] John Higham, *Strangers in the Land: Patterns of American Nativism, 1880–1925* (New Brunswick, 1955), 184.
[119] "It would mean everything to have a true friend for a colleague," La Follette wrote, in urging active work for Morris. La Follette to Charles Rosa, August 14, 1914, in the Rosa Papers.

which fact several of its own prelates have boasted. Its sole aim and struggle is to obtain complete power."[120]

Others besides Ekern feared the religious issue. A La Follette man in Waushara County wrote Ekern late in April, "Can you tell me of what religious belief our Governor is? And State Superintendent C. P. Cary? If they are Catholics do you know whether they belong to the Knights of Columbus?"[121]

Some McGovern men, on the other hand, regarded the question with satisfaction. In late May one of these reported to McGovern's secretary and political right hand, Harry Wilbur, that in his section, the heavily Scandinavian western part of the state, there was "Marked opposition to Morris on ac. Catholic connections." "To help Morris," he went on, "Ekern is calling the Gov. 'an apostate'—saying that he, the Gov. is at heart a Catholic."[122] Wilbur quickly replied, "I note what you say regarding the opposition to Morris and the ground on which it is based. Reports that come to me from different parts of the state indicate that that particular feature is going to play a large part in the campaign, though, of course, all the work along that line will be done quietly."[123]

As the campaign advanced the issue did not abate.[124] Ekern, long close to the editor of the *Skandinaven,* made every effort to keep that influential journal from opposing Morris. But he judged that the paper was subject to pressure from its readers.[125] He was apparently right, for early in August *Skandinaven* came out for McGovern, and later

---

[120] *Skandinaven,* April 22, 1914; translation in Ekern to Tom Morris, n.d., in the Ekern Papers.

[121] E. G. Keup to Ekern, April 22, 1914, in the Ekern Papers.

[122] F. A. George to Wilbur, May 22, 1914, in the McGovern Papers, Wilbur Correspondence.

[123] Wilbur to George, May 26, 1914, in the McGovern Papers, Wilbur Correspondence.

[124] H. J. Mortensen to Ekern, June 11, 1914; E. G. Keup to Ekern, June 23, 1914; Ole Eggum to Ekern, August 1, 1914, in the Ekern Papers; John S. Donald to James Makenzie, July 31, 1914, in the Donald Papers.

[125] Ekern to Tom Morris, June 10, 1914, in the Ekern Papers.

raised the religious issue in specific terms.[126] Several national journals and organizations both took advantage of and stimulated anti-Catholicism in Wisconsin. The leading anti-Catholic paper in the nation, *The Menace,* was read widely in the state, a pro-La Follette politician ruefully noted.[127] Both the Knights of Luther and the Guardians of Liberty were active.[128] The leaders of the Guardians of Liberty in the state were friendly to La Follette, but they were determined to pursue the political ends of the organization. This meant gathering information from candidates about their religious affiliations and passing it on to their local branches.[129]

Victory for McGovern was one of the fruits of bigotry. He polled 37,125 votes to 26,012 for Morris, with 26,156 for the leading anti-progressive candidate and about 25,000 scattered among three others.[130] Morris himself had no doubt that prejudice caused his defeat: "I ran into it everywhere."[131] John S. Donald, progressive secretary of state, conjectured that the closeness of his own renomination contest was due to the fact that many voters mistakenly believed him to be an Irish Catholic.[132]

McGovern was probably as good a progressive as Morris, perhaps better. The Catholic question had not worked directly to the advantage of stalwarts in this situation. The fact that such a question was important in 1914 indicated, however, that the attention of voters was not focused wholly on the political and economic issues of progressivism.

For McGovern, the windfall proved temporary, for he lost in the general election to the liberal Democrat Paul Husting, who probably benefited somewhat from the votes

---

[126] *Milwaukee Free Press,* August 4, 1914; Ekern to Ole Eggum, August 28, 1914, in the Ekern Papers.
[127] Ole Eggum to Ekern, August 1, 1914, in the Ekern Papers.
[128] John S. Donald to La Follette, September 22, 1914, in the Donald Papers.
[129] Ekern to Tom Morris, July 26, 1914, in the Ekern Papers.
[130] *Wisconsin Blue Book, 1915,* 233–235.
[131] Morris to Charles Rosa, September 12, 1914, in the Rosa Papers.
[132] John S. Donald to La Follette, September 22, 1914, in the Donald Papers.

of certain La Follette men who might have been called "fairminded Republicans." The battle between McGovern and Husting seemed personal and partisan rather than ideological. In any event, it was overshadowed by the notable triumph of Emanuel Philipp, which seemed to signal the end of progressivism in Wisconsin.

At long last, the stalwarts had accomplished their most cherished purpose—the downfall of the progressive Republicans. They owed their triumph in part to their own dogged persistence and to the intensified effort stimulated by Emanuel Philipp in sustaining William Howard Taft and redeeming the state from McGovern-style progressivism. They benefited also from the combination of circumstances that kept the socialists constantly aloof from the progressives. They owed something, too, to the Democrats, who largely abandoned La Follette with the revival of their own party's fortunes. In addition, they had capitalized on a variety of factors that had eroded progressive strength—jealousies, the toll of time, the diversion of attention to other questions, money troubles, and the limitations of the direct primary. Above all, the stalwarts had been able to capitalize on the basic conservatism of both the progressive ideology and the progressive electorate.

All this was so, at any rate, unless the stalwart victory of 1914 was simply an historical accident, occasioned by a chance confluence of events—the La Follette-McGovern schism, the economic recession of 1913, the emergency tax levy. Could it have been such a fluke? Only time and the 1916 elections would tell.

V

Emanuel Philipp and the Survival of Conservatism

THE YEARS 1915 and 1916 were a time of testing for Wisconsin's conservative Republicans. For more than twenty years the dynamic La Follette had warned the electorate that his political opponents were the self-seeking tools of predatory corporations. The actions of Old Guard leaders like Sawyer, Payne, Pfister, and the railroad lobbyists had lent substance to the charges. Emanuel Philipp was singled out by La Follette in his speeches and *Autobiography* as a typical corruptionist. Philipp's close associations through the years with the railroads and brewers made him particularly vulnerable to La Follette's attacks and voter suspicions. Now, through a combination of circumstances, Philipp had become governor of the state, with all the opportunity of that office to work his reactionary and corrupt schemes. The Philipp administration would demonstrate the true character of the conservative opposition. It would largely confirm—or greatly weaken—stereotypes integral to the progressive movement in the state. Progressives must have looked forward to the new administration with mixed feelings. The legislative and administrative fruits of twenty years of political battle were at the mercy of the enemy. On the other hand, should the Philipp administration act temperately, might it not consolidate its power and work still greater mischief in the long run?

At the outset, it seemed that the new governor would go forward with the all-out attack that he had promised during the primary. The University of Wisconsin had been his chief whipping boy in the primary campaign, and in the early months of his administration Philipp continued to voice strong criticism and threaten great changes. In March he revived fears that the university was teaching socialism.[1] At Marinette, in April, he said earnestly:[2]

I believe I voice the sentiments of every mother who sends sons and daughters to the university. We are American citizens and love American institutions and expect our children to return as good and loyal citizens, who can be relied upon to do their part in the perpetuation of our institutions, and we condemn in unmeasured terms the teaching, with the approval of any political system, of a theory of government that has a tendency to make them disloyal. If that demand is an interference with academic freedom, then let us interfere. . . .

The governor was fortified in his plan to revamp the university by a report by William Harvey Allen of the New York Bureau of Municipal Research. Allen had been engaged by the Wisconsin Board of Public Affairs in 1911 to do a survey of rural schools, and, in 1913, of the university. Given its progressive sponsorship, a favorable report might have been expected. Indeed, the conservative University Regent Granville D. Jones feared a whitewash, thinking Allen a tool of Charles McCarthy.[3] Jones was both right and wrong. Allen and McCarthy were of similar view and did work co-operatively together. But while McCarthy had crossed swords with Jones on issues of academic freedom, and was in sympathy with the "socialist" professors, he was also extremely critical of the university. McCarthy was at odds with Dean Russell and the College of Agriculture, was critical of what he considered to be the academic and aristocratic approach of the university, and was, primarily, an advocate of "practical" and "democratic" edu-

---

[1] *Milwaukee Journal*, March 17, 1915.
[2] *Milwaukee Sentinel*, April 11, 1915.
[3] Curti and Carstensen, *University of Wisconsin*, 2: 270.

cation.[4] He was not at all displeased when Allen's report proved critical of the university for not meeting the standards of efficiency spelled out by the investigators.

In 1914 the Board of Public Affairs decided to publish its own report, with Allen's as an appendix.[5] Allen responded by launching a little publication called *Everybody's Business* to defend the survey. When the new governor came to office, Allen was more than willing to ally with him in revamping the university. Philipp employed the disgruntled gentleman to draft legislation for him, chiefly the education and budget bills.[6]

The education bill appeared in innumerable forms during the spring of 1915. The key provision would have created a board of education superior to the university, normal schools, and common schools. The composition and powers of this board varied from bill to bill. Charles R. Van Hise, president of the university, led the opposition to the central education bill. Van Hise feared that Philipp had ulterior motives, that he wanted to gain control of the University by appointing the members of the board.[7] Alumni like Zona Gale and Evan A. Evans of Baraboo helped Van Hise in his fight.[8] The regents of the normal schools also swung their influence against the administration measures.[9] University and normal school people united with the brewery lobby to trade support during the session.[10]

During the course of 1915, Philipp moderated his position considerably. It was not the political weight of the opposition that caused the change, however; rather, Philipp shifted ground as a result of his own inquiries. Though he had taken a strong position in favor of a central board of education during the 1914 campaign, as governor he felt

[4] See McCarthy to Merlin Hull, May 7, 1915, in the McCarthy Papers.
[5] Curti and Carstensen, *University of Wisconsin*, 2: 277.
[6] McCarthy to Merlin Hull, May 13, 1915, in the McCarthy Papers.
[7] Curti and Carstensen, *University of Wisconsin*, 2: 285.
[8] *Ibid.*, 2: 289.
[9] William Titus to Emanuel Philipp, July 1, 1915; Marshall Cousins to C. A. Evans, April 3, 1915, in the Philipp Papers.
[10] Cousins to C. A. Evans, April 3, 1915, in the Philipp Papers.

impelled to inquire further. When educational authorities from throughout the nation argued with force and cogency against his scheme, Philipp became persuaded in favor of a more moderate course. He was probably influenced also by some of the young men he had recruited to his administration. Philipp's closest associates were moderate men who were in sympathy with the university. These included Michael J. Cleary, university alumnus and former assemblyman, who served as secretary to the governor until his appointment as insurance commissioner; Lawrence Whittet, another alumnus, speaker of the assembly, and later secretary to the governor; and George P. Hambrecht, a former assemblyman whom Philipp appointed to the Industrial Commission. The governor also came to rely heavily on the opinions of Halston J. Thorkelson, business manager of the university.[11]

The act that was finally adopted bore little resemblance to the original administration bill. The Board of Regents retained its powers while the new board of five members had limited financial responsibility.[12] Philipp, who had changed during these months and had shown his opponents that he was reasonable and disinterested, accepted it with good grace. Relations between he and Van Hise became almost cordial.[13]

Charles McCarthy judged that the university had not been hurt materially as a result of the fight, but that "today it does not hold the torch to the rest of the country." A general timidity with respect to the charge of socialism prevailed during the Philipp administration.[14] But McCarthy himself, another leading target during Philipp's primary campaign, marched jauntily through the legislative session

[11] Maxwell, *Philipp*, 96–100; Curti and Carstensen, *University of Wisconsin*, 2: 196.
[12] Curti and Carstensen, *University of Wisconsin*, 2: 291.
[13] Philipp to Van Hise, August 11, 1917, in the Philipp Papers; Curti and Carstensen, *University of Wisconsin*, 2: 292; Maxwell, *Philipp*, 100.
[14] McCarthy to J. W. McConaughy, October 1, 1915, in the McCarthy Papers; Curti and Carstensen, *University of Wisconsin*, 2: 71–76.

neither scathed nor cowed. In his first message to the legislature, Philipp asked that McCarthy be fired and the Legislative Reference Library abolished. The forthright McCarthy was called before a hearing of a legislative investigating committee in the office of the governor on April 8. For two days he was subjected to questioning about whether or not he had interfered in politics, professed socialism, or believed in the Constitution of the United States. McCarthy explained his behavior and opinions, raised some counterquestions as to what the governor meant by socialism, and judged, after it was all over, that Senators Platt Whitman and Edward T. Fairchild, conservatives both, took a fair view and that "finally the Governor himself got quite good humored."[15] Efforts continued in the legislature to curtail or transfer the functions of the Legislative Reference Library, but none of these succeeded. Indeed, McCarthy's relations with the governor took such a favorable turn that he was consulted on the education bill.[16]

Philipp, after close study of the matter, abandoned the idea of eliminating the Tax Commission. He did replace progressive appointees such as Insurance Commissioner Ekern and Dairy and Food Commissioner J. Q. Emery, among others. He abandoned reforestation efforts and revamped the Board of Public Affairs, which became simply a financial branch of the government, losing its grandiose planning functions.

State expenses continued to rise and gross tax receipts actually increased, but the state's share of the property tax was cut over two million dollars from the 1913–1914 figure. Moreover, no tax for general purposes was required.[17] Philipp had campaigned against the political character of progressive appointments, and he was very careful about his own. While the Philipp appointees were conservative,

[15] Memorandum, April 10, 1915, in the McCarthy Papers.
[16] McCarthy to Michael Cleary, May 3, 1915, in the McCarthy Papers.
[17] *Report of the State Treasurer for the State of Wisconsin for Fiscal Year Ending June 30, 1913 and June 30, 1914,* 17; *Report . . . For Fiscal Year Ending June 30, 1915 and June 30, 1916,* 13.

they did not subvert the laws they were appointed to enforce. Nor did the governor use his office to advance his own private interests. In fact, Philipp signed a bill to increase taxes on private car and equipment companies, his own line of business.[18]

The governor displeased some of his stalwart confreres. A few complained of his independence and failure to consult on matters of patronage and legislation.[19] He resisted Charles Pfister's efforts to guide his administration.[20] In his home territory of Milwaukee, Philipp disturbed some when he blocked a measure pressed by the liquor lobby,[21] and helped balk an effort to raise the railroad fare to two-and-a-half cents a mile.[22]

Philipp was not alone among conservatives in moving towards the middle of the road. John Whitehead, the patriarch of honorable stalwartism, had for several years been fearful of too radical a reaction against La Follette's works, some of which he acknowledged as worthwhile.[23] Other conservatives had sought to reunite Republicans across factional lines in the 1914 elections.[24] Upon being elected governor, Philipp received advice from a number of conservatives warning him not to destroy everything, not to give La Follette an issue for 1916.[25] The young men on whom he relied—Cleary, Hambrecht, the writer Charles Stewart, and especially Lawrence Whittet—astute and already experienced in business and politics, sustained and abetted the governor as he backed away from some of his earlier, more extreme ideas and pronouncements. Progres-

---

[18] Maxwell, *Philipp*, 94.
[19] Oscar Schoengarth to John J. Esch, April 2, 1916; Esch to John S. Roeseler, February 26, 1915, in the Esch Papers; Frank X. Boden to John J. Blaine, November 9, 1920, in the John J. Blaine Papers.
[20] Maxwell, *Philipp*, 94.
[21] L. C. Wagner to Philipp, June 8, 1915; John C. Voss to Philipp, June 9, 1915; John Whitehead to Philipp, June 26, 1915, all in the Philipp Papers.
[22] Philipp to E. S. Baker, March 2, 1915, in the Philipp Papers.
[23] Whitehead to Ralph Gabriel, May 15, 1914, in the Whitehead Papers.
[24] J. T. McGrath to John Whitehead, July 9, 1914, in the Whitehead Papers.
[25] Maxwell, *Philipp*, 94.

sives looking back on the Philipp administration agreed that the governor was "a big man," in character as well as body, one who did not hold grudges and who grew in office.[26]

During the years of Philipp's administrations, especially his first administration, La Follette men did not take so charitable a view of their old antagonist. The senator himself led the counterattack. Shortly after Philipp's election in 1914, La Follette wrote Ekern: ". . . We ought to start a lot of things. To begin with: Is there a man in our camp fit to take the job of building up La Follette's monthly, county by county *(and on the side incidentally making a good political organization in each township?)*. . . . In the meantime, we should be looking after *our own* in the legislature. What have we there that we can bank on? We should get a lineup in the Senate. We should have a candidate for Speaker. We must fight every minute to hold our own men and make an issue against the enemy."[27]

Through his secretary, John Hannan, Senator La Follette let it be known that he had the most at stake in the coming political contest and would take personal charge. He planned, in May of 1915, to return home in July and visit every part of the state personally to secure agreement among progressives on their primary candidates. In the meantime, he suggested that Ekern diplomatically block any meeting of progressives.[28] The La Follette tour was to involve speaking engagements as well as quiet conferences, and he sought from Ekern and others information about the last session of the legislature that he might use on the platform.[29]

A speaking tour in the southern and northwestern states,

---

[26] Interviews with Selig Perlman, December 8, 1953; William Kirsch, January 18, 1954; Charles Rosa, January 15, 1954; and William T. Evjue, January 18, 1954; Haugen, *Political and Pioneer Reminiscences*, 178–179.
[27] La Follette to Ekern, November 16, 1914, in the Ekern Papers. The emphasis is La Follette's.
[28] Hannan to Ekern, May 15, 1915, in the Ekern Papers.
[29] Hannan to Ekern, July 26, 1915, in the Ekern Papers.

his usual means of earning extra income, and the illness of his son Bobby, prevented La Follette from getting to Wisconsin until early September. Once back, he plunged into the job of mastering the follies and failures of the Philipp administration, aided by Ekern, Commons, Crownhart, Joseph D. Beck, and others.[30] His "educational campaign" finally got under way with a number of speeches late in November, and continued intermittently throughout the winter, whenever he could get away from Washington.

So far as generating a wave of progressive sentiment was concerned, La Follette's efforts were wasted. He concentrated on the charge that Philipp was undermining progressive legislation. But Philipp as governor was giving La Follette little new evidence and the senator was forced to rely heavily on twice-told tales of Philipp's past iniquities.[31] The true state of affairs was indicated when La Follette's candidate for speaker in the next session, Charles Rosa, wrote Speaker Lawrence Whittet, his prospective opponent and Philipp's chief adviser, "I do not believe but that you and I personally stand for pretty much the same things in legislation. Yet you are labeled a Philipp Republican and I a La Follette Republican."[32]

Craig Ralston, a political reporter for the *Milwaukee Journal,* later noted that the success of *La Follette's Magazine* was a barometer of progressive strength and that in 1915 the magazine yielded a gross income of only $11,781, as opposed to $36,495 in 1912. There was talk in 1915 of suspending publication.[33]

Ralston offered the new vitality of the Democrats in the state, inspired by the national Democratic administration, as a partial explanation for the decline of the progressive Republicans. Another factor was the relative suc-

[30] La Follette to Ekern, September 3, 1915, in the Ekern Papers; Belle and Fola La Follette, *La Follette,* 1: 547.
[31] Belle and Fola La Follette, *La Follette,* 1: 548; Maxwell, *Philipp,* 120.
[32] Charles Rosa to Lawrence Whittet, November 21, 1916, in the Rosa Papers.
[33] Craig Ralston, "The La Follette Dynasty" (unpublished manuscript), 141.

cess of the first Philipp administration. This, in turn, reflected and resulted from a fundamental weakness in the political fabric of progressivism: the anti-La Follette forces were neither so venal nor so reactionary as La Follette always wanted the voters to believe. They never had been. But there had been, in the early days, enough corporate influence and machine control to fuel a substantial reform movement. La Follette, at the head of that movement, had driven all his opponents together; a sort of Gresham's law, abetted by the aggressive La Follette, then worked against the reputation of each anti-La Follette man. But appearance and reality diverged. Emanuel Philipp was not a corporate corruptionist but an honest businessman of somewhat limited vision and education, yet highly able and capable of considerable growth. After 1914, Philipp had the opportunity to demonstrate the reality, and this he did to good effect. In so doing, he exonerated not only himself but many of his cohorts of the early days. Nor was this the whole of the matter. The fact that the stalwarts possessed considerable honesty and capacity meant that once in power they did a satisfactory job, instead of resupplying La Follette with new examples of corruption and reaction.

Many of the conservatives who proved their mettle in the Philipp administration were young men who had become politically active after La Follette's momentous 1904 victory. The fact that such men existed was of some importance. To be sure, many, probably a majority, of the younger men continued to enter politics on the progressive side. But by 1904 the upper rungs of the progressive ladder to office and influence were fully occupied, and even the lower steps were becoming crowded. The stalwart ladder, by contrast, seemed invitingly open. Here was a reversal of the situation that had worked to La Follette's advantage in the nineties. Also, there remained pockets of conservative Republicanism throughout the La Follette era, relatively prosperous older counties such as Rock and Walworth, in which conservative Republicanism remained socially proper for young businessmen or professionals, especially those of Yankee stock. Conservatively oriented business firms in the cities and towns, burgeoning in the prosperous pre-war years, provided an ample clientele for conservative Republican lawyers. True, it was difficult to consider oneself a regular Republican, as the conservatives did, without following the party's leader. But those who stood off from La Follette found highly acceptable patrons in Davidson and Taft—men who could promise not only office but respectability. (Probably Isaac Stephenson was himself a little too disreputable to serve in this way and few men thought of themselves as "Stephenson Republicans.")

For a variety of reasons, then, a new generation of conservative Republicans had come to maturity. When given the opportunity, they joined Philipp in redeeming the conservative image and providing a brand of state government much less vulnerable to attack than the administrations of Upham and Scofield had been. And because they demonstrated their responsibility while memories of progressive excesses were still fresh, the obstacles to progressive resurgence in 1916 were imposing.

A number of irons smouldered in the 1916 political fire. Another presidential election year had arrived, and no towering candidate overshadowed the favorite sons, of whom La Follette was perennially one. But to resume this role in any seriousness La Follette had to control the Wisconsin delegation, which was to be elected in April. The spring battle for convention delegates also involved control of the national committeemen posts. More important than that, as the first direct test between La Follette and Philipp since 1914, it represented a public test of progressive strength in Wisconsin. In September, both Philipp and La Follette would seek renomination and each was sure to oppose the other. Progressive success in the primary election depended in a number of ways on the April delegate battle.

As the La Follette men prepared for what many of the leaders regarded as a decisive contest with their archrivals, it was probably dismaying to some that extraneous issues continued to encroach on public attention and that, partly as a consequence of this new focus, apathy towards the progressive-stalwart contest seemed to be growing. While 1916 saw no statewide Catholic-versus-Protestant tests comparable in importance to the McGovern-Morris battle of 1914, the religious issue remained as prominent in politics as ever, especially in the western part of the state. Some observers felt that there were no other outstanding issues, and that the religious question was dominant in local contests throughout the state, and of importance even in the national election. The Guardians of Liberty once again led the anti-Catholic drive.[34] Attention was diverted also by news of the war in Europe and concern over American foreign and defense policy. On this issue, unlike the religious question, political leaders of all factions shared, and in many instances exceeded, voter anxiety. La Follette was one of those who was much concerned to prevent American involvement. He feared the effect of militarism and war on American democracy, and he made the issue prominent in the delegate election campaign.

Finding that the foreign situation commanded growing interest, La Follette had every reason to declare himself forthrightly. In his argument, he attempted to link the menace of involvement to the old familiar domestic concerns of progressivism. The senator expressed fear that powerful special interests, the eternal predatory pack, would gain dominance over the nation by means of army and navy expansion. He proposed, therefore, that the arms industries be nationalized. He proposed, further, an embargo on the shipment of arms and ammunition to belligerents. He sug-

[34] J. J. Irvine to Merlin Hull, March 17, 1916, in the Merlin Hull Papers; Anna Adams Dickie to Charles R. McCarthy, August 28, 1916, in the McCarthy Papers; Esch to A. E. Dudley, September 17, 1916; C. Rabenstein to Esch, September 9, 1916; O. G. Munson to Esch, September 12, 1916; Edward E. Browne to Esch, September 16, 1916; F. A. Cooper to Esch, October 2, 1916; Esch to Frank B. Woods, October 2, 1916; Esch to F. A. Cooper, October 3, 1916; Esch to W. F. Esch, October 12, 1916; Esch to Frank B. Oster, October 22, 1916; Esch to A. D. Dudley, October 30, 1916; N. B. Hood to Esch, November 1, 1916, all in the Esch Papers.

gested government-owned ships, partly in order to lessen the pressure of the shipping lobby. In short, La Follette sought to link the cause of progressivism with that of peace, and the forces of privilege with those of war.[35]

On the local level, progressives like Merlin Hull used the argument outlined by La Follette in the delegate contest. Hull sent voters a letter stating that La Follette was being opposed by the same elements as in the past. "The trusts and munition manufacturers are particularly active in politics at this time and will do all in their power to defeat him. . . . It is at once a contest for rule of the people and a protest against those who would use the government for private ends. . . ."[36] Hull tried to show that the delegate fight was an oldtime contest against the stalwarts and their Wall Street allies.[37]

Anti-German sentiment developed in Wisconsin late in 1914 and during 1915 as a result of the invasion of Belgium.[38] German submarine warfare during 1915 and early 1916 intensified this hostility, and gave point to the "preparedness" campaign led by Eastern Republicans like Roosevelt and Elihu Root, and finally joined in by President Wilson. While the President was campaigning for preparedness and against "hyphenated Americans," leading Democratic politicians of Wisconsin were swinging into line in a "Back the President" appeal.[39] They set it as their task to arouse public sentiment to the need for preparedness.[40] The campaign met with some success, even in heavily German Wisconsin. Staunch La Follette men like James Stone and A. W. Sanborn were among the major leaders

---

[35] *La Follette's Magazine*, 8: 3 (March, 1916).
[36] Form Letter from Merlin Hull, March 14, 1916, in the Hull Papers.
[37] Hull to Stone, March 13, 1916, in the Stone Papers; Hull to Crownhart, March 10, 1916, in the Hull Papers.
[38] McCarthy to Sir Courtenay Ilbert, April 1, 1915, in the McCarthy Papers.
[39] Husting to Gustave Alter, March 4, 1916, in the Husting Letterbooks.
[40] Husting to R. B. Kirkland, January 20, 1916; Husting to Richard F. Sortomme, February 12, 1916, in the Husting Letterbooks; *Milwaukee Journal*, February, March, 1916.

who disagreed with La Follette's stand in favor of an arms embargo and on other preparedness questions.[41]

For the most part, however, La Follette's outspoken neutrality stand was of advantage to him in 1916.[42] McCarthy noted early in 1915 that even while sentiment was swinging away from Germany, people generally feared American involvement.[43] The following year, all of Wisconsin's congressmen joined La Follette in supporting the Gore and McLemore resolutions, warning Americans to stay off armed merchantmen. Significantly, the conservative Republican *Milwaukee Sentinel* joined La Follette in favor of neutrality throughout 1916. Though Representatives Browne, Lenroot, and Stafford tended to differ with La Follette on the question of preparedness during 1915 and 1916, and such Republican papers as the *Wisconsin State Journal, Milwaukee Sentinel,* and *Superior Telegram* backed most preparedness measures, partisanship was not intense.[44]

While nationalists in Wisconsin were only mildly aroused by the preparedness campaign stimulated by the Democrats, Germans resented the belligerency of the Democratic administration and feared war.[45] Wilson antagonized them in 1915 with his stand against an arms embargo, reversal of his earlier position on loans to the Allies, and other measures that seemed unneutral. Their hostility was

[41] Stone to La Follette, February 23, 1916; Sanborn to Stone, March 13, 1916, in the Stone Papers. See also O. D. Whitehill to Stone, February 4, 1916, in the Stone Papers. A strong conservative who expressed the same view was Ellis B. Usher to John Esch, March 31, 1916, in the Esch Papers. For a full discussion of the preparedness movement in the state, see John P. Finnegan, "The Preparedness Movement in Wisconsin, 1914–1917" (unpublished master's thesis, University of Wisconsin, 1961).

[42] See *La Follette's Magazine,* 7: 3 (March, 1915), for La Follette's neutrality proposals.

[43] McCarthy to Sir Courtenay Ilbert, April 1, 1915, in the McCarthy Papers.

[44] James Ernest Jackson, "Wisconsin's Attitude Toward American Foreign Policy Since 1910" (unpublished doctoral dissertation, University of Wisconsin, 1934), 27–31.

[45] Husting to A. C. Bishop, February 14, 1916, in the Husting Letterbooks; Clifton James Child, *German-Americans in Politics, 1914–1917* (Madison, 1939), 64–110.

intensified by his campaign against "hyphenated Americans," begun late in 1915, and his drive to mobilize nationalist sentiment early in 1916.[46] The bellicosity of Theodore Roosevelt fortified their anger and fear.[47] The pro-German *Milwaukee Free Press* and the Social Democratic *Milwaukee Leader* led the aroused Germans.[48]

As matters stood in March of 1916, on the eve of the delegate election, nationalist sentiment had been mildly aroused to the disadvantage of La Follette, while neutrality sentiment, spearheaded by the large German population, was strong, to his advantage.[49] Most politicians were wary of the war issues and played them down. Merlin Hull, for instance, regarded the war talk as largely extraneous to Wisconsin politics. He found it the chief obstacle to getting the people to discuss their "real problems."[50] The fact was, however, that, as an astute politician observed in April, 1916, the war issues were "making quite a division in the state."[51] Emanuel Philipp himself inclined towards La Follette's side of the argument, so the issue was not clearly drawn between the Republican factions. Nevertheless, La Follette was generally regarded as the candidate of the neutralists. As such, he benefited from the preponderance of neutrality sentiment in the state.

Even so, there was much that was ominous for the Wisconsin progressive movement in the international situation. The danger that American involvement in the war would reverse majority sentiment with respect to La Follette was certainly serious. But there was another problem. The old lines of division were beginning to become scrambled,

[46] Child, *German-Americans in Politics,* 64–84.
[47] McCarthy to George Perkins, March 9, 1916, in the McCarthy Papers.
[48] Kronshage to Joseph Uihlein, February 15, 1915; Kronshage to C. J. Zaiser, August 20, 1915, in the Kronshage Papers.
[49] The correspondence of Congressman Esch during the first months of 1916 attests to the strong peace sentiment. See the Esch Papers, February through April, 1916.
[50] Hull to George Bennett, March 18, 1916, in the Hull Papers.
[51] Frank Winter to Esch, April 4, 1916, in the Esch Papers.

as some veteran progressives grew cooler towards La Follette while some stalwarts like Philipp leaned towards his point of view. The senator honestly viewed the international situation from the perspective of progressivism; he perceived no discontinuity. But many of the German-Americans of Wisconsin were influenced more by a natural sympathy for the Fatherland than by pre-war domestic ideological considerations. Thus, the rise of the new issue was beginning to render older questions politically obsolete, however much some of the oldtime champions like La Follette might temporarily benefit.

Meanwhile several congenital progressive ailments were once again combining to work against the reformers. The schism between La Follette and McGovern remained a fact of political life. And the La Follette progressives' continuing ideological commitment against conventions persisted, making it doubly difficult for progressive Republicans to resolve their differences quietly and then act in unison against the conservatives. Wherever La Follette spoke in Wisconsin in 1915, he took the opportunity to confer privately with progressives before each meeting. He always appreciated the value of unity and agreed with the warning from James Stone that the progressives were an independent lot who resisted dictation but would accept the advice of La Follette if personally given. La Follette tried to give the impression that all were being consulted, not dictated to.[52]

La Follette was trying to accommodate the progressive resentment of domination by the "Madison ring." All progressives agreed that unanimity was desirable, but all wanted to be included in consultations. Progressives from outside the Capitol resented the power exercised in La Follette's name by a few, notably Ekern, Crownhart, and Rogers. Many of them preferred the idea of a statewide conference of progressive leaders, which A. W. Sanborn, speaking for

---

[52] Stone to La Follette, October 29, 1915; La Follette to Stone, October 30, 1915, in the Stone Papers.

Emanuel Philipp and the Survival of Conservatism

a number of progressives, had advanced in the summer of 1915.[53] But La Follette remained leery of the conference idea.[54] He had always shied away from anything that looked like a convention. Perhaps he had a new reason to fear a conference now, for under the circumstances it implied the idea of a compromise with McGovern. While La Follette resisted the idea of a conference, at least until he had visited all parts of the state himself,[55] other progressives, including Chris Monson, Stone, Edward F. Dithmar, and A. W. Sanborn, were much concerned that a candidate for governor be agreed upon before internecine warfare should again break out.[56] La Follette fell ill in December, and, thus balked in his personal plans, apparently yielded to pressure and consented to a small conference, which Ekern arranged.[57] But no agreement emerged from the meeting.

January proved a busy month for Wisconsin's politicians. Both the Philipp and the La Follette factions chose a full slate of candidates for delegates to the national Republican convention. The Philipp men, in a full-scale Madison convention attended by about sixteen hundred delegates,[58] named a slate of candidates and created a body of 110 men, representing each congressional district, charged with selecting a candidate for United States Senator. The convention was pledged to back the candidate who emerged. In an effort to appear regular, the delegates promised to support whichever Republican nominee won out in the primary.[59]

[53] William Mauthe to Ekern, August 2, 1915, in the Ekern Papers.
[54] John Hannan to Ekern, May 15, 1915, in the Ekern Papers; La Follette to John S. Donald, October 20, 1916, in the Donald Papers.
[55] Otto Bosshard to Ekern, November 17, 1915, in the Ekern Papers.
[56] Chris Monson to Ekern, August 30, 1915; Bosshard to Ekern, November 17, 1915, in the Ekern Papers; Stone to La Follette, December 15, 1915, in the Stone Papers.
[57] Stone to La Follette, December 15, 1915, in the Stone Papers; John Ingram to Ekern, December 24, 1915, in the Ekern Papers.
[58] N. B. Hood to Esch, January 29, 1916, in the Esch Papers.
[59] Frank C. Meyer to Esch, January 29, 1916; Hood to Esch, January 29, 1916, in the Esch Papers.

Representative John Esch could probably have had the conservative Republican nomination for the asking, but he disavowed interest in it. Doubtless he shared his brother's opinion that even if La Follette could be defeated in the primary, the convention choice would lose in the general election due to defection of La Follette men to the Democrats.[60] The man ultimately chosen by the conservatives was a lesser vote-getter by far, Malcolm G. Jeffris, a Janesville lawyer and longtime foe of La Follette.

The progressives managed to put together a slate of candidates for convention delegates headed by A. W. Sanborn, Christian Doerfler of Milwaukee, Walter Houser, and James Thompson, a popular La Crosse Norwegian, for delegates-at-large. But they moved too slowly to pre-empt the field for a single candidate against Philipp in the September gubernatorial primary. As many had feared, Frank McGovern quickly filled the void. A group of McGovern men from throughout the state convened in Milwaukee on January 17, issued a call to the ex-governor to announce his candidacy, and heard their champion accept.

McGovern's candidacy was followed by a midnight meeting of a few of the inner circle at the home of La Follette, the result of which was the counter-candidacy of Otto Bosshard, a dedicated La Crosse progressive. The announcement was rushed to the newspapers in order to appear in the same issues that carried news of McGovern's candidacy. McGovern in turn denounced as false the efforts to show that the Bosshard announcement had come before his own. The responsibility for rival progressive candidates lay not with him but with his opponents, he asserted.[61]

Perhaps La Follette and his friends were too busy to give adequate attention to the McGovern problem. Before they could turn to the governorship matter, they had to make the delegate fight. Their opponents were formidable. Through George West of Milwaukee, the conservatives con-

---

[60] Will Esch to John Esch, January 31, 1916, in the Esch Papers.
[61] Pamphlet in the James Thompson Papers, 1916.

Emanuel Philipp and the Survival of Conservatism

trolled party machinery, including the voting lists; and their delegate-at-large candidates included two substantial leaders of statewide prominence in business and politics, Emanuel Philipp and S. A. Cook, as well as Emil Baensch and C. K. Ellingson, representing the German and Scandinavian elements.

The theme of the campaign of the conservative delegate candidates was "Republican Principles, Protective Tariff." They publicized La Follette's voting on schedules of the Underwood tariff as it affected the producers of each district. Complaints about business conditions and the tariff had been audible for some time.[62] The Philipp men adopted the national Republican strategy of laying the recent business slump at the door of the Democrats and their Underwood tariff. They hoped to anchor La Follette to the same charge because of his support of most of the Underwood schedules.[63]

While the progressives had a central organization, headed by Charles Crownhart, the chief organizational work rested with key local leaders. In the Seventh Congressional District, for instance, a meeting was held on January 24 at which two candidates for delegate were chosen and Assemblyman Merlin Hull, of Black River Falls, Jackson County, was chosen as campaign manager for the two. The obstacles confronting leaders like Hull were prodigious. Chief of these was the decline in progressive enthusiasm, remarked on by McCarthy and Hatton in 1914 and even more apparent in 1916. C. C. Gittings of Racine noted sadly the number of turncoats—former La Follette men—who had joined Philipp. County officials in his district tended to unite with whichever administration was in power.[64] A. W. Sanborn of Ashland commented that the progressives in his section were discouraged over the failure to unite on a

[62] Esch to Jerry A. Mathews, June 21, 1915; G. W. Hazelton to Esch, July 10, 1915, in the Esch Papers.
[63] Memo of action at meeting of candidates for delegate-at-large, February 28, 1916, in the Philipp Papers.
[64] C. C. Gittings to Stone, January 28, 1916, in the Stone Papers.

single candidate for governor, and saw little point in working politically.[65] Other progressives failed to see the importance of the delegate fight, thinking that La Follette had small chance to be nominated for President at the national convention.[66] The general apathy worried Crownhart, who believed that young men were needed in posts of responsibility in order to recapture the old enthusiasm.[67]

The keynote of the progressive campaign was struck at a statewide meeting in Madison on February 22. Attorney General Walter C. Owen emphasized the insurance situation in the state, saying that Wisconsin citizens were overcharged $1,500,000 annually on fire insurance premiums and $500,000 on other kinds of insurance, and that bills designed to give relief had been defeated by the pro-Philipp members of the legislature. La Follette addressed the meeting in the afternoon on the subject of past campaigns. In the evening, he discussed national issues and the international situation.[68]

The March issue of *La Follette's Magazine* was devoted chiefly to La Follette's speech indicting Philipp and his administration. La Follette rehearsed old charges involving lobbying by Philipp in 1901 and 1903, and again pointed out that as a businessman Philipp was dependent on the railroads and brewers for favors. Turning to the acts of his administration, La Follette criticized the governor for trying to reduce the tax commission to one man and to turn over income tax assessment to local assessors. He also scored the governor for his appointments to the industrial, railroad, and insurance commissions, and to the state supreme court. He pointed to Philipp's failure to reduce commissions or the gross tax burden as evidence of his hypocrisy. He explained reductions in state property taxes as being

[65] Sanborn to Stone, February 14, 1916, in the Stone Papers.
[66] John P. Lewis to Stone, March 16, 1916, in the Stone Papers; Frank B. Gesler to Merlin Hull, March 18, 1916, in the Hull Papers.
[67] Crownhart to James Stone, March 7, 1916, in the Stone Papers.
[68] *La Follette's Magazine*, 8: 3 (March, 1916).

the result of a surplus from the previous administration and a shift in the tax burden to the counties.

Philipp and his administration continued to enjoy considerable strength on the statewide issues, as events were to show. But the legacy of past progressive achievements remained in La Follette's favor. On balance, the neutrality issue also benefited La Follette. Thus, in the delegate election, the La Follette men were able to win a better than even division of the twenty-six national convention delegates. Fifteen men pledged to La Follette for President were chosen, as against eleven uninstructed delegates, headed by Philipp. The ballot provided a place at the top where the voter could indicate his preference as between a La Follette-instructed delegation and an unpledged one. In this contest, La Follette won by 110,064 to 70,813 votes. Both sides claimed the victory. But for neither was the victory complete. The spring elections showed that the issues were confused, the forces evenly divided.

One substantial advantage gained by the La Follette people as a result of the contest was the reconstruction of their battered political organization. The local lists and organizations that grew out of the contest remained in readiness for the fall election.[69] They would be used for the benefit of La Follette in his primary battle with Jeffris, and in the general election too, the progressives hoped. But what candidate for governor the progressive organization would aid remained an open and somewhat disconcerting problem. The hasty Bosshard candidacy was hardly calculated to heal the breach with McGovern or to win the hearty support of those La Follette men throughout the state who wished to participate in the choosing of candidates. La Follette had failed to bring unity through quiet methods, and the advocates of a progressive convention felt, in the spring of 1916, that only their plan could bring harmony and avoid another scattering of progressive votes such

---

[69] Crownhart to Hull, April 12, 1916, in the Hull Papers.

as occurred in 1914, when Hatton, Dahl, and others divided progressive support.[70]

A. W. Sanborn, a leader in the drive for a convention, regarded the pre-primary convention as not merely a temporary expedient, but a permanent necessity. He saw it not only as the vehicle for unity among progressives, but as the only way to enlist young men and give them a chance to show their abilities and get acquainted.[71] Jim Stone, less thoroughgoing in support of the convention gospel, saw it as a justifiable defensive measure against the conservatives, who had convened under the authority and by the call of the Republican State Central Committee.[72]

Walter S. Goodland headed the movement for the convention. In seeking signatures for the call, he expressed the hope that he could get ten from each county, "representing, if possible, all shades of Progressive thought."[73] On June 1, however, three weeks before the scheduled meeting, Frank McGovern served notice on the La Follette men and his own supporters that he would have nothing to do with the unity move. In an open letter to Goodland, released to the press on June 2, McGovern referred sarcastically to Goodland's use of the word "conference" rather than convention in his call. While admitting that a pre-primary convention was legal, he suggested that it violated progressive principles, and was a means of fostering "ring rule." Pressing this point, McGovern noted that there was no law at all to regulate the procedure of the caucuses and convention called for by Goodland. No way was provided to exclude chicanery. The former governor went on to say that his announced candidacy for governor rather than senator was a magnanimous gesture designed to avoid a primary battle with La Follette. On La Follette's side, all that was needed for unity, he said, was the withdrawal of Bosshard. Mc-

[70] Stone to W. S. Goodland, May 13, 1916; Goodland to Stone, May 18, 1916, in the Stone Papers.
[71] Sanborn to Stone, June 18, 1916, in the Stone Papers.
[72] Stone to Sanborn, June 16, 1916, in the Stone Papers.
[73] Goodland to Stone, June 1, 1916, in the Stone Papers.

Govern concluded his statement by alleging that the failure in 1914 was due not merely to disunity, but to a failure by many progressives to stand by their guns: "The canker of political cowardice was also at work; and in addition, let us say, a wish to see certain Progressives defeated. . . . The appeal must be for something deeper than a superficial and transient harmony."[74]

McGovern's statement presented his case in the most favorable light. He stood forth as a true progressive, reminding the leaders and voters of the traditional anti-convention position and of his own steadfast adherence to progressive principles, even when others had faltered before the conservative onslaught. At the same time, he suggested that since he had responded to the call of a representative conference, and had chosen not to oppose La Follette, his candidacy was in the interests of harmony.

McGovern's sincerity in denouncing the convention idea was open to serious doubt. He was probably moved to reject Goodland's harmony bid by the well-founded suspicion that the La Follette men would not countenance his candidacy unless it were forced on them.[75] In a convention, they would oppose McGovern with a La Follette man such as Bosshard, and then suggest that both withdraw in favor of a "harmony" candidate.

Though McGovern could not be tamed, the La Follette faction hoped to choose a candidate who would undercut his candidacy and force his withdrawal. Walter Owen was probably the strongest available candidate, but he was to be held in reserve for a spring race for the state supreme court against Justice Rouget Marshall.[76] Thus the field was open when over three hundred delegates assembled at the University of Wisconsin stock pavilion on June 22.

Proceeding quickly to business, the "conference"

---

[74] *Milwaukee Journal,* June 2, 1916.
[75] See, for instance, Stone to James K. Parish, June 16, 1916, in the Stone Papers.
[76] Owen to Stone, February 2, 1917, in the Stone Papers.

eschewed nominating speeches for governor and held an informal ballot instead. This first ballot showed William Hatton the leader with eighty-eight votes, McGovern second with eighty-six, Bosshard third with seventy, and the rest scattered. On the second ballot, Hatton polled 169 votes and on the third ballot achieved the necessary two-thirds, with 221 votes. Only the McGovern men remained steadfast to the end.[77]

Before the conference met, James Stone had expressed the generally felt view that above all the progressives should avoid the impression of a "slate prepared at Madison."[78] John S. Donald, the conference choice for secretary of state, later exhibited the same sensitivity to "the Madison bunch" charge. Reporting on the conference, *La Follette's* emphasized that the delegates themselves had developed Hatton's candidacy without solicitation.[80]

It appeared that a general understanding existed among La Follette men that they would indicate their preference on the first ballot, and then accept the pro-La Follette candidate with the highest total on the next ballot. Thus, the choice of Hatton was apparently a result of chance to a greater extent than was the case with most nominations. Faced by the candidacy of McGovern as well as Philipp, it was a choice that the ultra-La Follette men, those who backed Dahl in 1914, could hardly reject.

La Follette leaders like Hull, Tom Morris, and John McConnell found the platform approved by the conference weak on "Americanism." They continued to support the full La Follette slate, however, reserving their differences for private conversation.[81] The rift over foreign policy among progressives did not widen prior to the primaries and the November elections. *La Follette's Magazine* hailed

[77] Minutes of meeting of Wisconsin Progressive Republican Conference, June 22, 1916, in the Ekern Papers.
[78] Stone to Walter Houser, June 16, 1916, in the Stone Papers.
[79] Donald to La Follette, October 31, 1916, in the Donald Papers.
[80] *La Follette's Magazine*, 8: 8 (August, 1916).
[81] Frank Winter to Esch, July 24, 1916, in the Esch Papers.

the Madison conference as a bid for unity and reminded its readers of the fatal results of the 1914 rift. Praising Hatton as an able, unselfish unity candidate, the magazine implied that La Follette men should be content with their somewhat colorless candidate and that the McGovern men should abandon their champion in the interests of harmony.[82]

The cause was hopeless. McGovern had staked out the terrain in preparation for his own candidacy. He had avoided the trap of a convention and had strong ideological ammunition in defense of this course. But McGovern was no longer in a position to do more than work mischief against the La Follette men—he could not hope for victory. Yet he had reason to persevere, for a demonstration of what he could and would do might make the La Follette men more tractable in the future, and McGovern was still only fifty years old. Meanwhile the old problem of internal division, based on divided allegiances and compounded by the embarrassments related to the convention device, continued to work against the progressive Republicans.

La Follette's own popularity was as great as ever, and he easily defeated Malcolm Jeffris, 99,720 to 66,576. But though he everywhere endorsed Hatton, who conducted a surprisingly spirited campaign, Philipp won renomination. The governor received 83,769 votes to Hatton's 47,618 and McGovern's 35,846.[83]

Philipp's renomination was not solely the result of progressive division. The disunity among his opponents helped, but in addition the governor was able to capitalize on many of the issues that had served so well in 1914. The continuing potency of these issues was in fact recognized by the progressives, as the defensive tone of their campaigns testified. During the winter of 1915–1916, *La Follette's* gave considerable attention to the marketing of agricultural products.[84] The issue was not pushed by the magazine in

---

[82] *La Follette's Magazine*, 8: 7 (July, 1916).
[83] *Wisconsin Blue Book, 1917*, 188, 193.
[84] *La Follette's Magazine*, 7: 12, 8: 2 (December, 1915, February, 1916).

the 1916 campaign, however; explanations for high taxes and state expenses and proliferation of commissions were offered instead. The keynote of the progressive campaign was that administration of progressive laws already on the books required men in full sympathy with those laws. Hatton laid down this line in accepting the nomination, and *La Follette's* continued it. Walter Goodland, writing in *La Follette's,* rehashed past iniquities of the stalwarts to show their lack of trustworthiness.[85]

Progressive warnings of this sort were far less potent in 1916 than they had been earlier. The Philipp administration had given voters something concrete against which to measure progressive charges. It had shown the conservatives to be much more moderate and honest than the progressive rhetoric admitted, and in his campaign, Philipp was careful not to damage the new image, attempting instead to fortify it. The stalwarts launched their campaign with a July 12 convention at which they endorsed presidential candidate Charles Evans Hughes along with Philipp and Jeffris. Governor Philipp and his friends tried to show that the recent administration had cut taxes without reducing services.[86] They argued that the 1915 tax levy would have been still smaller had not the McGovern administration cut taxes late in 1914 in order to embarrass the incoming administration. Philipp also blamed progressives in the state senate for failure to lower taxes further.[87] In these efforts, Philipp benefited from his own improvement as a public speaker: "Wherever he spoke he left the impression of stability, truthfulness, responsibility and character. People, even old progressives, found that they liked Emanuel Philipp."[88]

[85] *Ibid.,* 8: 8 (August, 1916).
[86] James O. Davidson, an appointee of the administration as chairman of the State Board of Control, presented the popular argument to his Norwegian following through the *Skandinaven.* See John Benson to Davidson, August 20, 1916, in the Davidson Papers.
[87] *Milwaukee Sentinel,* July 13, 1916.
[88] Maxwell, *Philipp,* 127. Ralph Plumb, himself an orator, shared the view. Plumb, *Badger Politics,* 179.

La Follette's tremendous senatorial victory was due in part to the fact that the foreign policy issue continued to work in his favor. Malcolm Jeffris helped focus attention on the issue by denouncing La Follette's stand on preparedness, the arms embargo, and a referendum on war. La Follette responded squarely to the foreign policy questions in an automobile tour of the state, making much of his support of neutrality.[89]

The senator profited from the timing of the neutrality situation. German submarine warfare, the source of much of the bad feeling towards Germany and an embarrassment for neutralists like La Follette, came to a temporary end following the sinking of the unarmed American merchantman *Sussex* in April, 1916. In the months that followed, the tempers of those Americans who had advocated a firm stand against Germany cooled. Thus, a man who had criticized Representative Esch for his stand on the McLemore Resolution in the spring came to his support in September.[90] But for the neutralists, particularly the Germans, the issues of war and peace remained of paramount interest. In the general election, German voting as between Wilson and Hughes was determined by the degree to which Wilson was forgiven his early belligerency and credited for having "kept us out of war."[91] How many Germans deserted the Democratic primary in order to vote for La Follette was problematical.

Governor Philipp's faction found itself in control of the Republican state convention in September, 1916, though progressives had secured renomination for various state and legislative office. The Philipp men had the opportunity to write a reactionary platform, but they adopted a moderate one instead. In the campaign that followed, Philipp stressed

[89] Belle and Fola La Follette, *La Follette*, 1: 578–579.
[90] James O'Neill to Esch, September 2, 1916, in the Esch Papers.
[91] Husting to Ellis B. Usher, August 12, 1916, in the Husting Letterbooks; John Esch to George Esch, October 3, 1916; William Stafford to Esch, October 13, 1916; Esch to Stafford, October 14, 1916, in the Esch Papers; Haugen, *Political and Pioneer Reminiscences*, 180.

the idea that his administration "represented not standpatism or reaction but orderly progress, sound financing and moderation."[92]

Most progressive Republicans were willing to meet Philipp halfway. They contributed to the harmonious character of the state platform convention, and progressive candidates on the state ticket led in supporting their factional enemies against the Democrats.[93] A few maverick progressives backed the Democrat Burt Williams against Philipp, but they were the exception. La Follette, though he employed his own campaign manager, Crownhart, struck no blows at Philipp; and the governor reciprocated.

La Follette's neutrality appeal continued into the general election and again helped him. The lull in submarine warfare continued through November, so that no new wave of nationalism worked against the senator. But those who remembered President Wilson's anti-hyphenate campaign and other provocative actions had a chance to register their disapproval. This they did, giving La Follette an overwhelming victory. He defeated Democrat William Wolfe, 251,303 votes to 135,144. The rest of the Republican ticket swept into office without trouble, with Philipp, victor over Burt Williams by 227,896 to 164,633, trailing the ticket.[94]

The joint victory of Philipp and La Follette in 1916 was the anticlimactic conclusion of the all-out stalwart drive launched in 1912 and the progressive counteroffensive against Philipp. There were simply no statewide economic or political issues of sufficient magnitude to force a conclusive contest between the two factions. The neutrality questions cut across factional lines and rendered older issues less vital; subterranean currents of anti-Catholicism and prohibitionism added to the confusion and the seeming apathy

[92] George A. West to B. J. Castle, October 28, 1916, in the Castle Papers; Maxwell, *Philipp*, 125.
[93] Merlin Hull to Esch, September 21, 1916, in the Esch Papers.
[94] *Wisconsin Blue Book, 1917*, 287, 288.

towards other issues.[95] Insofar as the old issues remained operative, they tended to nullify one another. The national economy had recovered from the 1913 slump as a result of the European war. There was little general economic discontent as a springboard for progressive resurgence. Nor had the Philipp administration overturned popular progressive measures. Meanwhile, progressive "excesses" of 1913 and 1914 remained fresh in taxpayers' minds. On the other hand, years of "education" by La Follette and his friends, augmented by favorable national publicity from 1906 through 1914, had created a surplus of voter good will on which progressives were able to draw in the 1916 election.

It did seem, however, that the progressive movement had just about run its course in Wisconsin. Not that its accomplishments would be lost, for the permanency of progressive legislation had been confirmed by Emanuel Philipp and the more moderate position to which some conservatives had veered. Further innovations along progressive lines seemed likely in the future. But it was no longer inconceivable that such measures might have conservative sponsorship. Partly for these reasons, the dynamic force that made progressivism a "movement" was gone. Conservative moderation had made progressive intransigence quixotic and politically untenable. Then, too, conservative attacks and victories, depending as they did on the Jeffersonian rhetoric of progressivism, had made clear that progressive ideology itself imposed limits on the range of the movement and its potential endurance as a political entity. Though individual progressives might survive politically under such circumstances, it could no longer be on the crest of a "progressive movement."

Yet the political survival of the La Follette dynasty into the postwar period, the radicalism of the early 1920's, and

[95] Reflecting the prohibition issue were: Frank Winter to Esch, January 2, 1916; John J. Esch to W. F. Esch, May 15, 1916, September 1, 1916, in the Esch Papers.

the emergence of a powerful Progressive party in the 1930's would seemingly refute the contention that Wisconsin progressivism had run its course by the end of 1916. The explanation for this apparent contradiction lies in the circumstances preceding and surrounding the spectacular resurgence of La Follette's forces in the election of 1920.

VI

Loyalty, Loyalty, Loyalty

ON JANUARY 31, 1917, Germany announced the resumption of unrestricted submarine warfare. On February 3, President Wilson recalled the United States ambassador from Germany and the State Department issued the German ambassador his passports. On April 2, 1917, the Congress declared war against Germany. Nine of Wisconsin's eleven congressmen were among the fifty who voted "nay." Robert M. La Follette was one of six dissidents in the United States Senate.

President Wilson had begun making preparedness speeches in January, 1916. The Eastern press, influential leaders such as Theodore Roosevelt and Elihu Root, British propagandists, and the National Security League had been beating the drums for several years.[1] A month before American entry, the administration directed its preparedness shafts against members of Congress. It met a Senate filibuster against a bill to arm merchantmen by releasing the Zimmermann note, an intercepted German proposal to Mexico directed against the United States. The President then told the people that "A little group of willful men, representing no opinion but their own, have rendered the great Government of the United States helpless and contemptible."[2] The nationwide denunciation that fell upon La Follette, as leader

---

[1] See H. C. Peterson, *Propaganda for War* (Norman, 1939).
[2] *New York Times,* March 5, 1917, cited in Belle and Fola La Follette, *La Follette,* 1: 628.

193

of the "willful men," testified to the nationalistic feeling in the air. Even so, as the United States prepared to fight, the administration felt that there was not enough war sentiment in the land. As late as the end of May, 1917, Wilson's secretary, Joseph Tumulty, was perturbed that the people's "righteous wrath seems not to have been aroused. . . . A speech by Mr. Whitlock about German outrages in Belgium would help the American people to visualize just what poor Belgium has suffered and what our own people might suffer if German autocracy should triumph."[3]

The task of arousing public opinion fell to the Committee on Public Information, set up under the direction of journalist George Creel on April 14, 1917. During the months of war that followed, Liberty Loan campaigns provided the main occasions for the committee's patriotic exhortations. And the creation of opinion was but one side of the coin; suppression of opinion was the other. President Wilson "was never a man to take criticism calmly and his long-running reluctance to ask for war seems to have made him the readier to permit the crushing of criticism once he had made the decision. . . ."[4] The war extended into the most obscure corners of American life, and each man, woman, and child was asked to perform a service and to suffer the discipline of the soldier. America's shipyards, munitions works, government offices, training camps—indeed, the entire country—was thought of as part of the theater of war; an attack on the American cause was consequently viewed as an act of treason.[5]

The Espionage Act of 1917, amended by the Sedition Act in May, 1918, gave legality to the federal government's conformity campaign. Under the Espionage Act, the Justice Department confiscated motion pictures and raided the offices of anti-war organizations, while the Postmaster Gen-

[3] Joseph Tumulty to Edward M. House, May 31, 1917, in the Robert Lansing Papers, cited in Peterson, *Propaganda for War*, 324–325.
[4] Eric Goldman, *Rendezvous With Destiny* (New York, 1952), 254.
[5] Zechariah Chafee, Jr., *Free Speech in the United States* (Cambridge, 1941), 7–8.

eral guarded the mails. The more severe Sedition Act provided twenty-year prison terms for remarks intended to hinder the war effort. In practice, "the requirement of intention became a mere form since it could be inferred from the existence of the indirect injurious effect."[6] Socialist Victor Berger and progressive Republicans L. B. Nagler, Assistant Secretary of State, and J. M. Becker, a county judge, were among the Wisconsinites convicted under the act.

Wisconsin's preparedness forces had readied themselves for the larger challenge of war. Richard Lloyd Jones's *Wisconsin State Journal,* the liberal Democratic *Milwaukee Journal,* and Charles Pfister's *Milwaukee Sentinel* had been strong preparedness advocates. A chapter of the National Security League had been set up in Milwaukee in 1915 with the aid of the Merchants and Manufacturers Association, with August H. Vogel of the Vogel and Pfister Leather Company as president and Willett M. Spooner, son of the former senator, as secretary. The Milwaukee branch was the largest in the Midwest apart from Chicago and the heart of the organization in Wisconsin. A good deal of activity was generated in newly formed training camps, drill groups, and rifle clubs, culminating, on July 15, 1916, in a large preparedness parade in Milwaukee.[7]

The preparedness campaign revealed in microcosm many of the factors that were to make wartime life in Wisconsin so bitter and explosive. The German opposition to preparedness, conducted through the pages of the *Milwaukee Free Press,* which had been acquired by eighty businessmen of German stock, was "short sightedly chauvinistic," and served only to discredit the whole anti-preparedness movement.[8] Certainly, the large German community did nothing to disguise its sympathy for the Fatherland prior to the United States' declaration of war. The Wisconsin German-American Alliance, with 37,000 members, raised

---

[6] Chafee, *Free Speech,* 50.
[7] Finnegan, "Preparedness in Wisconsin," 37–59.
[8] *Ibid.,* 114.

funds for German, Austrian, and Hungarian war sufferers by selling pictures of the Kaiser and Franz Josef; and during March, 1916, some 175,000 Milwaukeeans contributed $150,000 to the Central Powers at a week-long bazaar. The socialists, many of whom were German-Americans, had neither a consistent position on preparedness nor much widespread appeal. They failed to improve the prestige of the anti-preparedness side.[10]

On the preparedness side, motives other than pure patriotism worked towards intensification of the conflict. The Democratic press and politicians had partisan reasons for supporting President Wilson in his preparedness appeal. For others, especially in the Milwaukee business community, the preparedness drive occurred in the context of the long-standing battle against the socialists. An editor of the *Milwaukee Sentinel* recalled in 1941 that the socialists had long been "considered fanatics, visionaries, utopians, and a good many other things by numerous business and professional people of the city."[11] The drive against the socialists that began in 1910 continued unabated into the municipal elections held in the spring of 1916. The Social Democrats were calling for public ownership of gas, electric lighting, and street railway companies. The incumbent mayor, Gerhard Bading, campaigned for re-election against "Socialism, with all its heresies and un-American ideas" and urged Milwaukeeans to send out the word to the rest of the United States that it would "never again allow the Red Flag to replace the Stars and Stripes on the . . . City Hall." But Daniel Hoan, the Social Democratic city attorney, defeated Bading for mayor.[12] Meanwhile, the pro-socialist labor unions of Milwaukee, quiet during the economic doldrums of the preceding years, became more aggressive in their organizational efforts.[13]

[9] Still, *Milwaukee*, 456.
[10] Finnegan, "Preparedness in Wisconsin," 114.
[11] Wachman, *Social-Democratic Party of Milwaukee*, 58.
[12] Still, *Milwaukee*, 522–523.
[13] Gavett, *Labor Movement in Milwaukee*, 126.

The preparedness drive gave employers and political anti-socialists an opportunity to embarrass and possibly weaken their adversaries. Under strong pressure, and probably anxious to defend himself and his party against the charge of "un-Americanism," Mayor Hoan agreed to march at the head of the July 15 preparedness parade, on the understanding that it pledged only undivided loyalty to America and not increased appropriations for munitions. The labor unions would not go along, but many workers marched—on orders from their employers, Victor Berger's *Vorwaerts* charged.[14]

With the onset of war, the power and opportunities of those who had led in the preparedness campaign greatly increased. These opportunities were by no means wasted. The whole of wartime hysteria was by no means attributable solely to the machinations of an interested minority, however. More important were the larger, impersonal forces of generalized patriotic emotion, intensified by special Wisconsin factors, notably the positions of La Follette and the Social Democrats on the war and the fact of Wisconsin's large German population. These were the factors that combined to make "loyalty" such a potent weapon. Doubtless even those who had economic or political reasons for trumpeting patriotism were themselves not invulnerable to the blood-stirring call. This was especially so because it was easy to subsume political ends, to promote the Democratic party or bury La Follette and the socialists, or economic ends, to check and perhaps push back the force of organized labor, under the larger category suggested by the war, "Americanism."

The Wisconsin legislature responded immediately to the declaration of war by authorizing a State Council of Defense to co-ordinate the state's wartime services. Governor Philipp appointed Charles McCarthy to do the preliminary organizational work. Later, Magnus Swenson, a Madison business leader, became chairman. Much of the work of

[14] Finnegan, "Preparedness in Wisconsin," 64–69.

the State Council of Defense was propagandistic. Governor Philipp wrote Swenson, "The main business of the Council of Defense is to supply men, money and crops. In the matter of securing men for the army the organization is useful in creating enthusiasm for the war, which is necessary under present conditions."[15] Publicity work was a major feature of campaigns to expand crop production, assist Liberty Loan drives, aid Red Cross fund raising, minimize food hoarding, and promote the canning and preserving of foodstuffs. The State Council of Defense published a weekly paper, *Forward*. It also supplied between eight hundred and a thousand speakers, known as the Four Minute Men, for Liberty Loan campaigns.[16]

More important than the federal and state governments in the loyalty campaign were semi-official and unofficial organizations. The Wisconsin Defense League was one. Organized prior to the war, it aided in recruitment once the war was on, chiefly by sponsoring mass loyalty meetings.[17] In September, 1917, it was succeeded by the Wisconsin Loyalty Legion, which soon had over three hundred chapters and several thousand members. The Loyalty Legion circulated loyalty petitions, became chief distributing agent for the Committee on Public Information, and helped the Red Cross, the Y.M.C.A., and United War Work. In addition, legionaires were pledged to "seek out and bring traitors to punishment" and "to hold up slackers to public contempt," which they did with enthusiasm.[18]

Wisconsin patriots drew heavily on Wilsonian phrases for their appeal. Slogans like "war to end war," "war to make the world safe for democracy," and "the United States has no ulterior objectives," gave a popular, democratic

---

[15] Philipp to Swenson, April 17, 1918, in the Philipp Papers.

[16] Draft of a report on the activities of the State Council of Defense, July 26, 1918, in the Philipp Papers; Karen Falk, "Public Opinion in Wisconsin During World War One," *Wisconsin Magazine of History*, 25: 399 (June, 1942).

[17] Falk, "Public Opinion in Wisconsin," 403.

[18] *Ibid.*, 404; Maxwell, *Philipp*, 164.

twist to aroused nationalism.[19] The champion loyalty advocate, State Senator Roy P. Wilcox of Eau Claire, portrayed the war as a death struggle between world democracy and world autocracy. He likened it to the American Revolution, the War of 1812, the Civil War, and the Spanish-American War as a battle for liberty.[20] Walter S. Goodland, a Racine progressive, appealed for the Loyalty Legion by writing that since Wisconsin had led in the patriotic cause of purification and popularization of state governments, it should now lead in the war of democracy against autocracy.[21] Thomas J. Mahon, a McGovern supporter, organized the Speakers Bureau for the Loyalty Legion, offering arguments and references that the speakers might use.[22] But speeches formed only a part of the loyalty arsenal. Loyalty was inspired also by the lyrics of song. Madison Episcopal Minister William Dawson rendered "The Battle Hymn of the Republic" as:[23]

Wisconsin's always loyal to the good old U.S.A.,
No matter what detractors or her enemies may say
All her sons both great and small, answer to their country's call—
For Wisconsin's always loyal to Old Glory.
Yes, Wisconsin will be loyal,
Yes, Wisconsin will be loyal,
Yes, Wisconsin will be loyal
Be loyal to Old Glory.

Six other verses followed. Inevitably, "On Wisconsin" was similarly transformed:[24]

On Wisconsin, On Wisconsin, You've always stood in line

---

[19] Falk, "Public Opinion in Wisconsin, 396–397.
[20] Unpublished manuscript speech by Roy O. Wilcox at the Opera House, Chippewa Falls, May 17, 1917, in the Roy O. Wilcox Papers.
[21] W. S. Goodland to James Thompson, September 13, 1917, in the Thompson Papers.
[22] Mahon to James Thompson, September 25, 1917, in the Thompson Papers.
[23] Dawson to John S. Donald, August 16, 1917, in the Donald Papers.
[24] From the program of the meeting of the Central Wisconsin Press Association, at Grand Rapids, April 15, 1918, in the Hull Papers.

Never wavered when danger threatened at your door.
On Wisconsin, On Wisconsin, Fight on for your fame!
Fight, citizens, fight. And we shall glorify the name.
On Wisconsin, On Wisconsin, Our boys are on the line.
Firing at the German tyrant. A victory shell each time.
On Wisconsin, On Wisconsin, Fight on for her fame.
Fight! fellows! Fight! And we shall win this game.

Excesses in the name of patriotism were not unusual in wartime, and they occurred in all parts of the United States during World War I. But Wisconsin probably exceeded other states in this regard because of certain special circumstances. To many, it seemed that the "unpatriotic element" was so large and menacing as to require the strongest countermeasures. Wisconsin Germans had shown sympathy for the homeland before the war, and Wisconsin had the largest proportionate German-American population in the nation.[25] In Milwaukee, where over 50 per cent of the population had German names, there flourished a German press, German clubs, German-language schools, and German restaurants.[26] The national Social Democratic party had met in St. Louis a day after the United States declared war and, after some deliberation, voted to oppose the war as one "which the capitalist class is forcing upon the nation against its will." This position was accepted by Victor Berger and the majority of Wisconsin's Social Democratic leaders. Though Milwaukee Mayor Dan Hoan did not endorse the St. Louis resolution, he adhered to the party's city platform, which blamed the capitalist class for American involvement and proposed that profiteers pay the cost of the

---

[25] *Fourteenth Census of the United States, 1920* (Washington, 1921), 1: 16, 3: 48.
[26] Still, *Milwaukee*, 455.

struggle.[27] The fact that Germans had always been the backbone of the party and that even non-socialist Germans were rallying to it during the war made it doubly suspect. And finally there was Robert La Follette, who followed up his Senate vote against the war with a continuing stream of criticism that seemed traitorous to some.

The intrepid La Follette continued to present matters in terms of the eternal struggle between men and money, the people and the interests, and to stress the importance of the domestic conflict as against the foreign. He warned in May, 1917, that "THE AUTOCRATIC CONTROL OF BUSINESS UNDER THE PRESSURE AND EXIGENCY OF WAR DOES NOT TEND TO PROMOTE DEMOCRACY BUT TO STRENGTHEN IMPERIALISM."[28] The next issue of his magazine pursued the idea further. La Follette wrote: "Every nation has its war party. It is not the party of democracy. It is the party of autocracy. It seeks to dominate absolutely. It is commercial, imperialistic, ruthless. . . . The American Jingo is the twin of the German Junker."[29] During the following months, La Follette's interest centered on the financing of the war. He regarded the floating of bonds as in the interest of the party of autocracy.[30] Such expressions were hardly calculated to unify the country in the war effort, nor to ingratiate La Follette with American "patriots."

The senator made a representative statement of his views before a gathering of the Nonpartisan League at St. Paul on September 20, 1917. La Follette told the farmer-labor gathering that "Twenty years ago this very season, at a little farmers' gathering in Ferndale, Wisconsin, I opened the fight against corporate power in the state." The kernel of the Ferndale speech had been "That the corporations in

---

[27] *Ibid.,* 524; Robert C. Reinders, "Daniel W. Hoan and the Milwaukee Socialist Party During the First World War," in the *Wisconsin Magazine of History,* 36: 48–56, 49, 52, (Autumn, 1952).
[28] *La Follette's Magazine,* 9: 5 (May, 1917).
[29] *Ibid.,* 9: 6 (June, 1917).
[30] *Ibid.,* 9: 8, 9 (August, September, 1917).

Wisconsin were not paying their fair share of the taxes, and that they ought to be made to pay up just as the farmers and owners of homes." The issue still existed in Washington, he charged; the fight was still for equitable taxation. La Follette cited the authority of "that wonderful man," Adam Smith, for his view that the war should be paid for out of current taxes. Tax levies were only 31 per cent on the average "upon the war profiteers." This after three years of "the richest pickings that was ever known in the history of mankind." Questioning the merits of the war itself, La Follette suggested that "it might be terminated with honor to the government."[31]

An error in reporting was picked up by the Associated Press, which told the country that La Follette had said "We had no grievances," instead of "We had grievances." A storm of troubles burst on the senator. Even without the misquotation, however, patriots were infuriated by La Follette's consistently voiced view. For self-styled patriots, Wisconsin's Germans, socialists, and senior senator had dual significance. First, their presence and activity suggested that the war effort in Wisconsin was in jeopardy. Second, they cast discredit on the entire state, putting even the patriots themselves under a cloud of suspicion before the nation. (The National Security League said that Wisconsin was 70 per cent below par in loyalty and a speaker for that organization told a Madison audience that "Wisconsin is under suspicion."[32]) Clearly, strong measures were needed both to support the war effort and to vindicate the state and themselves. For some, this meant redoubled activity of a noncoercive sort. For others, it meant increasing propaganda for loyalty. For still others, it meant coercive and repressive measures.

To these motives must be added the continuing interest of the Democrats, whose party controlled Congress and

[31] Quoted in full in Henry Huber, "War Hysteria," unpublished manuscript in the Huber Papers, 96–111. Rich excerpts may be found in Belle and Fola La Follette, *La Follette*, 2: 761–769.
[32] Falk, "Public Opinion in Wisconsin," 405; Huber, "War Hysteria," 143.

the executive and whose President had defined the war aims of the nation. Long habituated to minority status, some Wisconsin Democratic leaders probably found it a happy circumstance that an all-out crusade to back the administration and the war effort served also to embarrass the divided Republicans and the anti-war Social Democrats. While Democrats could hardly be held collectively guilty for all the instances in which personal rights were violated in the name of loyalty, yet the party, through its propaganda efforts, helped to charge the atmosphere with hatred and suspicion, a precondition for such encroachments.

The same and more could be said of segments of another interested element, the conservative business group, which had long been fearful of labor, the Social Democrats, and, to a lesser extent, La Follette. Charles Stewart, a Washington County writer and sometime secretary to Governor Philipp, observed that the centers of coercive patriotism were the cities and small manufacturing towns, and that the wealthier members of the community were the leading participants in what he termed "the rule by the rich." State Senator Henry Huber, one of the few who remained with La Follette, concurred.[33] Milwaukee was the center of patriotic activity and there much of the loyalty campaign was directed against the Social Democrats.

Though longtime enemies of La Follette and Social Democracy took advantage of wartime sentiment to strike at their foes, that was not the whole of the matter. Progressives, and even Social Democrats like A. L. Simons and William Gaylord, played prominent roles in the loyalty pageant. The effectiveness of the conservatives was only possible because of the universality of the patriotic appeal. Tom Morris, A. W. Sanborn, James Stone, Richard T. Ely, and John R. Commons were a few of the former La Follette backers whose sons served in the army and whose position on La Follette altered radically. Ely thought that La Follette was

---

[33] Charles D. Stewart, "Prussianizing Wisconsin," in the *Atlantic Monthly* (January, 1919), 99–105; Henry Huber, "War Hysteria," 60–70.

aiding the Germans; Stone split openly with La Follette when he said goodbye to his boy on October 3, 1917, and "made a little talk to him and his companions at Baraboo."[34]

The transition to anti-La Folletteism was not a complete reversal for many progressives. Even after breaking with the senator, promoting the Loyalty Legion, and asserting that loyalty was the paramount issue, Stone continued to back La Follette on the question of wartime taxation and payment for the war. His war rationale was not purely nationalistic, but involved the spreading of democracy in the world.[35]

One of the most interesting and important of the La Follette defectors was the editor of the *Wisconsin State Journal*, Richard Lloyd Jones. Jones was the son of Jenkin Lloyd Jones, a Unitarian minister and head of a social welfare center in Chicago. He attended the universities of Wisconsin and Chicago, went into journalism, and in 1910 became an editor of the muckraking journal *Collier's*. In 1911 he interested La Follette in the idea of buying the *State Journal* and using it as a progressive organ. A large, intellectual-looking man, Jones seemed to young William T. Evjue, his business manager on the *State Journal*, to be vain and egotistical, dictatorial and arbitrary. As La Follette persistently ignored his impassioned and perhaps threatening letters on questions of war and peace, Jones's pique grew. La Follette would not respond to rough treatment, and Jones hated to be ignored. Relations became strained during 1915 and 1916. With the war, Jones and La Follette drew further and further apart, until a complete break occurred in April, 1917, when Jones called La Follette halfbaked and insincere.[36]

Jones played a leading part in the creation of patriotic

---

[34] Ely, *Ground Under Our Feet*, 217–218; Stone to W. S. Pierce, March 16, 1918, in the Stone Papers.

[35] Stone to Frank Winter, January 24, 1918; Stone to La Follette, April 3, 1917, in the Stone Papers.

[36] Interview with William T. Evjue, January 18, 1954; Weissman, "Wisconsin State Journal since 1900," 107.

sentiment, in his own paper and through the Wisconsin Patriotic Press Association, which chose him president on September 4, 1917. Other progressive editors with him in the group were C. E. Broughton of Sheboygan, W. S. Goodland of Racine, A. M. Brayton of La Crosse, and Merlin Hull of Black River Falls.[37] Jones led in the vilification of La Follette and the drive to have him expelled from the Senate. So passionate was young Jones in his war views that he broke completely with his pacifist father. After the latter's death, he threatened to fight any resolution in his memory.[38]

Jones presented his war views in a series of letters to another independent-minded progressive. He wrote John Blaine in October, 1917, in response to Blaine's expressions of fear about repression of free speech, "I cannot see the guillotine to which you point." The fight was to spread democracy in the world: "Yes, we are using the tools of autocracy to defend democracy, and that too is inevitable. The foes that are working hardest for autocracy today are the fellows who are shouting loudest to perfect our own democracy before we attack autocracy. The fellows who point to the ills here at home and not the ills of the whole wide world are the arch reactionaries in America today and the greatest foe to peace in the future. Drastic measures are justified to meet drastic situations. . . ."[39]

Blaine persisted in his arguments and Jones resumed his defense in a most remarkable letter. He wrote:[40]

> As for your fear of reaction setting in, dismiss it. The arch reactionaries in Wisconsin today are the supporters of Bob La Follette. They are the cowardly pussy-footers who by their cheap and under-handed methods of weakening our national defenses are helping autocracy and not democracy; they are playing with the brewers and the kaiser's

[37] *Wisconsin State Journal,* September 5, 1917.
[38] Ada James Diary, April 22, 1919, in the Ada James Papers.
[39] Richard Lloyd Jones to John Blaine, October 6, 1917, in the Blaine Papers.
[40] Jones to Blaine, November 7, 1917, in the Blaine Papers.

disciples in America. They are no longer progressive; they are reactionaries of the worst and most dangerous kind. This war is advancing along progressive lines in economic and in industrial and commercial as well as educational avenues and is spiritualizing our American sense of communism as nothing has done since the days of 1776. Fall in.

The mind that welcomed the concentration of business, the expanding economic role of government, and the spiritual values of war was not in the mainstream of progressive thought. The anti-trust, anti-corporation, pacifistic orientation of Bryan and La Follette was a far cry from Jones's brand of progressivism and more truly represented the voting backbone. Yet Theodore Roosevelt had reflected a considerable body of intellectual opinion in the progressive camp that held to the Jones point of view. Such men found in war not the death of progressivism, but the opportunity for a new, efficient, spiritualized, and somewhat collectivized America.

Progressive desertion of La Follette probably resulted as much from social pressure as from conviction. La Follette men were ostracized as disloyal. Former La Follette men stood on lofty ground of patriotism and principle. Representative John J. Esch was warned by his closest political advisers that loyalty sentiment was high back home, that some of the political "outs" were trying to get in "under the claim of superpatriotism," and that patriotic speeches by him in his home district were in order.[41] The congressman, always an astute observer of constituent opinion, campaigned for the second Liberty Loan drive in October, 1917. He believed that this, together with his votes in favor of the Wilson Administration, would smooth his re-election road.[42] He was correct.

---

[41] Frank Winter to John Esch, July 23, 1918; Will Esch to John Esch, July 2, 1918, in the Esch Papers.

[42] John to Will Esch, July 5, 1918; John Esch to George Andrews, April 9, 1918; John Esch to William P. Welch, July 27, 1918; John Esch to W. B. Tscharner, July 27, 1918, in the Esch Papers.

Loyalty, Loyalty, Loyalty

The extent of patriotic excesses in wartime Wisconsin was considerable. Intemperate propaganda was part of it. For example, each day the *Madison Democrat* published this announcement on its editorial pages:[43]

> AMERICAN DEFENSE SOCIETY WARNING
>
> Every German or Austrian in the United States, unless known by years of association to be absolutely loyal, should be treated as a potential spy.
>
> Be on the alert. Keep your eyes and ears open. Take nothing for granted. Energy and alertness may save the life of your son, your husband, or your brother. The enemy is engaged in making war in this country, in transmitting news to Berlin, and in spreading peace propaganda, as well as lies about the condition and morale of American military forces.
>
> Whenever any suspicious act, or disloyal word, comes to your notice, communicate at once with the Police Department, phone number 12, or the State Council of Defense, phone Capitol 226.

The four Liberty Loan campaigns provided the chief occasions for speakers and mass loyalty meetings. The Reverend Newell Dwight Hillis told his Milwaukee audience: "The Germans slaughtered old men and matrons, mutilated captives in ways that can only be spoken by men in whispers, violated little girls until they were dead; finding a calfskin nailed upon a barn to be dried, they nailed a baby beside it and wrote 'zwei.'" These atrocities occurred with the approval of the German government, Reverend Hillis said.[44] The Liberty Loan campaigns also occasioned a quasi-official network that blanketed the state. Local organizations, part of the State Council of Defense organization, assessed each citizen a Liberty Loan subscription quota. Failure to meet the quota brought coercion of various sorts. In Milwaukee County, a phalanx of twenty-five automobiles with sixty to seventy community leaders and a banker to loan money where needed would bear down on a recalcitrant farmer

---

[43] *Madison Democrat*, March 5, 1918.
[44] Ada James Diary, October 16, 1917.

and demand subscription on the threat of putting yellow placards on his land reading, "The Occupant of these premises has refused to take his just share of Liberty Bonds. DO NOT REMOVE." Bluffs, threats, spurious legal warnings, all represented as coming from the government, were the stock-in-trade of these "flying squads."[45]

Councils augmented their own coercive force by encouraging neighbor to act against neighbor.[46] The State Council of Defense received many reports on "disloyalty" and often responded without further verification by dispatching letters like this one, directed to a small-town resident: "We understand that you are continually talking against Liberty Bonds and against the war in which your country is engaged. You are probably not aware of the penalty that such unpatriotic conduct deserves. We wish to know immediately if the representations made regarding you are true."[47] The Council of Defense used the Secret Service to intimidate. A letter directed to a Kenosha resident and signed "Secret Service" said: "Many complaints have reached our department relative to seditious remarks that you have made about our government. For your information, let me say that such an offense constitutes nothing less than treason."[48]

Under these circumstances it was not surprising that vigilante-like-elements sought to cover themselves with the mantle of Council authority. Thus, for example, an Augusta man wanted to promote a County Council of Defense to repress the opinion of Germans: "Quite frequently comes to our ears statements and sayings strongly anti-American. Some of which, in times of peace might be passed by with light censure, but in times of war should not be permissible.

---

[45] Stewart, "Prussianizing Wisconsin."

[46] B. C. Ziegler, County Chairman, to Dear Sir, n. d., in the Charles Stewart Papers.

[47] Karl E. Meyer, "The Politics of Loyalty: From La Follette to McCarthy in Wisconsin, 1918–1952" (doctoral dissertation, Princeton University, 1956), 33–34.

[48] Secret Service to Joseph Orth, July 10, 1917, "Secret Service" file, Council of Defense Papers, cited in Meyer, "The Politics of Loyalty," 35.

Can you procure for us blanks for organizing a Council, with instructions how to proceed, should occasion require our restraining efforts, along the lines indicated above?" Merlin Hull, the Secretary of State, assured him that councils would be organized in every county and township.[49]

Councils did not confine themselves to coercing Liberty Loan subscriptions. The Washington County Council of Defense set quotas for the War Chest Fund. A Committee on Appeals and Grievances judged complaints about excessively high quotas, but that committee's judgment was considered final.[50] Not surprisingly, private acts of intimidation and violence abounded. Thirty-five citizens of Hudson, in St. Croix County, told their congressman in Washington: "The Berger men . . . are growing reckless and unless something is done by Congress very soon, the people here will use part of Wisconsin's hemp crop to make neckties."[51] Socialist meetings were often suppressed.[52] Armistice Day, 1918, was celebrated in Evansville by hauling a seventy-two-year-old woman around in a lion's cage. (Her Liberty Loan subscription had been unsatisfactory.) Black River Falls was another site of Armistice Day hoodlumism. Earlier that year, a mob came by night to the home of a German farmer, put a rope around his neck, and beat him because he would not subscribe to his full Liberty Loan quota.[53]

One means of demonstrating loyalty was to castigate and repudiate the man who was, in the view of many, the chief cause of Wisconsin's disgrace, Robert M. La Follette. This simple course met with great popularity. The Wisconsin press had been largely neutral in sentiment, and rather

---

[49] G. F. Caldwell to Hull, March 7, 1918; Hull to Caldwell, March 7, 1918, in the Hull Papers.

[50] Committee on Collection, Washington County Council of Defense to Dear Sir, printed letter, December 3, 1918, in the Stewart Papers.

[51] Petition of thirty-five to Irvine Lenroot, April 10, 1918, in the Esch Papers.

[52] See the *Milwaukee Sentinel,* December 24, 1917, for a calm report of one such affair; see also Oscar Ameringer, *If You Don't Weaken* (New York, 1940), 359.

[53] Huber, "War Hysteria," 40–41, 84–85; Stewart, "Prussianizing Wisconsin," 103.

complacent about the distant war, until the end of January, 1917. Then came the break with Germany, and every English-language paper in the state except the Social Democratic *Leader* supported the President. When La Follette filibustered against the armed merchantship bill, the same papers joined in condemning him. All restraint was put aside. The *Superior Telegram,* for instance, ran a front-page picture of Benedict Arnold next to a picture of the eleven "willful men." Green Bay's *Press-Gazette* said of La Follette, "There is only one of two explanations applicable to his treacherous and preposterous course. His egotism and fanaticism have mentally unbalanced him, or he is acting for the German government." When La Follette joined with five other senators in voting against entry into war, in April, every paper but the *Leader* roundly condemned him.[54]

Richard Lloyd Jones, editor of the most important progressive paper, the *Wisconsin State Journal,* was after La-Follette's scalp well before the St. Paul speech of September. He began to wax superpatriotic in July, 1916. By February, 1917, he was characterizing La Follette's stand in favor of an embargo on munitions as "un-American." By July, the paper was among the strongest anti-La Follette journals in the state. Jones happily quoted the *New York Times* in denunciation of the senator. By August, Jones was impugning La Follette's motives.[55]

Curiously, the Wisconsin press did not pick up the St. Paul speech story until outsiders brought it to national attention. La Follette's old enemy, Theodore Roosevelt, took the lead by immediately denouncing La Follette in a series of speeches, one of them at Racine. "I abhor the Hun without our gates," the stern patriot said, "but more I abhor the Hun within our gates."[56] The Minnesota Commission of

---

[54] Jackson, "Wisconsin's Attitude Toward American Foreign Policy Since 1910," 34–50.
[55] Weissman, "The Wisconsin State Journal Since 1900," 106, 21.
[56] *Wisconsin State Journal,* September 29, 1917.

Loyalty, Loyalty, Loyalty

Public Safety and the Senate of the United States did La Follette more abiding damage than did the former President. The Minnesota group petitioned the Senate to expel La Follette as a teacher of disloyalty and sedition. The Senate referred the matter to a subcommittee, whose dilatory investigation provided a background for anti-La Follette activities throughout the war period. Not until the war was over did the committee and the Senate decide in La Follette's favor.[57] Meanwhile, La Follette weathered a storm that few could have borne.

The war fever found ready expression in the state legislature. Almost two months before United States entry into the war, Charles McCarthy found "a suppressed excitement in the legislature here this morning. . . . Last night the legislature, upon the motion of a man who voted against the resolution the other day, got up and sang 'America.'"[58] Three months later, the state senate expelled a Social Democrat for remarks "tending to show that he was disloyal."[59] Well before La Follette's September speech, the majority in the legislature felt called upon to show that La Follette did not truly represent Wisconsin, and that the state really supported the President. It passed the first of a series of resolutions backing Wilson on February 7, 1917, after Wilson broke diplomatic relations with Germany over the opposition of La Follette and four other senators. Veteran stalwart State Senator Timothy Burke took the occasion to say that Wisconsin had been disgraced by its national representatives.[60]

A year of wartime living plus the St. Paul speech vastly intensified feeling against La Follette. When the legislature met in special session late in February, 1918, another pointed loyalty resolution was inevitable. Senator Burke wanted to

---

[57] Belle and Fola La Follette, *La Follette*, 2: 770–779, 927–931.
[58] McCarthy to Sir Horace Plunkett, February 3, 1917, in the McCarthy Papers.
[59] Henry Huber to Fred Huber, May 12, 1917, in the Huber Letterbooks.
[60] Huber, "War Hysteria," 37.

denounce La Follette by name, but the plan was squashed by the Republican caucus in the interests of party harmony. As a compromise, the assembly adopted, by a vote of eighty to eleven, a resolution that recited Wisconsin's war record and condemned "all seditious utterances which, under the guise of free speech, are seeking to incite sedition and anarchy within or without our borders."[61]

An alternative resolution condemning La Follette by name was pending in the state senate, but there was little chance of any action on it. Then a small, mild-mannered La Follette partisan, Senator Henry Huber, threw a bombshell into the proceedings in the form of a long and impassioned address defending La Follette. The anti-La Follette men were furious. Senators who had left town were summoned back and the senate swiftly adopted a new resolution, known thereafter as the Wilcox resolution: ". . . We condemn Senator Robert M. La Follette and all others who have failed to see the righteousness of our nation's cause, who have failed to support our government in matters vital to the winning of the war, and we denounce any attitude or utterance of theirs which has tended to incite sedition among the people of our country and to injure Wisconsin's fair name before the free peoples of the world." The amendment was quickly adopted, twenty-two to seven.

In the assembly, Charles Rosa of Beloit fought a long delaying action. Finally, on March 6, Rosa agreed to permit a vote if he could offer a single amendment. The real test in the Assembly came on the Rosa amendment to the Wilcox resolution. The Rosa amendment called on the United States Senate, before which charges against La Follette were pending, "to at once hear and determine said question as in their judgement merit of said question demands, and if it shall appear that United States Senator Robert M. La Follette has been guilty of any traitorous or seditious conduct or has injured our country's cause we

[61] *Ibid.*, 91–92; *Wisconsin State Journal,* March 6, 1918.

Loyalty, Loyalty, Loyalty 213

condemn him for such conduct." The amendment was narrowly turned down, forty-five to forty-one. Once aside, the assembly quickly concurred in the Wilcox resolution, fifty-three to thirty-two. The senate promptly adopted the final draft with but three dissidents, Huber and two socialists.[62]

More stinging to La Follette personally, and perhaps in terms of effect, was the behavior of the faculty and student body of his alma mater, the University of Wisconsin. Wisconsin progressivism was distinguished by the extraordinary mutual esteem and co-operation between La Follette and the university. When President Van Hise and Professors Ely and Commons, among others, turned on him, it marked for La Follette a final shattering of the life and politics of the past.[63]

The university, nervous after years of attack on charges of socialism and extravagance, went out of its way to display its loyalty. Faculty members wrote pamphlets demonstrating Germany's war guilt; the university distributed these separately and as a book which was required reading at the university.[64] President Van Hise denied a student group the right to sponsor an address by Max Eastman early in 1917, after permission had already been granted and arrangements made.[65] Professor Richard Feise of the German department was dismissed following an irreverent remark to a colleague about a Liberty Loan button.[66] Van Hise, Dean Russell, and others participated in two meetings on October 9, 1917, that called for La Follette's expulsion from the Senate.[67] Faculty members joined in a loyalty rally at the gymnasium on December 12, 1917, following which students burned La Follette in effigy. Two weeks later, the Madison Club, in which university professors were prominent, expelled

---

[62] Huber, "War Hysteria," 91–92; *Wisconsin State Journal*, March 6, 1918.
[63] Belle and Fola La Follette, *La Follette*, 2: 842, 852–853.
[64] Jack Frooman, "The Wisconsin Peace Movement, 1915–1919" (master's thesis, University of Wisconsin, 1949), 274–275.
[65] Curti and Carstensen, *The University of Wisconsin*, 2: 73–74.
[66] Huber, "War Hysteria," 161.
[67] Belle and Fola La Follette, *La Follette*, 2: 793–794.

La Follette.[68] Finally, a move to formalize the whole procedure resulted in a "round robin" protesting the actions and utterances of La Follette as giving aid and comfort to Germany. All but four members of the faculty signed the memorial.

"Loyalty," in short, was the dominant fact of Wisconsin's political life during the war. It shattered the old political configurations beyond repair. Strange new alignments developed that bore little resemblance to the stalwart-progressive patterns. The outcome was exceedingly complex, in terms both of issues and of alignments. One complicating fact of wartime politics was this: The ultranationalist crusade did not bring the total destruction of either La Follette or reformism as political forces in Wisconsin. This was so largely because of the extensive discontent generated by wartime events. German sympathizers and victims of superpatriotism were disgruntled; so too were people with war-induced economic grievances.

The war brought expanded acreage and production and higher farm prices. Nevertheless, many Wisconsin farmers were restive. Dairying did not benefit from the war nearly so much as other forms of agriculture; dairy prices rose, but did not keep pace with feed-grain prices. Hay and bran were needed by many Wisconsin farmers for their hogs, horses, and cows, but efforts to secure price regulation on the skyrocketing feeds failed, while butter prices were controlled.[70] Irritation grew as the national food administration's promises of lower feed prices came to nothing.[71] Lessened butter output during the last two years of the war reflected widespread dissatisfaction among dairymen.[72]

---

[68] *Ibid.*, 2: 827–828.
[69] *Ibid.*, 2: 843; Huber, "War Hysteria," 171; *Wisconsin State Journal*, January 15, 1918.
[70] John Shinnick to Charles Lyman, November 12, 1917, in the McCarthy Papers.
[71] Lyman to McCarthy, December 20, 1917, in the McCarthy Papers.
[72] A. B. Genung, "Agriculture in the World War One Period," *1940 Yearbook of Agriculture* (Washington, 1940), 288.

The government promoted the organization of industry during the war, but when milk producers from Illinois, Indiana, and Wisconsin tried to fix milk prices their offices in Chicago were raided and anti-trust proceedings instituted. Wisconsin milk producers resented the apparent injustice and felt, too, that the federal government was withholding figures that would show the high cost of milk production.[73] At the same time that La Follette was being pilloried, in the fall of 1917, Wisconsin farm co-operatives were up in arms because a government regulation forced them to buy coal through the dealers rather than directly as before.[74] Charles McCarthy, on loan from Wisconsin to the food administration in Washington, was distressed to find on visiting Madison that "With conscription, high cost of fertilizer, insecticides, machinery, etc., etc., he [the farmer] is in a very bad humor."[75] Since the government appealed to farmers for crop expansion, farmers felt that the government should guarantee profitable prices and a good supply of labor. They wished, too, that imputations of farmer disloyalty should cease.[76]

Seeing businessmen in control of wartime machinery, and the huge profits being amassed by industry, farmers rejected wartime regulations, inconveniences, and price discriminations as the work of profiteers. The *Equity News* reflected discontent that focused chiefly on profiteers, labor shortages, mounting costs of manufactured goods, and ever-recurring charges of disloyalty.[77]

Some of this discontent found expression in demands formulated by a set of farm organizations, including the Wisconsin Society of Equity, early in the war. The farm representatives asked for creation of a commission representing producers and consumers to protect them from the machi-

---

[73] Miles Riley to McCarthy, October 1, 1917, in the McCarthy Papers.
[74] McCarthy to Harry Garfield, October 10, 1917, in the McCarthy Papers.
[75] *Idem.*
[76] Theodore Saloutos, "The Decline of the Wisconsin Society of Equity," *Agricultural History*, 15: 137 (July, 1941).
[77] *Idem.*

nations of profiteers; for the fixing of prices; the prohibition of speculation; the closing of boards of trade, stock exchanges, and chambers of commerce; and a graduated tax on all incomes over $25,000. They asked also for the nationalization of packinghouses, storage plants, terminal markets, and utilities to make speculation and profiteering impossible. None of these requests was met.[78]

The war greatly accentuated the Wisconsin farmer's tendency to organize. The most rapid expansion of the co-operative movement in Wisconsin occurred between 1912 and 1921.[79] The Wisconsin Society of Equity grew swiftly, and in 1917, the Nonpartisan League, fresh from political success in North Dakota, joined Equity in the Wisconsin field.[80] Under the new circumstances of war, the socialist-minded State Federation of Labor decided to co-operate with these farm organizations.[81]

The potency of wartime political forces came to a test in the spring of 1918. Senator Paul Husting met death in a hunting accident in October, 1917. Governor Philipp called a special session of the legislature and asked for power to appoint a successor, seeking to avoid the bitterness and distraction of an election. Anti-Philipp Republicans, Democrats, and Social Democrats blocked the plan, however, forcing a primary on March 19 and a special election April 2.

Superpatriots welcomed the election as an opportunity to demonstrate Wisconsin's loyalty. Irvine Lenroot, one of the two Wisconsin congressmen to vote for war, entered the Republican primary as a champion of loyalty. Lenroot had risen to prominence as a loyal La Follette man. He had served as speaker of the assembly under La Follette and

---

[78] *Equity News,* May 15, 1917, cited in Saloutos, "Decline of Wisconsin Society of Equity," 138–139.

[79] Frank G. Swoboda, "Agricultural Cooperation in Wisconsin," *Wisconsin Magazine of History,* 10: 164 (December, 1926).

[80] Lyman to McCarthy, July 11, 1917, December 7, 1917, in the McCarthy Papers.

[81] Executive Committee Minutes, Wisconsin State Federation of Labor January 1, 1918.

had dutifully opposed James O. Davidson in the 1906 primaries at the behest of La Follette. In 1908, Lenroot took his place among congressional insurgents as a La Follette man. But the years in Washington brought Lenroot power and respect and freed him from dependence on La Follette. His associations with friends of Theodore Roosevelt, his sympathy for the Roosevelt candidacy in 1912, and his ties with the national Republican leadership combined to draw him away from the senior senator. The two remained on friendly personal terms until the United States entered the war, however.[82] Then a complete break occurred. The break widened as a result of the personal animus that La Follette developed against his former protégé.

Lenroot's opponent in the Republican primary was the strongest Norwegian-American vote getter in Wisconsin since the heyday of James O. Davidson. "Big Jim" Thompson was a large, affable, handsome man, in his middle forties, a La Crosse lawyer of ordinary ability.[83] Thompson had always disclaimed ambition for office, but he had been quietly active in politics for some time.[84] As the "La Follette candidate," Thompson received little press support. But *La Follette's Magazine* was of course with him, as were a few papers that reached German voters. The most important daily to support him was the recently founded Madison *Capital Times*.

The *Capital Times* was born in revolt against the superpatriotism of Richard Lloyd Jones and his *Wisconsin State Journal*. Young William T. Evjue and three others left the *State Journal* in the fall of 1917 and started the rival paper behind an ice-cream parlor. Evjue sold stock to such La Follette men as A. T. Rogers, Charles Crownhart, Herman Ekern, Fred L. Holmes, and Charles Rosa. Banker Sol Levitan, a veteran La Follette man, helped several times.

[82] Gross, "A Political Grab Bag."
[83] Interviews with Charles Rosa, January 15, 1954; William T. Evjue, January 18, 1954; and William Kirsch, January 18, 1954.
[84] John Esch to Will Esch, July 26, 1916, in the Esch Papers.

In June, 1918, a former Wisconsin man, W. H. Dick, visiting from Mississippi, bought $5,000 worth of stock. Contracts to print the *Equity News* and *La Follette's Magazine* were valuable. Most important, the *State Journal* campaigned against profiteering by local merchants and drove them and their advertising to the new paper.[85]

Apart from the *Capital Times,* Thompson counted on farmers and workers. Henry Huber returned from his battle over the Wilcox resolution to find that farmers and laboring men approved his stand.[86] The proprietor of a stock farm near Milwaukee, in contact with farmers from all over the state, found them pro-La Follette almost without exception.[87] One of the anti-La Follette leaders of Mauston said that the local Equity men shouted patriotism, but quietly backed La Follette.[88]

Economic discontent alarmed Charles McCarthy. ". . . The whole country is in a ferment," he wrote. "We cannot win this battle in this country by merely shouting 'loyalty.' The battle is fundamentally an economic and social one. There are very few men with sinister motives on the side of Mr. Thompson and Mr. La Follette, but there is a good deal of muddle-headedness and a great deal of fear that the rich and the powerful may grow more rich and more powerful."[89] A supporter wrote Thompson that "We need men that will work for the interest of the people and not for the trusts. . . ."[90] Another volunteered to distribute literature, adding, "also tell me how many more millionaires we now have more than when the war started. . . ."[91]

[85] Kenneth Cameron Wagner, "William T. Evjue and the Capital Times" (master's thesis, University of Wisconsin, 1949), 31–67; Meyer, "The Politics of Loyalty," 39.
[86] Huber to William T. Evjue, March 7, 1918, in the Huber Letterbooks.
[87] Edward M. Schultz to Thompson, March 9, 1918, in the Thompson Papers.
[88] Frank Hanson to Esch, October 15, 1918, in the Esch Papers.
[89] McCarthy to H. M. Kallen, March 20, 1918, in the McCarthy Papers.
[90] Thomas H. Brehn to Thompson, March 9, 1918, in the Thompson Papers.
[91] George J. Brichen to Thompson Campaign Headquarters, March 11, 1918, in the Thompson Papers.

Thompson and La Follette stressed the economic arguments for all they were worth. La Follette attacked "the profiteers," and linked this appeal to the high cost of living and the taxation of war profits.[92] On the eve of the primary election the *Capital Times* and *La Follette's Magazine* tried to bring the profiteer question home by showing the large wartime profits made by twenty-one Wisconsin corporations.[93] The ace card in Thompson's campaign was a printed letter from La Follette to the voters, saying, "The tax dodging profiteers and the war-hogs are trying very hard to defeat him and I want to see them properly rebuked."[94] In his correspondence, his published statements, and his brief speaking campaign, Thompson ignored attacks on the loyalty question and gave full attention to economic questions.[95]

As the campaign developed, Thompson found that he could not choose the lines of battle. He was a captive candidate. He had apparently been urged to enter the race on the grounds that the economic issues were ripe. Sources all over the state pictured certain success. He announced his candidacy in the belief that it would be just another political campaign, fought on the issues of his platform. But La Follette supporters immediately rallied to him and, as Thompson explained, "Being that so many of his nearest supporters also supported me, and, in a way, stood sponsor to my candidacy, I could not take a position opposed to him. . . ." Afterwards he admitted ruefully that he would not have run had he foreseen that he would be labeled the "La Follette candidate."[96]

Thompson was trapped with the La Follette issue: "I took no part in that issue. I did not refer to it, nor to the Senior Senator, either in my literature or in my speeches."[97]

---

[92] *La Follette s Magazine*, 9: 2, 11, 12; 10: 1 (February, November, December, 1917; January, 1918).
[93] *Ibid.*, 10: 3 (March, 1918).
[94] La Follette to Dear Friend, March 13, 1918, in the Thompson Papers.
[95] James Thompson to Thompson, March 26, 1918, in the Thompson Papers.
[96] James Thompson to Thompson, April 11, 1918, in the Thompson Papers.
[97] James Thompson to Thompson, March 26, 1918, in the Thompson Papers.

But with the La Follette support came the issue of "La Folletteism," which the senator was content should be the issue. Thompson found himself in the middle, not knowing quite what had happened. The *Skandinaven,* which warmly supported him in the 1916 delegate contest, failed to back him, and other sources of strength vanished.[98] Lieutenant Governor Edward F. Dithmar bowed out earlier because of his German name and associations,[99] but the sacrifice was in vain. Even a Norwegian could not avoid the taint of Germanism that attached to La Follette. As Henry Huber described the situation, "Lenroot is the Stalwart and loyalty candidate. Of course, so far as loyalty goes, Mr. Thompson is just as loyal as Mr. Lenroot is, but as La Follette is backing Thompson, of course he is classed as disloyal."[100]

Poor Thompson could do nothing but swallow his medicine. After the campaign, he tried to repair some of the damage to his reputation by speaking at Liberty Loan meetings.[101]

Lenroot men neither knew nor cared that Thompson had not run in order to vindicate La Follette. La Follette's support was enough to mark Thompson in their eyes. The loyalty forces felt the eyes of the nation on them. The *New York Times* declared the election "a battle between Germany and the United States for possession of one of the United States."[102] President Wilson wrote a letter to the Vice President for public consumption, saying "I have no doubt that you have been following, as I have, with a good deal of anxiety the critical Senatorial contest in Wisconsin. The

[98] *Idem.*
[99] Herman C. Schultz to Thompson, February 28, 1918, in the Thompson Papers; Charles Crownhart to Charles Rosa, November 20, 1917, in the Rosa Papers. Crownhart judged Dithmar an unacceptable Senate candidate not only because of his German name but because in a published interview before American entry into the war he had indicated that he had relatives in the German navy.
[100] Henry to Fred Huber, March 14, 1918, in the Huber Letterbooks.
[101] James Thompson to Thompson, April 11, 1918, in the Thompson Papers.
[102] *New York Times,* March 13, 1918.

attention of the country will naturally be centered on it. And the question will be in every patriotic man's mind whether Wisconsin is really loyal to this country in this time of crisis or not."[103]

James Stone expressed the opinion of many when he wrote in January, 1918, that the big issue in the Senate battle would be "the all important question of loyalty to the nation in time of war."[104] That single theme dominated political thought and activity in the winter and spring of 1918. Before the Thompson-Lenroot primary battle developed, Victor Berger was regarded as the candidate of disloyalty. Some hoped to unite on a single candidate to oppose Berger.[105] When bipartisan efforts towards this end failed, and a primary battle against the La Follette forces developed, stalwart and progressive Republican patriots succeeded in uniting on Lenroot. As usual, Frank McGovern refused to accept the decision of a conference. But he could not hold his supporters against the force of the loyalty issue and had to withdraw in favor of Lenroot.[106]

Since Lenroot supporters hoped to "convince the nation of the loyalty of Wisconsin," and were unified on the basis of this issue alone, the candidate gave exclusive attention to it.[107] Campaign manager Alvin Peterson put the matter simply: "The issue is now loyalty versus disloyalty. Lenroot stands for America, Thompson for *La Follette*."[108] The *Wisconsin State Journal's* primary-day headline screamed, "DECIDE STATE'S LOYALTY TODAY."[109]

The loyalty question brought together a remarkable combination behind Lenroot. Progressive Jim Stone was glad that in his area "every ardent Stalwart" joined him in

[103] Meyer, "Politics of Loyalty," 29.
[104] Stone to Frank Winter, January 24, 1918, in the Stone Papers.
[105] Stone to Henry Campbell, February 25, 1918, in the Stone Papers.
[106] Stone to O. D. Whitehill, March 9, 1918, in the Stone Papers; *Wisconsin State Journal*, March 5, 1918.
[107] Stone to L. W. Nieman, February 28, 1918, in the Stone Papers.
[108] Printed letter, Alvin Peterson to James Stone, March 15, 1918, in the Stone Papers.
[109] *Wisconsin State Journal*, March 19, 1918.

backing Lenroot.[110] Stalwarts Platt Whitman and George Lines served on Lenroot's personal campaign committee. With them on the committee were such progressives as A. W. Sanborn, Otto Bosshard, W. S. Goodland, and E. F. Kileen, a former McGovern man.[111] Governor Philipp, who had been prepared to appoint Lenroot to the Senate vacancy if given a chance, took time off from his war duties and the problems of a special legislative session to deliver several effective speeches for Lenroot.[112] Even sectional loyalties broke down. John McConnell, Otto Bosshard, and A. M. Brayton, editor of the *La Crosse Tribune,* all deserted their La Crosse neighbor, Thompson.[113]

The unwitting victim of the loyalty crusade fell heir to considerable German support. The *Germania* and the *Free Press,* which had declined considerably since its days as a La Follette organ, backed Thompson. A longtime La Follette man confided that in Walworth County progressives had declined and the Germans gained, but "Between you and I, Thompson will get quite a sprinkling of German votes. . . ."[114] Germans, centered chiefly in the south and east of the state, had been Democrats to a large extent, but they blamed the national Democratic administration for the war and the loyalty fever. Judge J. M. Becker of Green County returned Thompson's nominating papers with the news that "It took me about ten minutes to obtain the signatures. About 50% of the former Democratic vote of this county will be cast for you as a La Follette candidate."[115]

The voting confirmed the existence of a new pattern, already suggested by the 1916 elections. The predominantly German areas, formerly anti-La Follette and Democratic for the most part, swung to the Republican party and the La Follette candidate; and the old La Follette strongholds,

---

[110] Stone to J. T. Dithmar, March 11, 1918, in the Stone Papers.
[111] Letterhead, Peterson to Stone, March 15, 1918, in the Stone Papers.
[112] Maxwell, *Philipp,* 162.
[113] J. E. McConnell to Stone, March 9, 1918, in the Stone Papers.
[114] S. C. Goff to L. E. Gettle, March 13, 1918, in the Thompson Papers.
[115] J. M. Becker to Thompson, February 28, 1918, in the Thompson Papers.

Loyalty, Loyalty, Loyalty 223

where the German population was sparse, gave the anti-La Follette candidate heavy support. Thompson carried Democratic and heavily German Dodge County against Lenroot by a vote of 2,328 to 901. He won Jefferson County by 1,657 to 760; Manitowoc by 1,778 to 541; Ozaukee by 1,000 to 143; Shawano by 1,401 to 560; Sheboygan by 2,160 to 970; and Washington by 1,699 to 233. He also carried Calumet, Columbia, Green Lake, Fond du Lac, Marathon, Milwaukee, and Outagamie counties. His vote exceeded the vote for the highest Democratic candidate in all but one of these chiefly Democratic and strongly German counties.[116]

Because the point is extremely important, statistical elaboration is warranted. Thompson carried twenty-four counties in the 1918 primaries, and "drew his largest percentage of the Republican vote in counties whose residents had responded with little enthusiasm to progressivism prior to the war."[117] The table on page 224 lists the twenty-four counties that Thompson carried against Lenroot in 1918, the percentage of Republican votes for Thompson, and the percentage of residents of German birth or parentage in these counties as of the 1910 census.[118]

Of ten conservative German-American counties that La Follette failed to carry in 1902 against the Democrat David Rose, all but two (Langlade and Taylor) were heavily for Thompson in 1918. The others (Dodge, Ozaukee, Jefferson, Kewaunee, Calumet, Fond du Lac, Green Lake, and Washington) switched. The hard-core Democratic counties, each with large German populations, were the five that had given John Aylward majorities against James O. Davidson in 1906. Each of these (Calumet, Dodge, Jefferson, Ozaukee, and Washington) was now in Thompson's column.[119]

Unfortunately for Thompson, the German support was

---

[116] *Wisconsin Blue Book, 1919* (Madison, 1919), 45.
[117] Meyer, "The Politics of Loyalty," 53.
[118] *Ibid.*, 54–55; the 1920 census gives no data on German parentage.
[119] See the *Wisconsin Blue Book, 1907*, 472, for the 1902 vote.

not enough. Lenroot won narrowly, 73,186 to 70,772.[120] The loyalty issue proved to be just too strong. An Eau Claire friend told him afterwards: "I think you made an astonishingly fine run. Just think of the circumstances. Even your best friends could not say a word without being 'disloyal.' Hardly to risk to speak for you. A regular terrorism seemed to prevail."[121] Even the Wisconsin Society

[120] *Wisconsin Blue Book, 1919*, 45.
[121] Waldemar Ager to Thompson, May 8, 1918, in the Thompson Papers.

County	Republican Percentage for Thompson	Percentage of Total Population of German Origin
Washington	87.9	42.8
Ozaukee	87.4	40.6
Calumet	86.0	37.0
Manitowoc	76.4	34.0
Dodge	73.3	40.5
Shawano	71.5	38.5
Sheboygan	69.0	37.8
Jefferson	68.7	41.5
Marquette	68.4	32.5
Outagamie	63.4	31.2
Milwaukee	63.0	44.1
Buffalo	60.5	27.2
La Crosse*	59.6	23.8
Kewaunee**	59.1	17.9
Green Lake	58.6	46.5
Sauk	57.6	29.6
Marathon	57.5	43.0
Fond du Lac	57.0	31.1
Adams***	55.6	13.1
Dane	52.4	16.1
Vernon	52.3	15.5
Columbia	51.3	22.7
Winnebago	51.0	34.4
Monroe	50.8	23.0
State average all counties:	48.8	27.0

*Thompson's home county.
**Kewaunee's largest foreign-born group were Austrian. Those of Austrian birth or parentage constituted 21.8% of the population.
***The smallest county of the group with a total population of 8,600.

Loyalty, Loyalty, Loyalty 225

of Equity, while aroused over economic questions, steered clear of Thompson.[122]

While Thompson and Lenroot fought it out, the Democrats had a primary contest of their own. The death of Husting, following soon after the demise of John Aylward and William Wolfe, the party's 1916 senatorial candidate, left the Democrats embarrassed for seasoned leadership. Charles McCarthy belatedly heard the voice that calls candidates and came forth to oppose Federal Trade Commissioner Joseph E. Davies. McCarthy feared the triumph of a La Follette man in the Republican primary; he believed himself stronger with farm and labor elements than Davies, and therefore more likely to ward off the national calamity of a La Follette victory.[123] Richard Lloyd Jones agreed. "The farmers and laborers are in revolt and will go to Thompson if Davies wins," Jones wired the wealthy Democratic reformer, Charles Crane. "McCarthy can surely win if he beats Davies but Davies cannot carry the mass of the people."[124]

McCarthy feared that Davies would be weak because his appeal followed the line set by the national administration, emphasizing loyalty and support for the President to the exclusion of all social and economic issues. Also, Davies was of an aristocratic caste, not cut out for the role of candidate. But Davies had the solid support of the Democratic machine, while McCarthy was new to party ranks. To his dismay, McCarthy was badly beaten by Davies, 57,282 to 13,784.[125]

The Democratic primary made it clear that the Democrats in Wisconsin were following the lead of the national administration in passing over controversial economic and social issues in favor of a "Back the President" loyalty

---

[122] John Hannan to Thompson, May 18, 1918, in the Thompson Papers.
[123] McCarthy to John Walsh, February 23, 1918; to Louis Wehle, February 24, 1918; to Vance McCormick, February 25, 1918; and to Charles Lyman, February 25, 1918, in the McCarthy Papers.
[124] Jones to Crane, March 15, 1918, in the McCarthy Papers.
[125] *Wisconsin Blue Book, 1919*, 45.

theme. The faction-ridden leadership united in trying to lure Republican patriots to their minority party with the popular song. Though McCarthy urged economic issues on Mr. Davies, "he seemed to think that there was only one great issue." The leading liberal Democratic paper in the state, the *Milwaukee Journal,* had "hardly a word . . . to counteract Mr. La Follette's appeal to workingmen and to toilers in general."[126]

The Democrats acted with their loyalty issue like a hungry child with a pound of candy: they gave no thought to saving it, or consuming it with moderation, but gnawed continuously on it and slapped any hand that reached for a piece. Even before the outcome of the Republican primary was known, the *Milwaukee Journal* was writing scornfully of Lenroot's war and preparedness record, condemning his stand on the McLemore resolution in particular.[127] After Lenroot was nominated, the party redoubled the challenge to his loyalty. The contest took on national significance when the *Milwaukee Journal* published a letter from President Wilson to Davies on the day following the primary. Wilson set forth the issues in writing: "The McLemore resolution, the embargo issue and the armed neutrality measure presented the first opportunities to apply the acid test in our country to disclose true loyalty and genuine Americanism. It should always be a source of satisfaction to you that on these crucial propositions you proved true."[128] Vice-President Thomas Marshall quickly pressed the attack with a Democratic "flying squadron" that included Governor James Cox of Ohio and Secretary of Labor William Wilson.[129] At Madison, Marshall goaded Republicans when he said, "If the vote at the primary is based upon the charges and counter-charges you have made against each other, you are about half for America, half for the Kaiser,

[126] McCarthy to Otto La Budde, March 23, 1918, in the McCarthy Papers.
[127] *Milwaukee Journal,* March 19, 1918.
[128] *Ibid.,* March 20, 1918.
[129] *Wisconsin State Journal,* March 31, 1918.

and all against Wilson. Having purified the stream in the primary you welcome the sewage in the election."[130]

Immediately after the primary, the Loyalty Legion tried to secure the withdrawal of Lenroot or Davies in order to present a solid front against Victor Berger. The unprecedented election of a socialist assemblyman in strongly German Marathon County in February perhaps stimulated fear of a Berger victory.[132] The *Milwaukee Journal* attempted to force the withdrawal of Lenroot,[133] and some Republicans favored the idea.[134] But the violent attacks on Lenroot's loyalty ruined any chance for such unity. Governor Philipp was infuriated by the efforts of some officials in Washington to identify Davies alone with loyalty to the war effort. His own efforts were indirectly inpugned by this approach and he was totally unwilling to see Lenroot honor the charge by withdrawing.[135] Republican State Chairman George West, a Philipp man, was able to point out that the attacks on Lenroot's loyalty made the request for his withdrawal an insult to the Republican party and a challenge to its future.[136]

Not only did the Democrats fail to pre-empt the loyalty issue, but they also succeeded in arousing the ire of Republicans and reinvigorating party feeling. The superpatriotic *Wisconsin State Journal,* almost always ready to back the President, felt impelled to criticize Wilson for his letter to Davies.[137] After the Vice-President's speech slurring the Republican party, the paper shifted its fire from disloyalty and the "Hun" to the Democrats. Republican patriots Lenroot, John Chapple, Cameron Fraser, and Otto Bosshard also expressed indignation at the President's words.[138]

[130] *Ibid.,* March 28, 1918.
[131] *Ibid.,* March 23, 1918.
[132] Meyer, "The Politics of Loyalty," 51.
[133] *Milwaukee Journal,* March 20, 1918.
[134] Stone to A. W. Sanborn, March 21, 1918; and to Richard Lloyd Jones, March 21, 1918, in the Stone Papers.
[135] Maxwell, *Philipp,* 163.
[136] George A. West to Stone, March 23, 1918, in the Stone Papers.
[137] *Wisconsin State Journal,* March 23, 1918.
[138] *Ibid.,* March 28, April 2, 1918.

Lenroot took full advantage of Democratic attacks in an all-out effort to unite the full Republican vote behind him. He departed from his primary strategy of relying exclusively on the loyalty issue. While defending his own loyalty against attacks, he left superpatriotism to Davies and concentrated on an appeal for Republican unity and the gathering of the Thompson supporters to his fold. In a form letter to Republicans, he asked for their time, effort, and vote. "I do not ask this as a personal matter but I ask it in behalf of the good name of the Republican party and the State of Wisconsin."[139] Lenroot brought in Representative John G. Cooper of Ohio, a passenger engineer on the Pennsylvania railroad and a strong union man, to speak for him.[140] He publicly acknowledged the loyalty of Thompson supporters and asked for their help.[141] Thompson and Edward Dithmar, among others, were only too glad to meet him halfway.

The success of the Republicans in closing ranks made the election of Lenroot certain. The Democrats tried to ride the loyalty horse to victory, but failed to win over enough Republicans. The first major election test of the loyalty issue in Wisconsin politics showed that traditional questions of partisanship and personality could not be lightly brushed aside. When Lenroot defeated Davies, 163,983 to 148,923, the only surprise was the closeness of the vote.[142]

The campaign to vindicate Wisconsin's loyalty fell short of complete success in another major respect. Victor Berger, the Social Democratic candidate, an avowed opponent of the war, stood on his party's St. Louis platform. His newspaper, *The Leader,* had lost its mailing privileges under the Espionage Act, and Berger was under federal indictment on charges of having made seditious remarks. Much more than La Follette or Thompson, whose records on the war were some-

[139] Lenroot to Dear Sir, March 28, 1918, in the Castle Papers.
[140] *Wisconsin State Journal,* March 31, 1918.
[141] *Milwaukee Journal,* April 2, 1918.
[142] *Wisconsin Blue Book, 1919,* 46.

what ambiguous, Berger was regarded and branded as the champion of disloyalty. The primary battles were only preliminaries; the main contest was against Berger. And in this contest, the Social Democrat emerged the winner in defeat. Despite the loss of his paper's mailing privileges, the intimidation of socialist speakers, and an intense campaign of vilification, Berger received 110,487 votes, almost three times the highest vote his party had previously recorded in Wisconsin. He received 34,490 votes in Milwaukee County alone, where the Social Democrat Hoan was re-elected mayor. In addition, Berger carried Calumet, Dodge, Green Lake, Manitowoc, Marathon, Ozaukee, Shawano, Sheboygan, Taylor, and Washington counties.[143]

The large Social Democratic vote in heavily German counties was interpreted as signifying preference for Germany against the United States. A minority, however, regarded the socialist vote, and to an extent the Thompson vote as well, as an expression of protest against the unreasoning attack on Germans by the *Milwaukee Journal* and the loyalty forces, and against the extreme social pressure exerted in the name of loyalty. The *Milwaukee Journal* had greeted the large Thompson vote in the March 19 primary with this comment: ". . . The great mass of German voters in typical German counties took the wrong road . . . They went as far as they could in making it clear that Germany, not America, is first in their affections and allegiance. . . ."[144] It was hardly surprising that Germans should have claimed that they were driven to the Social Democrats by the *Milwaukee Journal*.[145] A Watertown man was irate in explaining the strong Berger showing as "a protest against the past methods employed by our autocratic, self-styled leaders, who claim to have a patent on patriotism in this country, under which they are hiding to disguise their own

---

[143] *Idem.*
[144] *Milwaukee Journal,* March 20, 1918.
[145] J. E. Corrigan to McCarthy, May 6, 1918, in the McCarthy Papers.

selfishness for gain at the people's expense."[146] An astute socialist organizer, Oscar Ameringer, found deep resentment among conservative German farmers—not against the war itself, but against those who called them "Huns," "baby-killers," "kaiser-lovers," and "alien enemies."[147] The Germans of Wisconsin were loyal to the United States once the war was on, but resented the treatment accorded them.[148] Opposed by the force of government and social pressure, the Germans found it difficult to express their resentment except in the secrecy of the ballot box.

While the spring primary and general elections indicated a powerful ferment of discontent beneath the surface, they indicated also that loyalty was easily the major single issue. Still, the division of the loyalty forces, the failure to coalesce on a single candidate, showed that this single issue was not of sufficient strength to cement together widely disparate groups. The Republican gubernatorial primary bore this out and further widened the cracks in the loyalty wall.

Suspicion is dynamic, not static. It either grows or dies. Governor Philipp learned what Irvine Lenroot had already discovered: that the test of loyalty could be turned against the tester. Philipp had joined in the condemnation of La Follette. He had been greatly concerned, as war governor, to vindicate the reputation of his state. He had tried to make Wisconsin's war effort enthusiastic and efficient. Even so, when election time rolled around, he failed to meet the increasingly rigorous loyalty standards.

Roy P. Wilcox, the Eau Claire senator who had sponsored the resolution condemning Senator La Follette, led the attack against Philipp in an effort to wrest away the key to the executive mansion. The hostility between the two men ripened well before the 1918 primaries. Wilcox

[146] A. H. Hartwig to James Thompson, July 12, 1918, in the Thompson Papers.
[147] Ameringer, *If You Don't Weaken*, 328–329.
[148] Child, *German-Americans in Politics*, 85–86.

openly sneered at the governor's patriotism and opposed his measures, while Philipp nurtured his cordial dislike for Wilcox.[149] The primary campaign in the summer of 1918 brought the Wilcox-Philipp enmity into full blossom. Wilcox stumped the state attacking Philipp for his pre-war support for an arms embargo and his opposition to sending United States troops abroad.[150] As the campaign grew more heated, Wilcox told a Waukesha audience that most of those who had favored an embargo had bought German bonds. The same day, he virtually accused Philipp of spreading German propaganda.[151]

Wilcox, a relative newcomer to politics, had the support of a heterogeneous band of leaders from throughout the state. He was well suited to head such a combination, for on economic questions he was all things to all men.[152] He claimed to be a progressive, but few took him seriously.[153] Nevertheless, he had the support of most former La Follette men: Richard Lloyd Jones, Otto Bosshard, Walter Goodland, A. W. Sanborn, James Stone, Henry Lockney, D. W. Agnew, E. F. Kileen, John Chase, and D. O. Mahoney.[154] Wilcox was also supported by a number of men whose factional affiliations were not always clear. Among these were Levi Bancroft, W. D. Connor, Frank Gilbert, O. G. Munson, senators J. H. Bennett and David James, Rasmus B. Anderson, Alvin P. Kletzsch, Alvin Peterson, and young Alexander Wiley of Chippewa Falls.[155]

While one or two of these politicians had been close to Governor Philipp, most had been his political oppo-

---

[149] Maxwell, *Philipp*, 155–161; interview with William Kirsch, January 18, 1954. Kirsch was associated with the Legislative Reference Library and was in close contact with legislative and administrative people during the second Philipp administration.
[150] *Milwaukee Sentinel*. August 14, 1918.
[151] *Ibid.*, August 21, 1918.
[152] Interview with William Kirsch, January 18, 1954.
[153] *Idem;* Stone to John Chapple, August 13, 1918, in the Stone Papers.
[154] Jones to Stone, July 1, 1918; letterhead, Chapple to Stone, July 24, 1918, in the Stone Papers.
[155] *Idem.*

nents. The loyalty issue aside, they might well have preferred Wilcox to Philipp. More significant, therefore, was the group of oldtime stalwarts which broke away from the governor in favor of Wilcox. Among these were Theodore W. Brazeau, John Gaveney, Frank Bentley, John Whitehead, and Charles E. Pierce, former head of the Taxpayers League.[156] In Milwaukee, the governor's traditional stronghold, powerful stalwart forces swung to Wilcox. Willet M. Spooner led the rebels. Even the *Milwaukee Sentinel*, still owned by Philipp's most powerful backer, leaned as close to Wilcox as it could without openly endorsing him.[157]

The underlying causes of the revolt against Philipp remained obscure. The governor listed disappointed office-seekers among his opponents,[158] and certainly this source of dissatisfaction had been evident for some time. Philipp's refusal to replace capable progressive holdovers on the industrial and tax commissions caused comment in 1917.[159] A more important complaint, perhaps, involved the governor's failure to utilize the loyalty issue to clamp down on the rapidly growing Social Democratic party. Philipp antagonized Willet Spooner and others when he simply laughed at pleas for martial law in Milwaukee should the socialists win the spring elections.[160] For some, Philipp's brewer associations and his veto of a prohibition referendum bill were important.[161]

Governor Philipp's primary campaign consisted largely of a defense of his patriotism against the attacks of the *Milwaukee Journal* and Senator Wilcox.[162] At the same time, he made a strong bid for the German vote. At Chilton, in Calumet County, one of the eastern counties that had

[156] *Idem.; Milwaukee Sentinel*, August 21, 1918.
[157] *Milwaukee Sentinel*, September 3, 4, 1918.
[158] *Ibid.*, August 14, 1918.
[159] Frank Hammill to Philipp, January 23, 1917, in the Philipp Papers.
[160] *Milwaukee Sentinel*, August 24, 1918; interview with William T. Evjue, January 18, 1954.
[161] See also Maxwell, *Philipp*, 132–175.
[162] *Milwaukee Sentinel*, August 7, 1918.

recently been carried by Victor Berger, the governor said: "A patriot is a patriot regardless of his ancestry . . . as long as I am Governor of this state there shall be no discrimination. . . . There isn't going to be any tar and feathering in this state if we catch them at it. . . ." He went on to promise that there would be no curtailment of free speech or religious services in any language. Continuing through the strong Berger area, Philipp urged voters not to vote socialist unless they believed in socialism, implying, of course, that the German vote might find a more congenial haven in his column.[163] The bonds that held the loyalty forces together came further and further apart as Philipp grew increasingly angry at his tormentors. He denounced the fight against him as "the cheapest kind of political claptrap," and attacked his foes for offering nothing constructive, but dealing only in personal abuse of him.[164]

La Follette men had always found pre-primary coordination awkward and difficult. In 1918, it was almost impossible. An imperfect organization had been established in 1916 with Walter Goodland as chairman. The war quickly rendered this vehicle obsolete as Goodland and other leaders broke with La Follette on the loyalty question. As the gubernatorial primaries approached, the remaining La Follette men and some new volunteers needed leadership and guidance; but La Follette was preoccupied with the care of his son and with Senate business. Foreseeing no possibility of getting home to help with the campaign in August and September, moreover, he felt disinclined to dictate to those who would have to carry the load. La Follette did finally take a hand, through his secretary John Hannan, but not until delay had taken its toll.[165] Several La Follette men, acting on their own initiative, tried to

---

[163] *Ibid.*, August 25, 1918.
[164] *Ibid.*, August 25, September 1, 1918.
[165] John Hannan to Dithmar, June 22, 1918; Hannan to A. H. Hartwig, July 5, 1918, in the Rosa Papers.

persuade James Thompson to carry their colors in the gubernatorial primary,[166] but before they could get a commitment from him, an altogether unexpected event made it difficult for any La Follette man to enter the field.

A perennial officeseeker, three times unsuccessful candidate for Congress, and a progressive, J. N. Tittemore, had won a battle within the Wisconsin Society of Equity and had become president of that powerful farm organization early in 1917. He immediately flooded the *Equity News* with his writings and invaded Washington, seeking to effect a close working agreement between farmers and laborers. He then returned home again, spoke of the need for "farmers to represent farmers," and set a goal of 50,000 members for Equity. By "combining rhetoric, politics, religion and sophistry, he came close to achieving his goal."[167]

Powered by a host of grievances, Tittemore engineered farmers and laborers into a May 1 convention in Madison of five hundred delegates representing Equity, the Grange, the newly formed Nonpartisan League, and labor elements. The Nonpartisan Leaguers favored formulation of a platform, but opposed presentation of a statewide ticket, fearing that premature efforts would bring defeat and retard the movement. Tittemore was in control, however, and on May 2 the Wisconsin press announced that Mr. J. N. Tittemore had been nominated by a convention to run in the Republican primary for governor. A full ticket was offered, including two progressive politicians, Merlin Hull for secretary of state and John Blaine for attorney general.[168]

The convention's platform backed the war, declared for an eight-hour day—except for farms—and opposed child labor. It backed the initiative, referendum, and recall. For the farmers, demands focused on direct marketing and further co-operation between producer and consumer, greater

---

[166] William T. Evjue to James Thompson, April 23, 1918, April 30, 1918; Herman Sachtjen to Thompson, April 30, 1918, in the Thompson Papers.
[167] Saloutos, "Decline of the Wisconsin Society of Equity," 139.
[168] Madison *Capital Times*, May 1, 2, 1918.

state control over terminal facilities, and a larger voice for farmers in the National Food Administration. In addition, the platform scored war profiteers, called for further development of northern Wisconsin through higher taxes on unoccupied lands, and favored consolidation of rural schools.[169]

Though pleased that economic discontent was rising to the surface, the La Follette men were disturbed that the reform springs had gushed forth on Tittemore's land. Though a fluent talker, Tittemore had never been closely affiliated with the La Follette faction or any other.[170] Charles Rosa knew little of Tittemore, other than that he had been a progressive in former days and had been on the anti-La Follette side in the recent senatorial contest.[171] La Follette men therefore persisted in considering a ticket of their own, even after Tittemore's convention. Despite continued urging, James Thompson remained unwilling to offer himself again, but expressed dissatisfaction with Tittemore and urged that a fight be made by another La Follette man.[172] Lieutenant Governor Edward F. Dithmar was quite willing to run, and it was he who engineered a series of conferences of La Follette men in Madison in June.[173]

Despite the enthusiasm of some for a ticket, the general situation was far from favorable. John Hannan, through several conferences in Washington and by letter, brought home the negative arguments and warned against a fiasco that might discredit La Follette and his friends in the future. Organizational efforts were strong in Dodge and Jefferson counties, where new German friends were active, but the statewide organization had been shattered; pro-La Fol-

[169] *Ibid.*, May 2, 1918.
[170] Plumb, *Badger Politics*, 189.
[171] Rosa to James Thompson, May 6, 1918, in the Thompson Papers.
[172] James Thompson to Charles Rosa, May 4, 1918; Rosa to Thompson, May 6, 1918; Thompson to Rosa, May 10, 1918; Rosa to Thompson, May 13, 1918; Thompson to Evjue, May 24, 1918; and Thompson to Rosa, May 24, 1918, in the Thompson Papers.
[173] Dithmar to Rosa, May 27, 1918; Dithmar to Rosa, June 10, 1918; Minutes of the "Conference of the Progressive Republican party of the State of Wisconsin...," June 14, 1918, in the Rosa Papers.

lette congressmen, preoccupied with their own survival, were in no position to give much financial help to a statewide campaign; their general assessment of statewide prospects was pessimistic; farmers might be alienated by an anti-Tittemore ticket; La Follette could not come back to Wisconsin to campaign; and Dithmar would be handicapped by his German name.[174] By the end of June, the movement for a pro-La Follette slate was dead and Dithmar was resigned to another race for lieutenant governor.[175]

If the La Follette men could not field a candidate of their own, their obvious course was to support Tittemore. In so doing, they would preserve the semblance of progressive continuity and maintain friendly ties with the farmer movement that Tittemore headed. William T. Evjue, who had seen the Farmers and Laborers League convention in Madison, had favored such a course from the first.[176]

The La Follette men had other and perhaps even stronger reasons for supporting Tittemore. They knew that the real choice lay between Philipp and Wilcox; Tittemore had no statewide reputation.[177] Philipp was a man they had denounced as a lobbyist and tool of the interests for almost two decades; Wilcox was the framer of the resolution denouncing La Follette. Unhesitatingly, they decided on the governor. Amidst the struggle for political survival, past grudges were too costly to be indulged. It was not Philipp but Wilcox who wielded the heavy club of nationalism against them, a weapon far more potent and ominous than any they had encountered before. That threat, symbolized by Wilcox's candidacy, had to be repelled be-

---

[174] John Hannan to Dithmar, June 20, 1918, June 22, 1918, July 5, 1918; "Why Governor Phillip [sic] Was Unopposed For a Third Term," in the Gross Papers; Dithmar to James Thompson, June 29, 1919; Rosa to Thompson, August 2, 1918, in the Thompson Papers.

[175] Dithmar to James Thompson, June 29, 1918, in the Thompson Papers.

[176] Evjue to Rosa, May 6, 1918; Minutes of the "Conference of the Progressive Republican party of the State of Wisconsin. . . ," June 14, 1918, in the Rosa Papers.

[177] Interview with William T. Evjue, January 18, 1954.

fore it would again be safe or even possible to focus on traditional progressive men and measures. To support Philipp openly was to repudiate, or acknowledge as irrelevant, the progressives' past rhetoric, and might confuse their less sophisticated supporters in any case. The only thing La Follette's lieutenants could do, therefore, was to endorse Tittemore in the hope of drawing votes from Wilcox, who professed himself a progressive. Charles Rosa explained matters to James Thompson: "It makes me mad all over to find Progressives everywhere, down here, supporting Wilcox. He is also receiving almost the united support of the Stalwarts, and, unless we get busy, he is going to even defeat Philipp. This, to me, is going to be the last straw. I consider him five times as vicious as Governor Philipp, from the standpoint of Progressive Republicanism. I think that unless we do something, he is going to beat Philipp. The only thing that we can do now is to endorse Tittemore. Mr. Tittemore is not an ideal candidate, by a long ways. The way he went at the thing is disgusting to me. Yet if we endorse him, it will draw a lot of Progressive support to him, that will now go to Wilcox. If we do not succeed in nominating Tittemore, we will, at least, succeed in beating Wilcox. . . ."[178] A form letter soon went out to progressives throughout the state warning against Wilcox as a sympathizer of the interests and a man with private utilities connections, and soliciting signatures to a pro-Tittemore statement.[179] The *Capital Times* endorsed Tittemore and publicized his activities; various progressive leaders helped by speaking for him.[180] Some progressives were more direct. In strongly German areas especially, it was possible, even necessary, to back Philipp rather than Tittemore.[181]

---

[178] Rosa to Thompson, August 2, 1918, in the Thompson Papers; Evjue expressed a similar view in Evjue to Rosa, July 23, 1918, in the Rosa Papers.
[179] Rosa to Stone, August 12, 1918, in the Rosa Papers. The Rosa Papers for mid-August include a number of reactions to the solicitation.
[180] *Capital Times,* July 22, 25, August 16, 22, 1918.
[181] A. H. Hartwig to Rosa, August 17, 1918; C. N. Saugen to Rosa, August 14, 1918, in the Rosa Papers. Saugen was an assemblyman who had opposed

The outcome was influenced by two other factors: the rising liquor issue and the hardy religious question. On balance, both worked against Wilcox and to the advantage of Philipp. The Guardians of Liberty claimed a membership in the state of 150,000; Wilcox was a Catholic and therefore taboo for all Guardian voters.[182] "Drys" objected to Philipp. Since the prohibitionists were drawn largely from the non-German segments of the population, however, their impact was less than it might have been under other circumstances. Wilcox had to share "dry" support with Tittemore, moreover, while Philipp was strengthened by his position among the Germans.[183]

As returns began to come in, observers discovered that the primary contest was as close a battle as any could recall. For a week the lead seesawed back and forth between Philipp and Wilcox. At last, on September 11, final returns showed Philipp the winner. The governor received 71,614 votes to 71,164 for Wilcox and 45,357 for Tittemore.[184]

Philipp's renomination was clearly due to the same German vote that had been cast for Thompson and Berger earlier in the year. His large vote in heavily German counties such as Dodge, Green Lake, Jefferson, Milwaukee, Sauk, Sheboygan, in all of which he exceeded the vote for the leading Democratic candidate, was just enough to overcome heavy Wilcox support in the largely Yankee counties.[185]

The strong Philipp vote was based more on his position vis-à-vis the Wilcox loyalty people than it was on time-honored economic issues. This was made clear by the very close parallel in many counties between Philipp's vote and the support accorded Edward F. Dithmar, a veteran La

---

the Wilcox resolution. Due to the strong opposition to his renomination by Wilcox men, he found himself with the support of Philipp men and felt that he had to reciprocate.

[182] A. H. Hartwig to James Thompson, July 12, 1918; A. B. Wesner to A. P. Nelson, May 28, 1920, in the Adolphus P. Nelson Papers.
[183] William Kohn to Rosa, August 16, 1918, in the Rosa Papers.
[184] *Wisconsin Blue Book, 1919,* 93.
[185] *Idem.*

Follette man who was seeking renomination for lieutenant governor. Dithmar was opposed in the primary by candidates linked to Wilcox and Tittemore. Evidently, Dithmar was the unofficial running mate of Philipp. The following table reveals the similarity of their vote in certain counties.[186]

COUNTY	PHILIPP	DITHMAR
Calumet	296	290
Dunn	845	813
Grant	1,387	1,393
Green Lake	723	702
La Crosse	1,483	1,558
Lincoln	567	537
Milwaukee	16,402	16,288
Sauk	1,512	1,526
Sawyer	240	243
Washburn	343	347
Washington	698	690
Waukesha	1,335	1,356
Winnebago	1,841	1,821

In other counties, the votes of the two men were not so close. But the similarity was striking.

As a result of the war issues, the veteran progressive congressmen Henry Cooper, John M. Nelson, and William Cary were defeated in the primary. Under the circumstances, however, the La Follette progressives held the line quite well. La Follette men Dithmar and Blaine were nominated for lieutenant governor and attorney general, respectively. The renomination of Merlin Hull as secretary of state was also reasonably satisfactory to La Follette men, though the victory of Henry Johnson in his bid for renomination as treasurer was less so. At the Republican state convention a few weeks after the primary, a Philipp-Tittemore combination was in control, and this too was as much as the La Follette men could have hoped for.[187]

The anti-Philipp crusade continued into the general election. Philipp's veto of the prohibition referendum con-

---

[186] *Milwaukee Sentinel*, September 13, 1918.
[187] Maxwell, *Philipp*, 177–178.

tinued to rankle the "drys,"[188] and his war record remained unsatisfactory to many. The Loyalty Legion seriously considered endorsing Henry Mohlenpah, the Democratic candidate for governor, and did issue a scathing report on Philipp's war record.[189] A flu epidemic prevented the usual speaking campaign, but it did not curb the fervor of the Democrats, who used the loyalty and "Back the President" appeal to the fullest. President Wilson once more interfered, signing a personal appeal to voters for a Democratic Congress.[190] The Democratic candidate, Mohlenpah, headed his letters with the inscription "Americanism Must Prevail, Wisconsin Shall not Fail."[191] But, as in the spring, the Democrats found the Republican shell hard to crack. As soon as the primary results were known, Irvine Lenroot called for party unity behind Philipp. The *Milwaukee Sentinel,* which had hedged towards Wilcox in the primary, commended Lenroot and obliquely advised Wilcox to close party ranks.[192]

Along with the theme of united Republicanism, the Grand Old Party used other issues that were extraneous to the loyalty question. Economic discontent was played upon through a platform plank on the marketing question.[193] Philipp pointed to efforts by his administration to help farmers and laborers and to curb the cost of living. More boldly, so far as the loyalty issue was concerned, Philipp again defended his moderate course and appealed indirectly for German support.[194]

The ideological wall constructed by the Republicans against the Democratic battering ram proved strong enough. Philipp defeated Mohlenpah, 153,153 to 111,224. Social

---

[188] Adolphus P. Nelson to George A. West, October 30, 1918, in the Nelson Papers.
[189] Stone to Walter Davidson, October 15, 1918; Jones to Stone, October 15, 1918; Mohlenpah to Stone, October 19, 1918, all in the Stone Papers; *Milwaukee Journal,* October 23, 1918.
[190] *Milwaukee Journal,* October 25, 1918.
[191] Mohlenpah to Stone, October 19, 1918, in the Stone Papers.
[192] *Milwaukee Sentinel,* September 14, 1918.
[193] West to A. P. Nelson, October 7, 1918, in the Nelson Papers.
[194] *Milwaukee Sentinel,* October 23, 1918.

Democrat Emil Seidel received 57,163 votes, carrying five counties including Milwaukee.[195] The entire Republican state ticket rode into office and the party captured ten of eleven seats in Congress, despite the plea of the President. The most notable Republican victory was scored in the usually Democratic Second District, where Representative Voigt, an anti-war man, won out by 15,289 to 12,532. The only congressional district not carried by the Republicans was the fifth. There, Representative William Stafford encountered the same type of superpatriotic opposition that had plagued Philipp. When Stafford won in the primary, despite the opposition of the *Milwaukee Sentinel* and a citizens' loyalty group, unity against Victor Berger became impossible. Still under indictment for violation of the Espionage Act, Berger defeated his divided opposition. Moreover, the Social Democrats in Milwaukee County won all seven county offices, two of three senate seats, and eleven of nineteen assembly posts. The campaign had featured as main issues the popularity of the war and the treatment of dissent.[196] Elsewhere in the state, especially in heavily German counties, Social Democrats and Republicans took legislative seats from Democrats, reducing their delegation to two senators and five assemblymen, a loss of four seats in the senate and nine in the assembly. The Social Democrats emerged with four seats in the senate and sixteen in the assembly, a gain of one in the upper house and nine in the lower.[197]

For La Follette and his partisans, the outcome must have been encouraging. The showing of Republicans like Dithmar and Blaine on the state ticket, the victory of Voigt in the Second Congressional District, the generally dismal performance of the Democrats, and the excellent vote won by the socialists augured well for the future of La Follette, his faction, and the measures that he would espouse. The furi-

[195] *Wisconsin Blue Book, 1919*, 149.
[196] Olson, "The Milwaukee Socialists," 379–380.
[197] *Wisconsin Blue Book, 1917*, 292–299; *Wisconsin Blue Book, 1919*, 158–163.

ous storm of war hysteria had taken its toll, but some of the progressive craft had weathered it and were now within sight of land.

Yet things were not even approximately as they had been, and they would never be so again. The impact of the war on Wisconsin thought and politics was not simply jarring, but shattering. The factional alignments of the progressive years were destroyed and many of the older issues were subordinated or lost sight of when the emotion-packed loyalty issue cast its giant shadow over the state's life and politics. The La Follette organization broke beyond repair when progressives old and young rallied to the flag. The idealistic Wilsonian propaganda for war made the national cause the more appealing to progressives, who made common cause with their old enemies on the neutral ground of patriotism.

Gradually, out of the wreckage, emerged new political alignments, based on new issues. Both the La Follette progressives and the Berger socialists kept or regained some of their supporters on the basis of economic complaints. Both factions were decisively reinforced by new adherents: the conservative and formerly Democratic German-Americans, who shared with La Follette and Berger a common victimization at the hands of superpatriots and perhaps also some reservations respecting the war. On the other hand, the war-born loyalty group proved highly unstable, and by the spring of 1918 had subdivided into three segments—the Democrats, the superpatriotic Wilcox Republicans, and the moderate loyalty Republicans headed by Philipp and Lenroot.

While economic issues re-emerged, questions extraneous to pre-war progressivism were more important. The liquor and religious questions grew in influence and contributed to the outcome of the Republican primaries. Above all, the two-sided loyalty issue was controlling in politics. It was this issue that accounted for some of the strange relationships that sprang up between the new political factions, notably the covert and tentative mutual defense pact between the La Follette and the Philipp-Lenroot factions against the aggressive superpatriots. Factional relationships were influenced, too, by growing Democratic and Republican partisanship, a reversion to the post-progressive situation of 1916.

Neither La Follette nor reformism had been destroyed by the war. By the end of 1918, both were on their way back, soon to be stronger than ever. But their revival would be the product of the new era that the war had brought, not a continuation of a pre-war movement. Since United States participation in the war lasted just twenty months, and since La Follette and reformism surged back shortly thereafter, there is danger of viewing the war as an exciting but ephemeral interlude in an otherwise unbroken progressive era. That it was more than that, that it truly marked the end of one historical era and the beginning of another in Wisconsin, became evident in the reconstruction years that followed.

VII

Reconstruction and the New Progressivism

IN 1919 AND 1920 the La Follette faction rode back to power on the crest of a wave of angry sentiment generated by wartime quakes. The personnel and issues bore enough resemblance to the pre-war progressive movement to suggest that the war had merely interrupted the movement, not ended it. A closer review of reconstruction politics would show, however, that the reformist wave flowed directly from the war itself. The political alignments continued to seem strange, except in the context of the new conditions that war had brought; similarly, some of the important issues, such as the League of Nations and prohibition, had only tangential relevance from the standpoint of the pre-war progressive movement. If progressivism was again in the saddle, then it was a new progressivism, born of war.

The passions and problems of war echoed and re-echoed through American life long after the last gun fell silent. Deprived of a foreign foe, angry and fearful nationalism turned inward. The taint of "un-Americanism" clung to important and varied groups of discontented Americans, and the intense hostility of group against group continued into the postwar years. The high emotional pitch of the war was joined with the general conviction that the reconstruction period would see the making of a new world. In whose image would it be made?

Wisconsin nationalists were reluctant to abandon some of their wartime activities. The State Council of Defense, in dissolving, hoped to perpetuate its Americanization Committee through other agencies.[1] Governor Philipp encouraged the continued activity of the home defenders. In welcoming the formation of the American Legion, he wrote: "To protect our free institutions against alien influences will, I am sure, be the desire of every true American and the leadership that will be given by the soldier element will be welcomed by the people because it can be relied upon to be truly American and therefore safe."[2]

The Social Democratic party and the Industrial Workers of the World contained many members of European origin, including many Germans. The anti-war stand taken by these radical organizations made the transition from anti-Germanism to red-baiting a natural one. In the face of postwar unemployment, strikes, unionism, discontent and turmoil, the wartime nationalists and conservatives, out of fear and as a matter of strategy, mounted a furious drive against radicalism. Anti-German feeling, the focal point of a generalized xenophobia, served as a convenient vehicle for the transition.

Anti-Germanism remained particularly strong in Milwaukee, which by 1920 embraced 17.4 per cent of the state's population.[3] When the Milwaukee County central committee of the American Legion protested against the performance of a play in the German language, its stand received strong support.[4] In November, 1919, the *Milwaukee Journal* gave full publicity to a report from the New York City police department of a nationwide effort by the I.W.W. to organize Germans. The Milwaukee chief of police, who had broken up one I.W.W. meeting during the summer, promised that he would not tolerate such gatherings.[5] The *Journal*, leading Democratic paper in the state, linked pre-war strikes

---

[1] Wisconsin State Council of Defense Report, December 19, 1918, in the Philipp Papers.
[2] Philipp to John Turner, February 14, 1919, in the Philipp Papers.
[3] E. E. Witte, "Statistics Relating to Wisconsin From the 1920 Census," *Wisconsin Blue Book, 1923* (Madison, 1924) 17–40, 20.
[4] *Milwaukee Journal*, November 4, 1919.
[5] *Ibid.*, November 7, 1919.

with pro-Germanism, called Germany the leading nation in the new Internationale, and labeled postwar strikes as manifestations of Bolshevism.[6] A leader of the Knights of Columbus regarded Bolshevism and Socialism as "the greatest evil confronting the world today." Otto Falk, president of Allis-Chalmers, Milwaukee's leading manufacturing firm, made the dangers of "so many strange theories and doctrines" the keynote of his appeal for funds for Milwaukee colleges. In November, 1919, a "good government" league was formed in Milwaukee to fight socialism. Several months later, the American Constitutional League set up headquarters in the city to fight socialism, "hyphenism," and pacifism.[7]

Fear of "bolshevism" was a national phenomenon, fed in the first months of 1919 by news of the Seattle general strike in February, creation of the Third Internationale in March, and various assassination attempts in April. Fear, mingled with outraged patriotism, found ready outlet in all parts of Wisconsin. Wisconsin American Legion posts petitioned Congress to do something about the menace. Walker Sanborn, son of the old-line progressive A. W. Sanborn, spoke for his Legion post when he wrote conservative congressman Adolphus Nelson: "The I. W. W. and our unscrupulous foreign elements are arousing radicalism to acts of violence and treason against our country."[8] Nelson agreed; he told the Rhinelander Legion that "it is imperative that the United States should at once enact proper legislation that will deport all radicals, anarchists and un-American people."[9] This position had the full support of Wisconsin editors like Richard Lloyd Jones of the *Wisconsin State Journal,* who launched his anti-red campaign within two weeks of the end of the war.[10] The rapid rise in Wisconsin of the Nonpartisan League, combined with the growing

---

[6] *Ibid.,* November 2, 9, 5, 1919.
[7] *Ibid.,* November 3, 9, 8, 1919; *Milwaukee Sentinel,* February 22, 1920.
[8] Walker Sanborn to Nelson, December 4, 1919, in the Nelson Papers.
[9] Nelson to H. S. Crosby, December 19, 1919, in the Nelson Papers.
[10] *Wisconsin State Journal,* November 19, 1918.

strength and militancy of socialist labor, lent urgency to the cause.

Much of the agitation in Milwaukee late in 1919 was directed against the Social Democratic party, and Victor Berger in particular. Berger had been indicted and speedily convicted on charges of violating the Espionage Act. On February 20, 1919, Judge Kenesaw Mountain Landis sentenced Berger to twenty years at Leavenworth. While Berger was appealing to the Supreme Court, which ultimately overturned the conviction, the House of Representatives voted to unseat him. A special election was scheduled for December 19 to elect a new congressman. Berger declared his intention to ask a vote of confidence from his constituents. "Patriotic" forces combined on a single opposing candidate, conservative Republican H. H. Bodenstab.[11] Despite their efforts, however, Berger was re-elected by a vote of 24,350 to 19,566. The House of Representatives again refused to seat him, but Governor Philipp blocked another special election, rightly declaring that another victory for Berger would certainly result.[12]

The intense bipartisan campaign against Berger evidenced the continued strength of nationalist and anti-radical sentiments. But Berger's victory indicated that even stronger forces of protest were developing on the other side. Berger's victory was a clear protest against Congress for unseating him, against the high cost of living, against misgovernment from national to local levels, against prohibition, and against the war on Germany.[13]

Discontent was widespread and intense in the reconstruction period, springing from a variety of sources. Blame, too, was diffused. The "profiteers" and the superpatriots were prominent among the villains. But the common denominator among the scapegoats were the political "ins": the leaders of the national Democratic administration. Farmers,

---

[11] Olson, "The Milwaukee Socialists," 381–385.
[12] *Ibid.*, 386; Huber, "War Hysteria," 48–49.
[13] Olson, "The Milwaukee Socialists," 386.

laborers, consumers, socially oppressed Germans, and political liberals pooled their protests in a campaign against what seemed to be a common foe. As the drift of things became evident, even some conservative Republicans joined in the anti-Democratic phase of the protest movement.

The high cost of living was perhaps the most general and severe source of complaint. Early in 1919, Governor Philipp called it the chief problem of postwar reconstruction.[14] Milwaukee civic groups sponsored protest meetings against high prices in 1920.[15] Farmers felt the effects of rising costs acutely, as their bills for labor, fertilizer, implements, feed, and taxes went up.[16] For Wisconsin's farmers, increased prices were particularly painful, for higher costs had to be met out of lower income. Until the end of 1919, farm prices in the United States were somewhat above the general price average. In the face of shrinking markets and lapse of government supports, however, prices of farm commodities began to fall precipitously early in 1920.[17] The buying power of Wisconsin farm products fell in 1920 to 82 per cent of the 1910–1914 level.[18] Shortages of labor, coal, and sugar further aggravated farmers.[19] Led by the Wisconsin Society of Equity, many Wisconsin farmers continued to regard co-operatives as essential weapons against "middle-

[14] *Wisconsin Assembly Journal,* Fifty-fourth Session, January 9, 1919, "Message of the Governor," 62–82, 67.
[15] Still, *Milwaukee,* 477–478.
[16] A. B. Genung, "Agriculture in the World War Period," *Yearbook of Agriculture* (Washington, 1940), 287. A. H. Hansen's cost of living index, using 1913 as the base year, shows the cost of living rising from 104 in 1915 to 131 in 1917, 159 in 1918, 183 in 1919, and 208 in 1920. The figures of W. R. Burgess and Paul Douglas are similar. Bureau of Labor Statistics, *Historical Statistics of the United States, 1789–1945* (Washington, 1949), 235.
[17] Genung, "Agriculture in the World War Period," 289; Saloutos and Hicks, *Agricultural Discontent,* 100.
[18] McNall, Mortenson, Davidson, "Development of Wisconsin Agriculture," 5: 6 (June, 1934).
[19] U. S. Department of Labor, U. S. Employment Service, to Philipp, April 14, 1919; H. T. Christenson to Philipp, March 21, 1919, in the Philipp Papers.

men," particularly meatpackers and the Chicago Livestock Exchange.[20]

Discontented labor elements were led by the powerful railroad brotherhoods. The railwaymen, whose unions had grown and conditions improved during wartime federal operation of the railroads, were bitterly opposed to turning the roads back to private hands. They championed their own "Plumb Plan" for continued government operation both before and after passage of the Esch-Cummins Act in February, 1920. Hoping to bring about the repeal of the bill, they launched vigorous efforts to defeat those who had supported it.[21]

Other groups among laboring men were well provided with economic complaints and fears. They were hurt by high prices and fearful of employer efforts to lower wages, break strikes, and block organization. Industry had been developing steadily in Wisconsin between 1910 and 1920, especially the metal and machinery, and the paper and paper-products groups. By 1920 those classified as workers constituted 34.1 per cent of the state's gainfully employed, exceeding for the first time the number engaged in agriculture. Labor discontent was therefore a more significant political factor than ever.[22]

A bipartisan middle-class liberal element which included such veteran progressives as C. B. Ballard, Ada James, Zona Gale, Henry Krumrey, and A. J. Schmitz joined together in the Wisconsin branch of the Committee of 48. They were chiefly concerned with the preservation of democracy and liberty; Ada James expressed considerable bitterness against President Wilson for his seemingly dicta-

---

[20] Charles Lyman to McCarthy, February 23, 1920, in the McCarthy Papers; Saloutos, "The Decline of the Wisconsin Society of Equity," 144.

[21] For a brief discussion of trends in railroad union membership in this period see Leo Wolmen, *The Growth of American Trade Unions, 1880–1923* (New York, 1924), 53–55.

[22] Witte, "Statistics Relating to Wisconsin From the 1920 Census," 29, 25.

torial methods: "With the Kaiser it was me & Gott, with Wilson it is God and I. This is the only difference in attitude of 2 rulers on a question of authority."[23]

Liberty was more than a pious abstraction for Wisconsin's Germans, whose wartime experience was not soon forgotten.[24] Nor was the question of liberty merely academic to farmers, laborers, and their representatives. They were aware that repression had political and economic as well as social aspects. Following the lead of Samuel Gompers, they joined in attacking legislation that seemed to threaten freedom of speech and assembly.[25] A major issue for the Germans of Wisconsin, as throughout the United States, was the League of Nations. Many Germans associated it with what they considered a harsh peace imposed on Germany; linked it, too, with President Wilson, whom they blamed for the entry of the United States into the war and for wartime repression.[26]

Out of the general ferment of 1919 and 1920 arose a new Left in Wisconsin politics. Farm and labor organizations became stronger, more radical, and more willing to co-operate with one another. To a considerable extent, they proved willing to work through the La Follette group in politics, which in turn lent strength and political experience to the coalition.

Following its 1916 electoral success in North Dakota, the Nonpartisan League had sent organizers into a number

---

[23] Ada James Diary, February 14, 1920.

[24] Herman Bilgrien to James Thompson, February 8, 1920, in the Thompson Papers; William Stafford to John J. Esch, April 15, 1920; Will Esch to Esch, April 10, 1920, in the Esch Papers; Lenroot to Stone, April 27, 1920, in the Stone Papers; McCarthy to J. S. Cullinan, April 9, 1920, in the McCarthy Papers.

[25] *Capital Times*, January 19, 1920; Henry J. Bohn to Esch, January 22, 1920, in the Esch Papers; Representatives of the Wisconsin Society of Equity, the Nonpartisan League, the federations of railroad brotherhoods, and shop crafts to Adolphus P. Nelson, January 23, 1920, in the Nelson Papers. This petition against the Graham and Sterling bills was typical of a number to be found in the correspondence of Wisconsin congressmen.

[26] Thomas A. Bailey, *Woodrow Wilson and the Great Betrayal* (New York, 1947), 23–24.

of states, including Wisconsin. By early 1920, with over twenty thousand members in Wisconsin, a newspaper in Madison, and eighty organizers working on a commission basis in the field, the NPL was ready to take a strong hand in state politics.[27] During the course of the year, it augmented its strength with over $100,000 in dues and initiation fees and almost six thousand new members.[28]

The NPL drew some support in the economically backward northern counties, but its main strength, in terms of membership, was in the southern and eastern parts of the state, especially among German farmers.[29] It benefited from a serious breach in the Wisconsin Society of Equity, when an ex-Populist, D. Weller Long, led in opposition to what he considered the conservative and self-interested policies of J. N. Tittemore.[30] Tittemore remained adamant against the new farmers' organization, but Long allied his forces with the Nonpartisan League.

In Milwaukee, the union movement had been reviving since 1916. Prosperity made it possible for labor organizers to mount a new drive to enroll the city's workers. In 1919 alone, twenty-eight new unions were organized, and membership swelled in existing unions. By the end of 1920, union membership in Milwaukee had reached 35,000, an increase of 15,000 in seven years.[31] In Milwaukee, as elsewhere, the labor movement shifted to the left, grew more militant and more vocal.[32]

---

[27] Theodore Saloutos, "The Non-Partisan League in the Western Middle West," *Agricultural History*, 20: 235–251 (October, 1946); *Capital Times*, January 5, 1920; letter addressed "Gentlemen," April 27, 1920, Wisconsin Nonpartisan League Papers.

[28] Financial summary, January 1, 1920 to February 28, 1921, in the Wisconsin Nonpartisan League Papers.

[29] Walter A. Ebling, "Recent Farmer Movements in Wisconsin" (master's thesis, University of Wisconsin, 1925), 7–8. Membership distribution probably relates as much to the economics of organization as to the incidence of discontent.

[30] Saloutos, "The Decline of the Wisconsin Society of Equity," 143–147.

[31] Gavett, *Labor Movement in Milwaukee*, 131, 135, 126.

[32] *Ibid.*, 131.

In the state as a whole, the pro-socialist Wisconsin State Federation of Labor had over 41,000 members by the end of 1919, including 461 affiliated unions. There were also another 361 unaffiliated unions, many of them small but including the strong and militant railroad brotherhoods.[33]

Representatives of the Nonpartisan League, dissident Equity elements, the Committee of 48, the State Federation of Labor, the railroad brotherhoods, and a few Social Democrats met in Milwaukee in March, 1920, to plot joint strategy.[34] Nothing came of efforts directed towards creation of a national third party, but substantial farmer-labor unity was forged on a statewide basis. That summer, the new unity resulted in a farmer-labor convention, a platform, and a slate of candidates in the Republican primary. The more immediate result was to give La Follette the support of the groups represented in his fight to control the Wisconsin delegation to the Republican national convention. Even Victor Berger was belatedly persuaded to permit socialist support for a slate pledged to La Follette for President.[35] The farmer-labor-liberal elements were probably drawn together, and then to La Follette, by three things: a common outrage over the wartime treatment they had received at the hands of the Wilson Administration and local reactionaries; fear of continuing offenses from the same quarters; and the prospect of positive results as a reward for unity and zeal.

The La Follette men were well situated to benefit from this resurgence and co-operativeness on the Left. For the most part, they were in thorough sympathy with both the

---

[33] 1919 Financial Statement, in the Wisconsin State Federation of Labor Papers.
[34] Ada James Diary, March 20, 1920; *Milwaukee Sentinel*, March 17, 1920.
[35] Minutes of the Executive Committee, Wisconsin State Federation of Labor, January 21, March 7, March 24, March 28, March 29, in the Wisconsin State Federation of Labor Papers; Gross, "A Political Grab Bag." La Follette was not a serious contender for the presidential nomination but he was concerned to control his state's delegation. This was generally understood by both sides.

complaints and the nostrums of the Nonpartisan Leaguers, Equity, the State Federation of Labor, the railroad brotherhoods, the Committee of 48, and even the socialists, and could give sincere representation to these elements in politics. They were the bearers of the already venerated tradition of progressivism, chiefly due to the continuity that La Follette gave. Moreover, they had already shown their ability to appeal to ordinarily conservative Democratic Germans on the issues raised by the war. This new association was one that, by judicious handling, might well be perpetuated.

As they approached the first postwar test of political strength, the April election of delegates to the Republican national convention, the La Follette men set out to mold the various segments of protest into a new political coalition. Their chief task was to relate the many complaints one to another. They sought to show, for instance, that the Esch-Cummins bill was of concern not only to railroad workers but to farmers and consumers as well. They argued that the bill guaranteed a 6 per cent return to the private owners and would result in higher freight rates for farmers and higher prices for consumers.[36] Senator La Follette's chief attack in 1919 was directed against the League of Nations. The primary appeal in this campaign was to German voters, but the issue was related to economic complaints as well. Wisconsin press opinion had been generally favorable to the League of Nations idea until President Wilson's return to the United States in February, 1919, with a concrete plan for the League. Most papers remained favorable, but *La Follette's Magazine* and the socialist *Milwaukee Leader* condemned it. The *Milwaukee Sentinel* and the *Wisconsin News*, a Hearst paper that resulted from a merger of the *Milwaukee Free Press* with two other papers in 1918, saw the League as likely to be controlled by England and her dominions and distrusted the broad powers of the Executive Council, wherein the United States had but one vote

---

[36] *La Follette's Magazine*, 12: 1, 2, 3 (January, February, March, 1920); Madison *Capital Times*, March 4, 1920.

among nine. The Republican *Superior Telegram* feared that the League might interfere in American domestic affairs or control American foreign policy.[37]

When the full terms of the treaty were revealed in May, 1918, the German-language papers denounced their severity towards Germany, especially the territorial claims, the war-guilt clause, and the reparations provisions. By July, 1919, several of these papers, sympathetic to the League earlier, turned violently against it as an instrument of British domination. Meanwhile the League to Enforce the Peace, whose leaders in Wisconsin included a number of stalwarts and such superpatriots as Roy Wilcox and Fred Vogel, Jr., exerted little influence on opinion.[38]

The La Follette men took the lead among those prominent in politics in denouncing the League of Nations. Henry Huber, Charles Crownhart, and James Thompson, among others, took part in an anti-League speaking campaign late in 1919.[39] Though apathy towards the League issue had begun to set in by the end of 1919, La Follette persisted in stressing the opposition to it during the preconvention months, apparently to good political effect. Governor Philipp declared against the League in general terms in March, 1919, and more explicitly in July, and Senator Lenroot took an increasingly harsh position against it.[40]

With such irreconcilables as Hiram Johnson of California, La Follette attacked the League from a progressive point of view. In the opinion of these men, the League was an alliance of the victors against the vanquished, an antidemocratic, imperialistic union designed for exploitation. The League would guarantee the profits of the imperialists and remove the power of decision-making from the hands

[37] William Spellberg, "Wisconsin Reaction to the Versailles Peace Treaty as Revealed in Newspapers, Letters and Resolutions of Organizations" (master's thesis, University of Wisconsin, 1953), 19–41.
[38] *Ibid.*, 81–116.
[39] Thompson to Crownhart, October 2, 1919; A. T. Rogers to Thompson, October 9, in the Thompson Papers.
[40] Spellberg, "Wisconsin Reaction," 116–163; Maxwell, *Philipp*, 204; Frooman, "The Wisconsin Peace Movement, 1915–1919," 286–288.

of the American people. It represented a further extension of the autocracy and profiteering that had emerged during the war, under the aegis of President Wilson. In one of many editorials on the subject, La Follette wrote that the people "are shocked to witness the readiness with which he [Wilson] traded off his principles—fourteen points and all—for the League Compact to enforce by the sword the terms of a treaty which surrenders every moral issue and sets up a supreme, imperialistic and financial dictatorship in the world." The League compact, La Follette continued, "surrenders control of this government to an armed autocracy and betrays American independence to the great European powers; and appalling to contemplate, it puts liberty in chains; it rivets the shackles of bondage on subject nations forever; it is the death knell of hope for Ireland, India and Egypt."[41]

With his campaign against the League and his drive for convention delegates, La Follette fought his way out of the wartime corner. The powerful force of nationalism was now at least partly on his side. While the *Milwaukee Journal* remained strong for Wilson, conservative Republican papers like the *Milwaukee Sentinel* and the *Janesville Gazette* dropped their "Back the President" plea of wartime days as the League issue developed.[42] Doubtless Republican politics also played a part in this shift. In any event, La Follette returned to the fold of Republicanism on the League issue and on the question of opposition to Wilson.[43] Certain national events also helped La Follette to regain much of his respectability in Wisconsin. Following the 1918 elections the United States Senate was divided forty-

[41] *La Follette's Magazine*, 11: 7 (July, 1919). See also *La Follette's Magazine*, 11: 3, 4 (March, April, 1919).
[42] Jackson, "Wisconsin's Attitude Toward American Foreign Policy Since 1910," 115, 124.
[43] La Follette attacked Wilson as a high-handed autocrat. *La Follette's Magazine*, 11: 3, 4 (March, April, 1919). Governor Philipp and the *Milwaukee Sentinel* made extensive attempts to capitalize on the President's lack of popularity. *Milwaukee Sentinel,* March 20, 21, 23, 24, 25, 27, 1920.

nine to forty-seven in favor of the Republicans, and the G. O. P. needed La Follette's co-operation to organize it. Under these circumstances, party leaders mellowed markedly towards the senator and in January, 1919, defeated the long-pending attempt to expel him on charges of disloyalty.[44]

With some of the sting withdrawn from the wartime nationalism, discussion of social, economic, and political issues had much freer rein. An early sign of the times came in June, 1919, when Richard Lloyd Jones, harried by the competition of the rising young *Capital Times,* summarily sold the *Wisconsin State Journal* and quit the state.[45] By September, 1919, the prominent Milwaukee La Follette man Edwin J. Gross, who just five months earlier had despaired that "Somehow our old 'La Follette' organization has gone to pieces and with it possibly the forward movement of the progressive cause," had a more encouraging report for the senator. Gross had found "that the major number of our fellows, while silent for the last two years, never faltered in their old belief. Many of those who lost their heads and quit are quietly coming back on this theory: 'After all Senator La Follette represents the progressive idea and that is the important thing.' "[46] In the months that followed, former La Follette men such as John S. Donald, Duncan McGregor, and James Stone reinforced Gross's impression as they shied away from their new stalwart associates.[47]

The circumstances of war had produced a tacit and highly tentative alliance between La Follette and Philipp, the archrivals of earlier days. The basis for a continuation and strengthening of these ties persisted into the reconstruction period, for recollections of common wartime grievances

[44] Belle and Fola La Follette, *La Follette,* 2: 910–917, 927–931

[45] Weissman, "Wisconsin State Journal Since 1900," 120–124. A. M. Brayton, editor of the *La Crosse Tribune and Leader Press,* persuaded the Lee Syndicate to buy the paper and establish him as editor. Under Brayton, the paper took a much milder tone than formerly.

[46] Gross to La Follette, April 17, 1919, in the Gross Papers.

[47] John S. Donald to John McConnell, February 27, 1920, in the Donald Papers; Stone to Lenroot, March 16, 1920, in the Stone Papers.

remained fresh, the ardent nationalists remained on the scene, and the Wilson Administration provided a common enemy against whom these two Republican leaders might unite. George A. West, a wealthy Milwaukee businessman, Republican chairman and a Philipp man, suggested to Edwin Gross early in 1920 that a compromise ticket for delegates to the Republican convention be formed. The notion was not at all farfetched, for at this time some men in the La Follette camp were commenting favorably on supporting Philipp against Lenroot for the United States Senate.[48]

By early 1920, however, the La Follette men felt strong enough to be able to reject the proposal. With the war over and the national administration under fire, with a strong farmer-labor movement developing in the state and the Germans coming into the open politically, La Follette's prospects seemed excellent. For La Follette, participation in a coalition with Philipp represented a safe means of regaining political respectability, but it also involved the risk of losing control of the farmer-labor element, which over the long haul would be the foundation stone for the La Follette faction's power and the nucleus of any coalition it might form. The result was that the original wartime stalwart-progressive coalition against La Follette was patched together to enter a slate of twenty-six unpledged candidates against twenty-six pledged to support La Follette for President. Former La Follette men Otto Bosshard and William Hatton joined Governor Philipp and George West as candidates for delegate-at-large on the uninstructed slate. Senator Irvine Lenroot issued a statement in support of the ticket.[49]

Even so, relations between the La Follette and the Philipp factions remained remarkably good. Indeed, Edwin Gross found that "The Madison group . . . seemed to be hesitant about waging any real campaign against Governor Philipp." For his part, the governor refrained from assailing

---

[48] Gross to Evjue, January 10, 1920, in the Gross Papers; Plumb, *Badger Politics*, 193–194.
[49] *Milwaukee Sentinel,* March 29, 1920.

La Follette on "patriotic grounds," instead associating himself with La Follette's complaints against the Espionage Act, the high cost of living, and war profiteers. The chief conservative argument was the old-fashioned contention that the uninstructed delegates would remain loyal to the Republican party and would be more effective in the national convention. While treating La Follette with moderation, Philipp took time out from the delegate fight to deliver a verbal attack on Roy Wilcox. And George West, campaign manager for the anti-La Follette slate, did his Milwaukee rivals a valuable and sportsmanlike service in making them aware of certain defects in their nomination papers that might have kept them off the ballot.[50]

While the unpledged slate adopted a somewhat defensive tone and offered no platform, the La Follette men took the offensive with a nineteen-point platform calculated to please disgruntled farmer, labor, liberal, and German elements, and perhaps even some whose main idea was simply to chastise Democrats. The platform called for "the immediate conclusion of peace and resumption of trade with all countries," opposed the League of Nations, advocated repeal of the Esch-Cummins law and ultimate public ownership of the railroads, and demanded "the immediate restoration of free speech, free press, peaceable assembly, and all civil rights and liberties guaranteed by the Constitution," repeal of the Espionage and Sedition Acts, abolition of the injunction in labor disputes, collective bargaining for labor and farm organizations, promotion of co-operatives, progressive taxation, and various direct democracy measures.[51]

Public opinion was so fluid, mixed, and confused that few would predict the outcome with any confidence. Politicians of every faction awaited the results as the first concrete indication of what might be expected thereafter. It was the La Follette men who rejoiced on April 7. Wisconsin's voters had welcomed La Follette back from wartime

[50] Gross, "A Political Grab Bag"; Madison *Capital Times,* March 26, 1920; *Milwaukee Sentinel,* March 20, 29, 23, 1920.
[51] Belle and Fola La Follette, *La Follette,* 2: 993–994.

exile with a tide of votes for the delegates pledged to him. They elected twenty-four of his twenty-six candidates, including all four of his delegate-at-large candidates. Philipp led the uninstructed slate with 70,747 votes, while James Thompson led the La Follette ticket with 117,647. Henry Krumrey polled the fewest votes of the La Follette delegate-at-large candidates with 107,044.[52]

The delegate contest had been regarded by the La Follette faction as a test of whether or not they could afford to offer a slate of candidates for state office in the upcoming primaries.[53] Encouraged by the result, they determined to conduct the summer primary campaign with the same general strategy they had used in the April delegate contest. This they did, by putting forth a full slate of candidates independent of Emanuel Philipp; by continuing to work in tandem with the aroused farmer-labor elements with respect to choice of candidates and issues stressed; by continuing to appeal to Germans on the League of Nations and liberty issues; and by continuing to co-operate as much as possible with Emanuel Philipp.

Complete unity among the forces of the Left proved impossible. At a time when the prospects of the Social Democrats seemed bright, Victor Berger was unwilling to throw away a lifetime's effort by subordinating the interests of his party to those of the Nonpartisan League and the La Follette faction. He resented, moreover, the fact that two Nonpartisan League congressmen together with progressives had voted for his expulsion, and he regarded the League as representing the "bourgeoisie." In this, he adhered to his party's view as expressed in its 1917 St. Louis platform. Thus, despite the urging of William Zumach, a prominent labor organizer and Social Democrat, and other socialist leaders, Berger drew back from further collaboration following the delegate elections. At the Social Democratic party's state convention in June, one of the platform planks called

---
[52] *Wisconsin Blue Book, 1921*, 16–17.
[53] Gross, "A Political Grab Bag."

for the right of voters to elect their representatives and specifically condemned "the congressmen of the Nonpartisan League and the so-called La Follette progressives for voting against the principles of representative government to unseat Victor Berger." The party also resolved in favor of expelling any member supporting the candidates of other parties.[54] Though the leaders of the Milwaukee Federated Trades Council and Wisconsin Federation of Labor continued their flirtation with the "bourgeois" reformers into May and June, Berger's stand limited the extent and duration of the attachment.

J. N. Tittemore, President of Equity, was still more virulent in his opposition to the Nonpartisan League, which was cutting the ground from under his organization and his political ambitions. He kept his dwindling forces out of the hands of the Nonpartisan Leaguers by running in the Republican gubernatorial primaries himself.

A breach also occurred within La Follette's own ranks as a result of the rival ambitions of John J. Blaine and Edward F. Dithmar, each of whom sought the designation of the La Follette and Nonpartisan League leaders for governor. Dithmar was a veteran progressive who had served as lieutenant governor since 1915. He had powerful support from many progressive politicians, and had established friendly relations with Governor Philipp. His candidacy was backed particularly by his fellow Germans. Dithmar had stepped aside several times because of his German name; he was in no mood to be sidetracked again.[55] Blaine, initiator of the Stephenson investigation in 1909 and independent candidate for governor in 1912, had been elected state attorney general in 1918. He had established close

[54] William Zumach to H. G. Teigan, November 14, 1919, cited in Saloutos, "The Nonpartisan League in the Western Middle West," 235–251, 246; Olson, "The Milwaukee Socialists," 403; Madison *Capital Times*, June 19, 21, 1920.
[55] O. G. Munson to John J. Esch, April 2, 1920; John Esch to George Esch, August 2, 1920, in the Esch Papers; G. H. Geweke to James Thompson, August 2, 1920, in the Thompson Papers; interview with William T. Evjue, January 18, 1954.

relations with farm leaders, and had presented Equity's marketing proposals to the 1918 Republican platform convention. In addition, he was friendly with Fred Holmes, who, as proprietor of a statewide news service and a man close to the La Follette inner circle, was in a position to help him.[56] The most important factor in Blaine's favor was the fear, expressed by La Follette's law partner, Alfred T. Rogers, that La Follette men would have to fight the war all over again if they backed Dithmar.[57] The fact that Dithmar had indiscreetly committed himself to the prohibitionists weighed against him, too, for La Follette hoped to dodge the nettlesome liquor issue.[58] And Dithmar's earlier unwillingness to run for delegate-at-large on the La Follette slate could hardly have strengthened him among La Follette's lieutenants.[59]

The La Follette men decided on Blaine. But Dithmar remained adamant, and persisted in his campaign for governor. He continued to claim progressive support, but denounced the Nonpartisan League.[60] The effect of his candidacy was to cut from the progressive coalition a number of Germans who were angered by wartime repression but were not attracted to the economic program of the Nonpartisan League.[61]

Despite the loss of Social Democratic support and the independent candidacies of Tittemore and Dithmar, the La Follette faction benefited from unusual unity and strength on the political Left. Spearheaded by the State Federation

[56] Interview with William T. Evjue, January 18, 1954.
[57] A. H. Hartwig to James Thompson, January 30, 1920, in the Thompson Papers.
[58] Gross, "A Political Grab Bag"; Dithmar to Rosa, May 21, 1920, in the Rosa Papers.
[59] Dithmar to Rosa, February 19, 1920, in the Rosa Papers.
[60] Dithmar to Progressive Republicans, July 17, 1920, in the Thompson Papers; Madison *Capital Times,* July 23, 1920.
[61] John Esch to George Esch, August 2, 1920, in the Esch Papers; J. H. Geweke to James Thompson, August 2, 1920, in the Thompson Papers. Dithmar's 31,399 votes were drawn chiefly from such heavily German counties as Dodge, Jefferson, Marathon, Milwaukee, Sauk, and Shawano. *Wisconsin Blue Book, 1921,* 70.

of Labor and the Nonpartisan League, a Farmer-Labor League convention was held in Madison in late May that produced a platform, of which 100,000 copies were printed.[62] The platform bore a marked resemblance to the earlier La Follette platform, probably evidencing more similarity in thinking than in design.[63] Several weeks later a Nonpartisan League convention in Madison endorsed a full slate of candidates in the Republican primaries. Conferences with labor leaders on congressional candidates were planned in areas of labor strength.[64]

The farmer-labor ticket, if not in fact devised in consultation with leaders of the La Follette faction, was certainly calculated to effect an easy union with that group. The ticket was headed by Blaine for governor and Thompson for senator, and included another La Follette man for treasurer. The other three on the state ticket more directly represented the Nonpartisan League. Blaine addressed the convention and accepted its platform, adding that, though a lawyer, he had worked at farming most of his life.[65] The *Capital Times* endorsed the Nonpartisan League and its candidates,[66] and a Progressive Republican Campaign Committee run by La Follette men Charles Crownhart, Fred Holmes, and L. E. Gettle went on to conduct a statewide campaign for the ticket.

The unity forged between the La Follette men and the Nonpartisan League was not something that could have been taken for granted. In other states, such as North and South Dakota, the League arose in opposition to progressive Republican forces quite as much as against stalwarts. The League was suspicious of non-farmers, while professional politicians, progressives included, were often leery of League

[62] Executive Committee Minutes, June 4, 1920, in the Wisconsin State Federation of Labor Papers.
[63] Farmer-Labor League platform, enclosed in Ingalls to Blaine, November 5, 1920, in the Blaine Papers.
[64] Madison *Capital Times,* June 15, 1920.
[65] *Ibid.,* June 16, 1920.
[66] *Ibid.,* June 16, 17, 1920.

programs, dictation, and rivalry for office.[67] In Wisconsin, the candidacy of Dithmar expressed the divergence between progressive and Nonpartisan Leaguer. But Blaine, acting on his own, had met the farm protest movement and the League more than half-way since 1918. Most important were two other factors: The La Follette progressives were somewhat more radical than their counterparts in nearby states, making alliance with the Nonpartisan League easier; and the La Follette men encountered the League at a time when they were struggling against their conservative-nationalist opponents. They could ill afford to reject any allies, even at the cost of a few offices. It might be added that since the old progressive organization had been thoroughly shattered, and the La Follette people were rebuilding in any case, alliance with the farm group and others entailed less of a blow to the faithful than would have been the case in more stable times.

The new farmer-labor unity continued through the primary campaign. Even on the local level, the Nonpartisan League sponsored joint political meetings with labor.[68] At the same time, the railroad unions, the Milwaukee Trades and Labor Council, and the State Federation of Labor exerted unprecedented political efforts on their own, matching the extraordinary activity of the new farmers' organization.[69] The nature of the opposition probably helped to strengthen the new progressive coalition. The chief opposition candidate for the gubernatorial nomination was Roy Wilcox, framer of the resolution denouncing La Follette.

[67] Robert Morlan, *A Political Prairie Fire* (Minneapolis, 1955).
[68] Esch to A. P. Nelson, July 17, 1920, in the Esch Papers.
[69] John Esch to George Esch, August 23, 1920; John Esch to Will Esch, August 10, 1920; John Esch to C. M. Bright, July 17, 1920; Stone to John Esch, August 6, 1920; John Esch to George Esch, August 9, 1920; John Esch to Will Esch, September 3, 1920, in the Esch Papers; Frank Sullivan, Chairman, Wisconsin Legislative Board Brotherhood of Railroad Trainmen to Officers and Members of the Brotherhood of Railroad Trainmen, August 30, 1920, enclosed in Sullivan to Thompson, August 30, 1920, in the Thompson Papers; Executive Board Minutes, Wisconsin State Federation of Labor, June 4, 1920, in the Wisconsin State Federation of Labor Papers.

Running for attorney general was another superpatriot, William J. Morgan of Milwaukee, who based his candidacy on opposition to the Nonpartisan League as a dangerous, un-American organization.[70] Irvine Lenroot, regarded by the La Follette men as a renegade and opposed by the railroad unions as a strong defender of the Esch-Cummins Act, was again a candidate for the Senate as his short term drew to a close. Some of the incumbent congressmen were natural targets too, especially John J. Esch of Esch-Cummins fame.

The Nonpartisan League, the labor elements, and the La Follette Republican candidates gave major emphasis to the issues of the Esch-Cummins Act and the League of Nations during the primary campaign.[71] The high cost of living was the central and unifying economic complaint. A timely increase in freight rates gave point to reformers' charges.[72] The keynote of the campaign, linking friends and pinpointing enemies, was the familiar theme that the elections were part of the age-old contest between the producers and the non-producers, the farmers, laborers, and consumers on the one hand and the "profiteers" on the other.[73] Many anti-La Follette men acknowledged the strength of these issues and feared the unrest arising from economic conditions. "Big business is still big business," James Stone warned his friend Lenroot in April. "We have to show labor that the Republican party is its friend. At the present time there is distrust and suspicion everywhere."[74] Lenroot agreed. "If big business does not wake up and content itself with moderate profits," he replied, "we are riding to a fall just as surely as the sun shines."[75]

[70] *Milwaukee Sentinel*, September 15, 1920; William J. Morgan to John Whitehead, August 2, 1920, in the Whitehead Papers.
[71] *La Follette's Magazine*, 12: 7, 8, 9 (July, August, September, 1920).
[72] Madison *Capital Times*, July 31, August 16, 1920.
[73] "The New Day," Nonpartisan League Primary pamphlet, 1920, n.p.; A. W. Barney to Esch, August 30, 1920, in the Esch Papers; see the 1920 campaign circular in the Joseph Beck Papers for a fuller sample of a typical reform appeal.
[74] Stone to Lenroot, April 19, 1920, in the Stone Papers.
[75] Lenroot to Stone, April 27, 1920, in the Stone Papers.

Lenroot represented himself as a believer in a progressive, not a destructive policy, a loyal progressive who attempted to work within his party and the bounds of the possible, not an ineffectual lone wolf like La Follette.[76] While defending and attempting to explain the complicated Esch-Cummins Act, he also spoke at length on the extravagance and thievery practiced during the war, for which he denounced President Wilson. He reminded one amused auditor of La Follette, the *Capital Times,* and Hiram Johnson.[77]

Even ardent conservatives paid full respect to the new issues. The *Milwaukee Sentinel,* strongly supporting Lenroot, tried to present him in a progressive light.[78] A convention inspired by Governor Philipp adopted a platform that made particular and sympathetic reference to the issues of the cost of living, profiteering, and the plight of agriculture.[79] The gubernatorial candidate chosen by that convention issued his own platform, calling for drastic action against profiteering, aid to farmers in storage and marketing, an extension of the recently created state marketing division, the eight-hour day, collective bargaining, and a voice for labor in the management of industry.[80] In the general election, even the archnationalist Republican candidate for attorney general acknowledged that the cost of living was "outrageously high" and promised to stop profiteering, promote marketing reform, and improve farm prices.[81]

As interest in the League of Nations receded, the economic issues grew in relative importance. But even in 1920, when the lines of division on economic questions were very sharply drawn, issues largely extraneous to, or different from, the progressive issues of pre-war days played important roles. The war-born grudges of the Germans and of Governor

[76] Lenroot to Stone, April 20, June 30, 1920, in the Stone Papers.
[77] E. H. Coulson to Thompson, August 11, 1920, in the Thompson Papers.
[78] *Milwaukee Sentinel,* August 13, 31, 1920.
[79] Madison *Capital Times,* July 15, 1920.
[80] *Milwaukee Sentinel,* August 7, 1920.
[81] *Ibid.,* September 15, 1920.

Philipp fell in this category; so did the liquor issue. The temperance question had never been totally absent in Wisconsin even in the heyday of progressivism. But by 1920, following enactment of the Eighteenth Amendment, itself a product of war circumstances, and with enforcement legislation and administration still at issue, it had a greater prominence than ever before. The powerful "wet" forces, which included beer and liquor interests and most Germans, took up defensive positions in favor of 2.5 per cent "near beer" and light wines. The Order of the Camels, an anti-Prohibition fraternal group, took the question into politics, where it clashed with the Anti-Saloon League, spearhead of the "dry" forces. Neither side of the controversy would accept evasion by candidates. Each regarded the issue as of paramount importance.

Secretary of State Merlin Hull, a progressive of the more independent sort, had long been associated with the prohibitionists. He ran for the Republican gubernatorial nomination in 1920 as a "dry" and attracted his major support from this element.[82] Edward Dithmar had also made himself acceptable to the prohibitionists. But the leaders of the Anti-Saloon League wanted to concentrate their support on the strongest "dry" candidate. For this reason, they recommended Roy Wilcox, the "patriot" candidate, as most likely to defeat the unacceptable La Follette man, John Blaine.[83] The leadership of the "dry" forces of 1920 were quite similar in ideology and social composition to the anti-La Follette nationalists. Manufacturers were prominent among the Anti-Saloon Leaguers and Germans were few.[84]

[82] See the Hull Papers, July and August, 1920.
[83] R. P. Hutton to Dear Brother Pastor, August 28, 1920, in the Hull Papers; R. P. Hutton to Dear Brother Pastor, August 31, 1920, enclosed in L. E. Gettle to Thompson, August 31, 1920, in the Thompson Papers; R. P. Hutton to The Leaders of the State, September 2, 1920, in the Hull Papers; John Strange, "Autobiography," 45.
[84] A. D. Campbell to Hull, April 22, 1918, in the Hull Papers. The Anti-Saloon League had a manufacturers committee that included such business leaders as Judson Rosebush of Appleton, John Strange of Menasha, F. J. Vea of Stoughton, J. J. Phoenix of Delavan, and others.

With Roy Wilcox, William Morgan, and other archnationalists, the Anti-Saloon League warned against the red menace and free love.[85] Thus, a good portion of the "dry" vote against pro-La Follette candidates would probably have been lost even without the liquor question. "Dry" Norwegians were the chief exceptions.

John Blaine, while not making too great a point of it, sided with the "wets." But James Thompson, representing La Follette and the Nonpartisan Leaguers in the Senate race against Irvine Lenroot, feared to commit himself. His fellow Norwegians throughout the state were almost unanimously "dry" in sentiment, if not always in practice, and they feared that he would lose some progressive support unless he sided with the prohibitionists.[86]

Danger to Thompson from the "wets" was even more grave. In March, Thompson was worried by rumors that Mayor A. C. McHenry of Oshkosh would come forth as the candidate of the Order of the Camels to divide votes with him. He was troubled too by questionnaires and threats from the Camels.[87] Thompson's natural inclination was towards a "near beer" and light wine plank, which he believed would satisfy them.[88] But the Madison La Follette leaders clung to the hope that La Follette could persuade the mayor not to run.[89] Crownhart, in charge of the Madison headquarters, was reluctant to give up the strategy of neutrality on the liquor issue that had been so successful in the past.[90] Thompson was in no position to defy the inner circle,

[85] Anti-Saloon League pamphlet, enclosed in Frank B. Metcalfe to Blaine, April 16, 1920, in the Blaine Papers.
[86] C. C. Wayland to Thompson, March 16, 1920; O. G. U. Siljan to Thompson, August 10, 1920, in the Thompson Papers.
[87] Thompson to Alfred T. Rogers, March 10, 1920; C. R. Diegle to Thompson, June 11, 1920, in the Thompson Papers.
[88] Thompson to Crownhart, June 14, 1920; Thompson to A. T. Rogers, June 25, 1920; Thompson to Fred Holmes, June 26, 1920, in the Thompson Papers.
[89] L. B. Nagler to Thompson, May 22, 1920, in the Thompson Papers.
[90] Crownhart to Thompson, June 15, 1920, in the Thompson Papers.

and remained uncommitted respecting prohibition to the last.

The strategy of neutrality on the liquor question crashed resoundingly. By 1920 the issue was too prominent to be put aside. The La Follette men regarded it as extraneous to the main issues, but many others disagreed. By remaining neutral, Thompson alienated both sides. The Anti-Saloon League came out strongly for Lenroot in the last stages of the primary contest.[91] Even more important, Mayor McHenry declared his candidacy, remained in the race, and polled 46,952 votes. Thompson received 149,442 votes, and Lenroot won with 169,296 votes.[92] Thompson's defeat was clearly due to McHenry's candidacy.[93]

Absent from the state for the most part, Lenroot had managed to retain the friendship of both the Philipp and the Wilcox factions. He was therefore able to come forth as the only "loyalty" candidate for the senatorial nomination. But no other politician of prominence duplicated his remarkable achievement. Nor did Lenroot see any hope of personally bringing about unity on an anti-La Follette nominee for governor.[94]

Roy Wilcox represented the ardent nationalists in the 1920 campaign. As candidate for the Republican gubernatorial nomination he set out to defend the state against the ravages of the Nonpartisan League, which he denounced as an un-American carrier of the alien doctrines of socialism and free love. In this appeal he was ably seconded by William J. Morgan, candidate for attorney general, and by the

[91] E. J. Onstad to Thompson, September 9, 1920; R. P. Hutton to Dear Pastor, August 31, 1920, enclosed in Gettle to Thompson, August 31, 1920, in the Thompson Papers; Anti-Saloon League Leaflet, August 30, 1920, in the Huber Papers.
[92] *Wisconsin Blue Book, 1921,* 75.
[93] E. J. Onstad to Thompson, September 9, 1920, in the Thompson Papers; Charles McCarthy to Gifford Pinchot, September 15, 1920, in the McCarthy Papers; J. W. Carow, Republican State Central Committee, to A. P. Nelson, October 2, 1920, in the Nelson Papers.
[94] Lenroot to Stone, July 2, 1920, in the Stone Papers.

Milwaukee Sentinel.[95] With Wilcox in the race, there was no prospect of anti-La Follette unity. The enmity between Wilcox and Philipp, developing through the 1917 and 1918 legislative sessions and the close and bitter 1918 gubernatorial primaries, reached a peak at the Republican state convention in September of 1918. A meeting of Republican leaders was held in the governor's office one night during the convention in an effort to hammer out an acceptable platform. In the presence of Philipp, Wilcox strongly objected to endorsement of the Philipp administration's war effort and delivered a scathing personal denunciation of the governor. Philipp responded with deep emotion, comparing his own war record with Wilcox's. When the meeting ended, as the men were leaving the room, Philipp was heard to say, "As I live that man will never be elected to any office in Wisconsin if I can help it."[96]

Philipp, deeply wounded at repeated aspersions on his patriotism, had his opportunity for revenge in 1919 and 1920. The impact of war was such that even benefiting the La Follette men seemed to Philipp a small price to prevent Wilcox succeeding him as governor. In the midst of his springtime campaign for delegate-at-large against the La Follette candidates, Philipp made clear his abiding hostility towards the Eau Claire patriot. Denying any combination with Wilcox, Philipp publicly said, "I would not go into a political combination with a man who, a year and a half ago, went all over this state, misrepresenting and maligning me. Perhaps I ought to forgive my enemies, but I cannot forget them, and I am not going to forget them."[97] In the middle of July, with Wilcox already in the field, Philipp engineered a convention of conservative Republi-

---

[95] A. H. Clark to Esch, August 5, 1920; Roger Y. Flanders to John Esch, August 9, 1920, in the Esch Papers; *Milwaukee Sentinel,* August 15, 18, September 4, 5, 1920.
[96] Madison *Capital Times,* August 21, 1925.
[97] *Milwaukee Sentinel,* March 23, 1920.

cans in Madison. Addressing the assembled delegates, the governor said, "There are some candidates running for governor without any principle. Mr. Roy P. Wilcox, the drum major of the stay-at-home division of the state, is out again." Philipp surprised many delegates by declining the convention's nomination, but praised the gubernatorial candidate selected by the nominating committee, Gilbert Seaman of Milwaukee.[98]

Seaman's nomination was immediately hailed by the *Capital Times* as a great blow to the Wilcox candidacy. Seaman had just returned from military duty. Years before, he had served in the Philippines and Cuba. Back in Milwaukee, he had taken a leading role in "patriotic" activities. He was a former University of Wisconsin Regent and a friend of Francis McGovern. Though little known in the state, he had a "vigorous, forceful personality." The *Capital Times* rejoiced that Seaman would surely detach from Wilcox much of the soldier and patriotic vote, as well as some of the "university vote."[99] A week after the Madison convention, Seaman announced that he would run. His motives remained in doubt. Clearly, however, he was brought into the field through the urging of his friend Philipp, and Philipp was bent chiefly on wrecking Wilcox.[100]

Wilcox attacked the Seaman candidacy as directed against himself, not Blaine.[101] The Milwaukeean's campaign confirmed the truth of the charge. In his opening speeches, Seaman attacked Wilcox, scoffing at his pose as savior of

[98] Madison *Capital Times,* July 15, 1920.
[99] *Ibid.,* July 15, 1920.
[100] Philipp's confidant and secretary wrote in 1954: "I think the Governor was instrumental in his being a candidate." Lawrence Whittet to author, March 3, 1954. Other contemporaries had no doubt that Philipp was responsible for the candidacy and that he was motivated by hostility to Wilcox. Interviews with William T. Evjue, January 18, 1954; William Kirsch, January 18, 1954; and Charles Rosa, January 15, 1954; Craig Ralston, "The La Follette Dynasty," 225.
[101] Madison *Capital Times,* July 18, 1920.
[102] *Ibid.,* August 11, 1920.

Wisconsin.[102] Philipp plunged into the campaign with charges that Wilcox was spending in excess of statute limitations, and Seaman echoed the allegation.[103] With the end of the primary race, Seaman and Blaine exchanged compliments on the courtesy of their campaigns.[104] (Wilcox's candidacy was weakened by another factor. Anti-Catholicism was experiencing a postwar resurgence and Wilcox was a Catholic.[105])

On election night, William T. Evjue later recalled, he, Fred Holmes, and other La Follette men gathered in Governor Philipp's office to await the primary returns. It proved a happy occasion for all, for the governor shared their jubilation when Blaine forged ahead of Wilcox. Blaine kept the lead and won by 113,001 votes to 102,199 for Wilcox. While Dithmar drew 31,399 votes, chiefly at the expense of Blaine, Gilbert Seaman more than offset this by polling 59,008. Wherever nationalist sentiment was strong, as in Milwaukee, Racine, Rock, and Walworth counties, Seaman shared support with Wilcox. Merlin Hull drew 45,308 votes and J. N. Tittemore polled 27,348.[106] But the effect of these candidates on the Blaine-Wilcox contest was probably slender, for Tittemore and Hull each had some appeal in both of the major camps. Tittemore had some farmer support, of course, but his strong anti-Nonpartisan League stand duplicated Wilcox's appeal. Hull had some strength among old-line progressives, but he too had a foot in the Wilcox camp as a loyalty advocate and a "dry." It was the Seaman candidacy that tipped the scales towards Blaine.

[103] *Milwaukee Sentinel,* August 19, 1920; Madison *Capital Times,* August 27, 1920.
[104] Madison *Capital Times,* September 10, 1920.
[105] A. B. Wesner to Nelson, May 22, 1920; Nelson to Wesner, May 28, 1920, in the Nelson Papers. The superintendent of the Anti-Saloon League had enough respect for the issue publicly to defend Wilcox against charges that he did not send his children to public schools. Madison *Capital Times,* August 27, 1920.
[106] *Wisconsin Blue Book, 1921,* 70.

The other primary results were generally encouraging to the La Follette progressives. Two Nonpartisan Leaguers, Elmer Hall and George Comings, won places with Blaine on the state ticket. Even more significant, only one Wisconsin congressman who had supported the Esch-Cummins bill survived. Esch himself was defeated. On the anti-La Follette side, however, Lenroot, Treasurer Henry Johnson, and William J. Morgan, most rabid of the anti-Nonpartisan Leaguers, all won; and a majority of the Republican legislative candidates were anti-La Follette men.[107]

If anything, the bitterness of the conflict increased with the general election. Though nominated to the same ticket with Blaine and the other Nonpartisan League candidates, Morgan did not drop his attacks after the primary. The Lenroot-Philipp elements urged Republican unity and succeeded in electing Lenroot's primary campaign manager, Alvin Peterson, for chairman of the State Central Committee,[108] but Morgan pressed his attack on the Nonpartisan Leaguers at the platform convention. After a twelve-hour fight in the resolutions committee, Morgan brought his case to the floor of the convention where he won inclusion of the following platform plank: "We denounce the leadership of the Nonpartisan League, the I. W. W., the Communist party, and all other agencies seeking to undermine the principles of democracy and advocating a program of state socialism, bolshevism or anarchy. We denounce the attempt of non-residents of Wisconsin through the leadership of the Nonpartisan League to control the Republican party in Wisconsin."[109] The platform also withheld endorsement of Blaine and the rest of the state ticket. Though many of the economic issues were recognized by the platform framers, they also backed the Esch-Cummins Act and made no concessions on the issues of free speech, press, and assembly, or the use of foreign languages.[110]

[107] Plumb, *Badger Politics*, 196–204.
[108] Madison *Capital Times*, October 21, 1920.
[109] *Ibid.*, September 22, 1920.
[110] *Idem.*

The La Follette faction struck back with vigor. Two days after the convention, La Follette called for the defeat of all those who had supported the Esch-Cummins bill.[111] The most prominent of these was of course Irvine Lenroot, Republican candidate for the United States Senate. Accordingly, and at the solicitation of La Follette, James Thompson declared his independent candidacy for the Senate against Lenroot.[112] Thompson offered the betrayal of Blaine by Morgan and others as justification for his own bolt.[113] Though the Milwaukee labor elements were lost to the Social Democrats, he retained full and enthusiastic support of the railroad brotherhoods and the Nonpartisan Leaguers.[114]

Blaine did not openly endorse Thompson. Neither, however, did he endorse his running mate, Lenroot. Furthermore, he repudiated the party platform.[115] The lines became even more sharply drawn when several La Follette men on the state central committee resigned during October.[116]

Roy Wilcox had been balked by Gilbert Seaman in efforts to launch an independent candidacy against Blaine,[117] but the Democratic nominee, R. B. McCoy, was eminently satisfactory to nationalists. Led by Morgan and Wilcox, many anti-La Follette Republicans openly bolted the ticket and continued their all-out campaign for Americanism.[118]

[111] Madison *Capital Times,* September 24, 1920.
[112] E. J. Onstad to Thompson, September 16, 1920; Thompson to Onstad, September 18, October 4, 1920, in the Thompson Papers.
[113] Madison *Capital Times,* October 6, 1920.
[114] Evjue to Thompson, September 30, 1920; E. J. Onstad to Thompson, October 5, 1920; Thompson to Onstad, October 6, 1920; Onstad to Thompson, November 17, 1920, in the Thompson Papers.
[115] J. W. Carow to Nelson, October 2, 1920, in the Nelson Papers; Blaine to Alvin Peterson, October 13, 1920, in the Blaine Papers; Madison *Capital Times,* September 22, 1920.
[116] Madison *Capital Times,* October 12, 15, 1920.
[117] *Milwaukee Sentinel,* September 12, 1920; Madison *Capital Times,* September 17, 1920.
[118] *Milwaukee Sentinel,* October 23, 1920; A. W. Prehn to Blaine, October 30, 1920, in the Blaine Papers.

Milwaukee business leaders intensified their campaign to save the state from radicalism. Two hundred and fifty individuals and firms supported the American Constitutional League of Wisconsin, whose alleged purpose was to "conduct an educational campaign in Milwaukee in behalf of Americanism and in opposition to revolutionary radicalism." The organization, founded in February, 1920, claimed, by the end of October, to have published thirty separate pieces of literature, distributed to every home in Milwaukee, and to have held over five hundred meetings, mainly among workers in factories.[119]

The anti-radical crusade was not restricted to Milwaukee. In a state that was habituated to intense political conflict, the 1920 battle set a new record for bitterness and took on the aspects of full-scale class warfare. A Lincoln County lawyer discovered that a Blaine man in the lumber district had to "bear the jeers and jibes of the emissaries of the big interests. . . ." He was "counted a Bolshevik and an I. W. W. . . . shunned socially, ridiculed professionally, and running the gauntlet of being broken financially."[120] Even anti-Blaine men acknowledged that the campaign was remarkable for the amount of vilification and falsehood directed against Blaine.[121]

But all the passion was not on the nationalist side. The La Follette leaders found an angry resentment in the electorate that matched their own bitterness. A Chippewa Falls assemblyman told Blaine after the election that "all the aristocrats and semi-aristocrats seem to be against you. Also most of the Preachers and lawyers here, I don't know why, but the laboring man, skilled or not, and the Farmers were for you."[122] Other politicians observed that though "con-

---

[119] American Constitutional League of Wisconsin to E. O. Henderson, October 28, 1920, in the Blaine Papers.

[120] C. M. Sheldon to Blaine, November 17, 1920, in the Blaine Papers.

[121] A. C. Bishop to Blaine, November 7, 1920; Frank H. Hanson to Blaine, November 11, 1920, in the Blaine Papers. Charles Rose expressed the same view in Rosa to Blaine, November 3, 1920, in the Blaine Papers.

[122] F. W. Bartingale to Blaine, November 6, 1920, in the Blaine Papers.

servative" pressure remained heavy in the towns and cities, strong "progressive" efforts among the farmers met with a good response.[123] Economic and social complaints far more severe than those of the early progressive days provided fertile political soil for bold, aggressive leadership. In the 1920 campaign, the La Follette men continued to link the twin issues of the Esch-Cummins Act and the League of Nations with the cost of living, the designs of the "money power," and the "profiteers."[124]

La Follette pressed home the issues on which the reformers counted when he launched his speaking campaign in Milwaukee on October 21. Encouraged by an enthusiastic audience, La Follette lashed out at his enemies:[125]

... Shops and factories are beginning to slow down or close down, workmen by the thousands are being thrown out on the streets all over the country, farmers are being driven to distraction by a collapse of the prices of their wheat, corn, cotton, wool and milk, far below the cost of production, while the consumers of the cities, far from benefiting from the hardships of the farmers, are still paying profiteers war prices for everything they consume and householders are panic-stricken with the fear that they will not at any price be able to secure the coal to keep their wives and little ones from freezing when the bitter winter comes upon us.

The chief causes of all the trouble, La Follette continued, were the Treaty of Versailles, with its "diabolical league of nations," and the Esch-Cummins Act. "Behind them both," he argued, "are the great exploiting interests of the United States and the world—the international bankers, with their deposit boxes full of worthless foreign securities and bonds which they seek to have the United States

---

[123] F. E. Carswell, secretary of the Independent Progressives, to Blaine, November 3, 1920; G. M. Follensbee to Blaine, November 5, 1920, in the Blaine Papers.

[124] Madison *Capital Times*, October 6, 9, 15, 19, 22, 1920; *La Follette's Magazine*, 12: 10 (October, 1920).

[125] *Milwaukee Sentinel*, October 22, 1920.

guarantee by dragging us into the league of nations, and of watered railroad securities which they have already had the government guarantee by the iniquitous terms of the Esch-Cummins railroad law."[126] The appeal was especially effective among consumers, workingmen, farmers, and small merchants.[127]

The extent of disgruntlement in certain quarters was testified to by the tactics of the conservative, nationalistic *Milwaukee Sentinel,* still the leading conservative Republican organ in the state. Concerned for the fate of Lenroot, the *Sentinel* reverted to the defensive tactics of the primary campaign. It gave wide publicity to endorsements of Lenroot from progressives and did the same for Warren G. Harding. Most of its space was devoted to an all-out assault on President Wilson; but the attacks were vaguely worded, in apparent deference to Wilson's progressive opponents.[128]

Election returns proved what was evident to observers during the campaign: though McCoy would be strong in the larger towns and cities, Blaine would run well in rural areas and labor centers. As it turned out, Blaine carried such railroad centers as Superior and La Crosse but lost most other cities and larger towns. His rural support was tremendous. It was indicated by returns from a number of counties in which McCoy carried the only city while Blaine carried the county. For instance, Blaine lost Prairie du Chien but carried Crawford County, 2,853 to 1,898. He lost Menominee but carried Dunn County by almost two to one. He lost the city of Eau Claire, but won the county, 5,449 to 3,972. The same pattern held in Iowa, Marathon, Outagamie, Portage, Richland, Sauk, Sawyer, Shawano, and Taylor counties. Variations on this pattern were evident everywhere.[129]

[126] *Idem.*
[127] J. D. Beck to Blaine, February 20, 1920; Eugene Meyer to Blaine, November 5, 1920, in the Blaine Papers. See also Fred Wylie to Huber, form letter, October 29, 1920, in the Huber Papers.
[128] *Milwaukee Sentinel,* October, 1920; see especially October 3, 4, 16, 23, 24, 28, and 29.
[129] *Wisconsin Blue Book, 1921,* 165–208.

Though the conservative-nationalist coalition remained strong, the tide was running for the La Follette men. Blaine defeated McCoy decisively, 363,608 to 246,890.[130] Along with Blaine, the La Follette group saw Hall and Comings elected to state office, veteran progressives John M. Nelson and Henry A. Cooper restored to Congress, and other La Follette men sent to Washington with them, one of these being Joseph Beck, primary victor over Representative Esch.

Despite all this, the overriding and complicating fact about the 1920 election in Wisconsin is that Warren G. Harding carried the state by a tremendous margin. Harding won every Wisconsin county, polling 498,576 votes to 113,422 for Democrat James Cox, and 80,635 for Social Democrat Eugene V. Debs.[131] Harding had, by accident or design, been positioned at the confluence of countless streams of discontent and had sailed to victory on the angry current that resulted. His overwhelming triumph, of course, benefited all other Republican candidates, especially since women were voting for the first time and were generally felt to be reluctant to jeopardize the effectiveness of their ballots by splitting their votes.

Among those who contributed heavily and significantly to Harding's triumph in Wisconsin were most of the state's German voters, many of whom had voted Democratic prior to the war. The German-language press left little doubt where it stood. Despite Wilson's hope for a "solemn referendum," the League of Nations issue was no longer of major concern to the German-language papers. But wartime wounds remained open and Cox stood as the unfortunate symbol of "an extravagant and autocratic party" and a party "that interfered with the constitutional rights of the German-Americans."[132]

German-Americans had been sensitized to the issue of personal liberty in pre-war days by means of the liquor

[130] *Ibid.*, 209.
[131] *Idem.*
[132] *Appleton Volksfreund*, cited in Spellberg, "Wisconsin Reaction to the Versailles Peace Treaty," 176.

question and, for some, the influence of nineteenth-century German liberalism. This issue of personal liberty had brought the Germans into close and sympathetic association with La Follette, a fellow victim and a forthright champion. Thus, much of the German-American vote for Harding reflected not simply undifferentiated discontent but a definite pro-La Follette kind of discontent. This was evident in the statistics of the other main contests, for governor and senator.

Contributing to Blaine's victory was a strong showing in many counties that were heavily German and had formerly voted Democratic. For example, in Calumet County the vote was Blaine 3,325, McCoy 930; in Dodge it was Blaine 8,554, McCoy 4,911; and in Washington, Blaine 5,194 to 1,980 for McCoy.[133] In each of these counties, the percentage of people of German ancestry was at least 10 per cent over the state average, as of the 1910 census; each had been among the five counties that had voted for the Democrat John A. Aylward in 1906.[134]

James Thompson failed in his independent candidacy, but his vote of 235,029 (as against 281,576 for Lenroot, 89,265 for Democrat Paul Reinsch, and 66,172 for Social Democrat Frank Weber) was remarkable in the light of Harding's tremendous Republican vote, the reluctance of voters to split their ballots, the opposition of the national and state Republican machinery, the unwillingness of some Blaine men to jeopardize the entire ticket by bolting on the senatorship, and the strength of Lenroot's campaign.[135] Among those who contributed to the Thompson total were many Germans; and in so doing, they clearly marked themselves not just as anti-Democrat but as pro-La Follette—in the sense that La Follette symbolized a certain segment of discontent. The five hard-core Democratic counties that

[133] *Wisconsin Blue Book, 1921*, 169, 173–174, 204.
[134] Meyer, "The Politics of Loyalty," 54–55; *Wisconsin Blue Book, 1907*, 472.
[135] Wallace Ingalls to Blaine, November 5, 1920, in the Blaine Papers; Plumb, *Badger Politics*, 196–197.

had backed Aylward in 1906—Calumet, Dodge, Jefferson, Ozaukee, and Washington—with populations of German birth or parentage ranging from 37 to 42.8 per cent as of the 1910 census, all backed Thompson against Lenroot.[136] Though Thompson carried only seventeen of seventy-one counties, of the ten counties whose German population exceeded the state average by 1910, he out-polled Lenroot in eight.[137] These included all of the major German counties in the state, headed by Milwaukee. There Thompson surpassed Lenroot, but the county was carried by Social Democrat Frank Weber, who polled 41,393 votes to 38,319 for Thompson, 36,456 for Lenroot, and 21,459 for Reinsch. Weber did not carry any other county. Thirteen counties, most of them predominantly German, had voted Democratic at least twice in gubernatorial contests from 1892 to 1900. Of these, Thompson carried ten.

Blaine's victory was not a clear-cut triumph for the new reform forces. The big factor that worked against Thompson, the Independent, benefited the Republican Blaine: straight party voting. The presence on the ticket of Harding, Lenroot, and sundry conservatives at the local level made many anti-Blaine Republicans leery of an overt ticket-splitting strategy, lest their candidates suffer retaliation. Harding's landslide victory in Wisconsin then brought votes to the whole Republican slate, including Blaine.[138] In large part, however, the Blaine victory came out of a contest between the new nationalist-conservative force, and the new Left that had likewise formed since 1917. Blaine's triumph revealed the strength of the latter.

The new progressive coalition that La Follette headed

---

[136] Meyer, "Politics of Loyalty," 54–55; *Wisconsin Blue Book, 1921*, 209.
[137] For the senate vote, see the *Wisconsin Blue Book, 1921*, 209.
[138] John Gompin to Blaine, November 6, 1920; David Atwood to Blaine, November 7, 1920; Frank X. Boden to Blaine, November 9, 1920, in the Blaine Papers; Robert S. Shields to Nelson, September 8, 1920; Shields to Nelson, September 11, 1920; Nelson to Shields, September 30, 1920, in the Nelson Papers; Fred Holmes to Thompson, November 22, 1920; E. J. Onstad to Thompson, November 10, 1920, in the Thompson Papers.

did not win control of the Wisconsin legislature until 1922. In that year also La Follette won an overwhelming re-election to the Senate. In 1924, when the aging warrior ran for President on the ticket of a new Progressive party, he easily carried Wisconsin. He died in 1925, but his death did not stem the tide. The La Follette name, borne in political battle by the sons of "Old Bob"—Robert, Jr., and Philip—remained a focal point and unifying force for the discontented.

In Wisconsin at least, and perhaps elsewhere, those who voted for Harding expressed more than a weariness with Wilsonian idealism and nostalgia for the *status quo ante bellum*. In many ways the 1920 election seemed to show a resurgent progressivism. The old progressive leader, La Follette, was again riding high, and with him rode at least some of his pre-war lieutenants and allies, men like Blaine, Huber, and Crownhart. The old ideology, updated with words like "profiteer" but still based on suspicion of large corporations and a Jeffersonian distinction between the people and the "interests," seemed born again. Certainly, among the electorate at large, there was an ample voting basis for a new reformism: German-Americans, farmers, and laborers were up in arms. The latter two, moreover, were better organized for protest than ever before through the Nonpartisan League and the railroad brotherhoods. In certain circumstances, the socialistic State Federation of Labor and the Milwaukee Trades and Labor Council could be counted on to co-operate with the others; and, on some matters, even the Social Democratic party was prepared to join with "bourgeois" allies.

That reformism was again strong in Wisconsin was clear. But the strength of the forces of protest in the reconstruction period and their links with the pre-war progressive movement should not obscure the fact that the pre-war decline, so evident in the elections of 1914 and 1916 especially, was real—not merely an interlude in an otherwise prolonged and uninterrupted progressive continuum extending from the 1890's into the 1920's and beyond. The war so jarred society in Wisconsin as to generate new issues, new alignments, and, as compared to 1915 and 1916, a new mood of anger and bitterness. In 1917 and 1918, nationalistic progressives made common cause with nationalistic conservatives; conservative Democratic Germans were driven, largely on the issue of personal liberty, to La Follette and Victor Berger; and the archenemies of another era, La Follette and Philipp, likewise united against common enemies. With the termination of the war in Europe, the relative power of the various factions changed, but otherwise the war situation continued.

While some of the ex-progressives grew uncomfortable with their conservative associates, still others saw in the rise of radicalism—typified by the Wobblies, the Nonpartisan Leaguers, the Social Democrats, and, much in the news, nameless anarchists—something very different from the Jeffersonian progressive movement for which they had fought earlier. The conservative nationalists were even more alarmed at the postwar situation. The fact that many radicals had opposed the war and that some were of European, even German background, confirmed their worst fears and spurred their determination to press on with the militant wartime campaign for Americanism.

As wartime inflation burgeoned into a still greater postwar inflation, irate farmers, laborers, and Germans of all classes lent support to the Nonpartisan League, the railroad brotherhoods, the Wisconsin State Federation of Labor, the Social Democratic party, and the La Follette progressives. This coalition on the Left flowed naturally from war circumstances, when reformers, dissidents, and progressive political leaders were thrown together in mutual self-defense against common oppressors. But it was a broader coalition than those of pre-war days, and, on balance, a good deal more radical as well. The issues of 1920 were not only new but in some ways were different from those of pre-war days. This was especially so of questions of foreign policy and personal liberty, both of which sprang naturally from the impact of the war on German-Americans, socialists, farmers, laborers, and Robert M. La Follette himself.

As Arthur Link has contended with reference to the nation,[139] a species of progressivism, bearing many similarities to the pre-war movement, did exist in Wisconsin during the postwar period and later. But the similarities were more apparent than real, and in truth the postwar movement was substantially a new and different phenomenon, born, bred, and shaped by the war. The original Wisconsin progressivism—the vibrant, grassroots progressivism of Congressman La Follette and the "university boys"—had faded and died of internal contradictions and external pressures by 1916.

[139] Arthur S. Link, "What Happened to the Progressive Movement in the 1920's?," in the *American Historical Review*, LXIV: 833–851 (July, 1959).

Conclusion

WISCONSIN'S PROGRESSIVE MOVEMENT declined for a variety of reasons. Part of it had to do with the stalwarts. For one thing, these anti-La Follette Republicans were always more numerous and more powerful than the national fame of the progressives suggested. They were, moreover, wrathful against La Follette and united in their determination to oust him and his faction. This feeling was in large part due to resentment against La Follette's tactics. The stalwarts were never so venal as La Follette represented them and were able, through the progressive years, to renew themselves and replenish their ranks with honest and energetic young men. Thus, once in power, under the leadership of Emanuel Philipp, they steadily improved their image and undermined efforts towards progressive revival.

Most of the progressives' difficulties lay with themselves, and resulted in disastrous internal division and ultimately defeat at the hands of conservatives. Factional schism stemmed from a number of things. Ambitious progressive leaders like James O. Davidson, W. D. Connor, Isaac Stephenson, and Francis E. McGovern had independent sources of power within the progressive coalition that they could detach in time of personal need. Put another way, the voting backbone of progressivism was not wholly reliable so far as the La Follette group was concerned. While they would not repudiate progressivism, that concept was sufficiently flexible for the Norwegians in good conscience to support one of their own, Davidson, against La Follette's choice, Lenroot. Voters and leaders within the progressive coalition also responded to regional considerations, so that McGovern, from populous Milwaukee, was a power in his own right. Money and business connections gave Stephenson and Connor their special influence.

A fundamental disagreement among progressives as to the nature of the movement and the strategy that was required also contributed to factional schisms. La Follette viewed the fight as eternal, between the people and the "interests," and believed that constant political strife, focusing on ever new issues, was essential. By contrast, most progressives identified the movement with certain specific ends. To them, disruption in party and community life was a necessary evil in the attainment of these ends, not a way of life to be embraced on a permanent basis. The placid and friendly Davidson was especially well suited to appeal to progressives on this basis, and he detached many from the coalition. Wisconsin's relative prosperity in these years, with the rise of dairying and of industry, doubtless helped him.

Embarrassments relating to La Follette's commitment to the primary and to a simplified democratic ideology constantly worked to the benefit of dissidents and promoted schism. The primary device and the anti-boss commitment encouraged rivalry among progressive leaders and groups. Davidson benefited most spectacularly from this limitation in 1906, but it was McGovern who put it to his advantage most frequently, beginning with his senatorial bid in 1908 and running through the 1916 primaries. Occasionally, progressives of the "inner circle" felt compelled to ignore the anti-boss, pro-primary commitment and to meet in "conferences" or pass the word downward from La Follette. These steps were taken with awkwardness and embarrassment, and were exploited by schismatics like McGovern, who on such occasions could present himself as the authentic progressive who resisted boss dictation.

Internal weaknesses within progressivism worked di-

Conclusion 285

rectly to the advantage of the stalwarts. The most serious limitation of all, perhaps, was the strong Jeffersonian strain in progressive thought. Such ideological underpinnings were adequate for the legislative purposes of the La Follette administrations, when focus was on anti-bossism and the primary, equitable taxation, honesty in government, and railroad regulation. But when the McGovern administrations went beyond these measures, the strain on Jeffersonian rhetoric proved too great. Stalwarts were able to woo progressive voters with criticism of heavy taxing and spending, bureaucracy, and meddling by university professors. Progressive dependence upon relatively conservative voters was the greater for the fact that so much of the laboring population was already committed to the Social Democratic party, especially in Milwaukee. Democrats were more useful to the progressives than Social Democrats in the pre-war days, yet dependence on them proved to be another source of weakness, for with the revival of Democratic fortunes in 1912 the "fair-minded" Democrats largely returned to their own party in both primaries and general elections. In the same period, declining zeal, the toll taken by the passing years, became evident among the progressives. A younger generation had come on the scene, heralded by the independent gubernatorial candidacy of Blaine in 1914. But the new progressives could not immediately assume the top factional posts as their predecessors had in the early days, and their enthusiasm waned. Yet another factor in the progressive decline was the diversion of public attention to issues extraneous to progressivism. For the La Follette group, the liquor question had always been a red herring, but it did count for something among the electorate. Anti-Catholicism, another sub-surface constant, emerged to compete strongly for voter attention in 1914 and after. In 1914 the war in Europe and national foreign policy considerations also began to divert attention from traditional progressive concerns. Finally, the need for money was a constant problem and source of weakness to the progressives. To get it, damaging concessions were made to Isaac Stephenson. When that source dried up, the La Follette forces came to depend a great deal upon what La Follette could raise on the national lecture platform. This had the effect of draining his energies and health and keeping him out of the state at critical times.

The various weaknesses evident in the decade 1906 through 1916 were foreshadowed from the start. The pre-1900 roots of progressivism were in many ways conventional and conservative. Party loyalty remained strong, and the factional wars of the nineties, however intense, were fought largely within the context of an overriding Republicanism. The reform leaders, headed by La Follette, Haugen, Hoard, and Bryant, were all tested party men of "sound" principles. On the national level, they espoused sound money and the protective tariff as against the radicalism of the Populists and the Bryan Democrats. On the state level, the reforms they sought, though important, were unimpeachably moderate. Hoard and his dairymen followers wanted protection against oleomargarine, state aid in the improvement of dairy products, and state enforcement of the high dairy standards that were earning Wisconsin a place in the national market. La Follette campaigned more generally for fuller democracy and an end to corporate domination, for honesty and economy in government, and for equalization of the tax burden as between farmers and corporations. Farmers, ethnic groups, and middle-class elements throughout Wisconsin could easily respond to such a program. Especially was this so because the reformers offered fuller recognition to Scandinavians, patronage to disgruntled old-line politicians, and positions of leadership and opportunity to bright young businessmen and professionals.

That Wisconsin was able to gain recognition as the leading progressive state on the basis of so conventional a foundation was cause for wonder. Part of the explanation rested with the Old Guard politicians. They opened the door to the reformers by permitting too brazen an exercise of corporate influence, by using heavy-handed and corrupt tactics, and by ignoring the interests of those to whom La

Follette appealed. Some of this could be explained with reference to the rise of corporations, especially railroads, in the state. But that factor was hardly unique to Wisconsin. What was unusual in Wisconsin was the combination of circumstances that created a virtual vacuum of Old Guard leadership during the critical years of the rise of progressivism. Philetus Sawyer was semi-retired during most of the nineties, yet he kept the reins of power; Henry Payne and John Spooner were more interested in national than state affairs, and Spooner had no stomach for politics. Death took Sawyer in 1898, but no plans for an orderly succession had been made. Not until the emergence of Emanuel Philipp after 1910 did conservative Republicans again have capable leadership.

At least as important as Old Guard shortcomings in accounting for the strength of Wisconsin progressivism was the quality and character of the reform leadership. Robert M. La Follette was extraordinary in many ways. He had tremendous determination and energy; he was willing to give of himself without concern for wealth or health; he had a flair for the dramatic and a strong sense of righteousness; and he was a magnetic and compelling public speaker. He had, in short, great abilities to lead. These he chose to use not simply for the limited ends suggested by the general character of his support and of the times, but in a fuller and above all a more long-lasting way. His own tendency to moralize and simplify crystallized in a larger view and strategy—the belief that the corporate wolves would always be at the gate and that the people must be constantly mobilized against them.

In addition to the extraordinary leadership given by La Follette, Wisconsin's progressive movement had another unusual advantage: the character and influence of the University of Wisconsin. Much of the excellence that inhered in progressive legislation and administration, including the labor legislation during the McGovern administrations, may be explained in part with reference to the direct and indirect influence of the university faculty.

Given the conventional roots of the movement, extraordinary achievement, whether through the influence of the university or the efforts of La Follette, was bought at a heavy price. La Follette's polarizing techniques were effective; yet they contributed to stalwart unity and aroused internal discord. The use of experts and commissions, and the increase in state spending, made the progressive movement relatively more effective and wide ranging than elsewhere; yet both opened the door to successful stalwart attacks. Much of the story of the decline of progressivism related to the tension between the movement's methods and achievements on the one hand and its conventional political base on the other. Had it been otherwise, the decline would have been less precipitous and spectacular—but only because the movement would have been less notable and significant.

We have treated of Wisconsin politics during World War I and the reconstruction period with an eye towards what went before, in order to make clear the discontinuity and to justify the assertion that while progressivism may have survived the war, the progressive movement had ended. One is tempted to range beyond this primary purpose, and to draw comparisons of several sorts. By viewing Wisconsin progressivism in the postwar period, it may be asked, for example, whether the new progressivism was not the beginning of the New Deal's reform coalition. This analogy could be supported in Wisconsin by the greater radicalism, the fuller participation of organized labor, the greater division along class lines, and the stronger ethnic and civil-liberties appeal—all qualities which are generally acknowledged to characterize the New Deal and to distinguish it from the pre-war progressive movement. But there are serious flaws in this theory. The Democratic party was to be the vehicle for the New Deal nationally; but enmity towards the Democratic party was one of the cohesive factors in postwar Wisconsin progressivism. The New Deal made a strong appeal to ethnic groups; so did postwar Wisconsin progressivism, but this was hardly a new departure—nor

Conclusion

was Wisconsin's German population very suitable material for a national coalition that would, in the late 1930's, move strongly away from isolationism.

To speculate spatially instead of temporally, one might conjecture that Wisconsin's experience was typical of the nation's, and that a substantial new wave of reformism encompassed the states in the early 1920's. But generalizing about the nation in the postwar period on the basis of Wisconsin politics is hazardous. True, Wisconsin's new progressivism sprang from certain fundamental causes which were common to the Middle West and even to the nation; but equally true, Wisconsin had certain advantages that were both unique and important. The strong progressive tradition; the continuing leadership of Robert M. La Follette; the fortuitous alliance of progressive politicians with Nonpartisan Leaguers, workingmen, and socialists; and the large number of German-Americans: all of these were crucial and distinctive factors in postwar reformism in Wisconsin.

What is true of postwar politics in Wisconsin is true of progressivism in general: easy generalizations, whether about the rise, nature, or decline of the movement in America, simply cannot be made on the basis of the experience of a single state. The country is too diverse for that. At the same time, however, no adequate picture of the national progressive movement can be drawn without reference to Wisconsin.

Select Bibliography

PRIMARY SOURCES

Manuscript Collections

All manuscript collections listed are on deposit at the State Historical Society of Wisconsin:

William J. Anderson Papers.
John A. Aylward Papers.
A. O. Barton Papers.
John Blaine Papers.
Harry Bolens Papers.
Bryan J. Castle Papers.
Henry A. Cooper Papers.
James O. Davidson Papers.
John S. Donald Papers.
Herman L. Ekern Papers.
John J. Esch Papers.
E. J. Gross Papers.
Nils P. Haugen Papers.
Henry Huber Papers.
Merlin Hull Papers.

Paul Husting Letterbooks.
Paul Husting Papers.
Ada James Diaries.
Elisha Keyes Letterbooks.
Elisha Keyes Papers.
Robert M. La Follette Papers.
Charles R. McCarthy Papers.
Francis E. McGovern Papers.
O. G. Munson Papers.
Adolphus P. Nelson Papers.
Emanuel L. Philipp Papers.
Charles Rosa Papers.
Charles Stewart Papers.
James A. Stone Papers.
Charles S. Stout Papers.
John Strange Papers.
James Thompson Papers.
John M. Whitehead Papers.
Wisconsin State Federation of Labor, Executive Committee Minutes.
Wisconsin Nonpartisan League Papers.

Newspapers and Periodicals

Capital Times (Madison), 1918–1920.
Eau Claire Telegram, 1906–1914.
Green Bay Press-Gazette, 1906–1916.
Janesville Gazette, 1901–1914.
La Crosse Tribune, 1906–1920.

Select Bibliography 293

La Follette's Magazine (Madison), 1909–1920.
Milwaukee Free Press, 1906–1910.
Milwaukee Journal, 1912–1920.
Milwaukee Sentinel, 1901–1920.
Oshkosh Northwestern, 1906–1916.
Racine Times, 1906–1916.
Superior Telegram, 1906–1914.
Wisconsin State Journal (Madison), 1901–1920.

Autobiographies and Memoirs

Ameringer, Oscar. *If You Don't Weaken.* New York, 1940.
Anderson, Rasmus B. *The Life Story of Rasmus B. Anderson.* Madison, 1917.
Commons, John R. *Myself.* New York, 1934.
Ely, Richard T. *Ground Under Our Feet.* New York, 1938.
Haugen, Nils P. *Political and Pioneer Reminiscences.* Evansville, 1930.
La Follette, Robert M. *La Follette's Autobiography: A Personal Narrative of Political Experiences.* Madison, 1913.

Government Publications

Legislature of Wisconsin. *Assembly Journal,* Thirty-ninth Session, Fiftieth Session, Fifty-fourth Session.

————. *Report of the Senate Members of the Joint Senatorial Primary Investigation Committee,* 1911.

United States Census Reports, 12th, 13th, and 14th, 1900, 1910, 1920.

United States Department of Commerce, Bureau of the Census. *Historical Statistics of the United States, 1789–1945.* Washington, 1949.

Wisconsin Blue Book. Madison, 1889–1921.

Wisconsin Highway Commission. Bulletin No. 3: *The State Highway Aid Law,* 1913.

Wisconsin State Treasurer. *Report of the State Treasurer of Wisconsin,* 1914, 1916.

Interviews

Herman L. Ekern. May 6, 1953.

William T. Evjue. January 18, 1954.

William Kirsch. January 18, 1954.

Selig Perlman. December 8, 1953.

Craig Ralston. January 20, 1953.

Charles Rosa. January 15, 1954.

O. A. Stolen. January 4, 1955.

George R. Taylor. February, 1954.

SECONDARY SOURCES

Books and Articles

Bailey, Thomas A. *Woodrow Wilson and the Great Betrayal.* New York, 1947.

Barton, Albert O. *La Follette's Winning of Wisconsin.* Des Moines, 1924.

Blegen, Theodore C. "The Scandinavian Element and Agricultural Discontent." *Annual Report of the American Historical Association, 1921.*

Bordner, John S. "The Use of Wisconsin Land." *Wisconsin Blue Book, 1935.*

Chafee, Zechariah, Jr. *Free Speech in the United States.* Cambridge, 1941.

Child, Clifton James. *German-Americans in Politics, 1914–1917.* Madison, 1939.

Select Bibliography 295

Current, Richard Nelson. *Pine Logs and Politics: A Life of Philetus Sawyer, 1816–1900.* Madison, 1950.

Curti, Merle, and Vernon Carstensen. *The University of Wisconsin: A History, 1848–1925.* 2 vols., Madison, 1949.

Dearing, Mary. *Veterans in Politics: The Story of the G.A.R.* Baton Rouge, 1952.

Deutsch, Herman J. "Railroad Politics." *Wisconsin Magazine of History* (June, 1932).

Epstein, Leon D. *Politics in Wisconsin.* Madison, 1958.

Falk, Karen. "Public Opinion in Wisconsin During World War One." *Wisconsin Magazine of History* (June, 1942).

Fowler, Dorothy Ganfield. *John Coit Spooner, Defender of Presidents.* New York, 1961.

Fries, Robert. *Empire in Pine.* Madison, 1951.

Gavett, Thomas W. *Development of the Labor Movement in Wisconsin.* Madison and Milwaukee, 1959.

Genung, A. B. "Agriculture in the World War One Period." United States Department of Agriculture, *1940 Yearbook of Agriculture.*

Groves, Harold. "The Wisconsin State Income Tax." *Wisconsin Blue Book, 1933.*

Hechler, Kenneth W. *Insurgency: Personalities and Politics of the Taft Era.* New York, 1940.

Higham, John. *Strangers in the Land: Patterns of American Nativism, 1860–1925.* New Brunswick, 1955.

Kennedy, Padraic. "Lenroot, La Follette and the Campaign of 1906." *Wisconsin Magazine of History* (Spring, 1959).

Kinsman, D. O. "The Genesis of the Wisconsin State Income Tax." *Wisconsin Magazine of History* (September, 1937).

Korman, Adolph G. "Political Loyalties, Immigrant Traditions and Reform: The Wisconsin German-American Press and Progressivism 1909–1912." *Wisconsin Magazine of History* (Spring, 1957).

La Follette, Belle Case and Fola. *Robert M. La Follette, 1855–1925.* 2 vols., New York, 1953.

Link, Arthur. "What Happened to the Progressive Movement in the 1920's?" *American Historical Review* (July, 1959).

Lovejoy, Allan O. *La Follette and the Direct Primary in Wisconsin.* New Haven, 1941.

McNall, P.E., W. P. Mortenson and R. D. Davidson. "Development of Wisconsin Agriculture." *Economic Information for Wisconsin Farmers* (June, 1934).

Maxwell, Robert S. *Emanuel L. Philipp: Wisconsin Stalwart.* Madison, 1959.

————. *La Follette and the Rise of the Progressives in Wisconsin.* Madison, 1956.

May, Henry. *Protestant Churches and Industrial America.* New York, 1949.

Merrill, Horace S. *William Freeman Vilas, Doctrinaire Democrat.* Madison, 1954.

Morlan, Robert. *A Political Prairie Fire.* Minneapolis, 1955.

Mowry, George. *Theodore Roosevelt and the Progressive Movement.* Madison, 1946.

Olson, Frederick I. "The Socialist Party and the Unions in Milwaukee." *Wisconsin Magazine of History* (Winter, 1960–1961).

Peterson, H. C. *Propaganda for War.* Norman, 1939.

———— and Gilbert Fite. *Opponents of War, 1917–1918.* Madison, 1957.

Phelan, Raymond Vincent. *The Financial History of Wisconsin.* Madison, 1908.

Plumb, Ralph. *Badger Politics, 1836–1930.* Manitowoc, 1930.

Select Bibliography

Raney, William. *Wisconsin: A Story of Progress.* New York, 1940.

Reinders, Robert C. "Daniel W. Hoan and the Milwaukee Socialist Party During the First World War." *Wisconsin Magazine of History* (Autumn, 1952).

Ross, Sam. *The Empty Sleeve: A Biography of Lucius Fairchild.* Madison, 1964.

Saloutos, Theodore. "The Decline of the Wisconsin Society of Equity." *Agricultural History* (July, 1941).

————. "The Nonpartisan League in the Western Middle West." *Agricultural History* (October, 1948).

————. "The Wisconsin Society of Equity." *Agricultural History* (April, 1940).

———— and John D. Hicks. *Agricultural Discontent in the Middle West 1900–1939.* Madison, 1951.

Schafer, Joseph. *History of Agriculture in Wisconsin.* Madison, 1922.

Still, Bayrd. *Milwaukee: The History of a City.* Milwaukee, 1948.

Thelen, David Paul. *The Early Life of Robert M. La Follette, 1855–1884.* Chicago, 1966.

Thompson, Alexander M. *The Political History of Wisconsin.* Milwaukee, 1902.

Vance, Maurice M. *Charles Richard Van Hise: Scientist-Progressive.* Madison, 1960.

Wachman, Marvin. *History of the Social Democratic Party of Milwaukee, 1897–1910.* Urbana, 1945.

Weibull, Jorgen. "The Wisconsin Progressives, 1900–1914." *Mid-America* (July, 1965).

Wight, William W. *Henry Clay Payne.* Milwaukee, 1907.

Witte, E. E. "Labor in Wisconsin History." *Wisconsin Magazine of History* (Winter, 1951).

————. "Statistics Relating to Wisconsin From the 1920 Census." *Wisconsin Blue Book, 1923.*

Wolmen, Leo. *The Growth of American Trade Unions, 1880–1923.* New York, 1924.

Unpublished Works

Finnegan, John P. "The Preparedness Movement in Wisconsin." Master's thesis, University of Wisconsin, 1961.

Frooman, Jack. "The Wisconsin Peace Movement, 1915–1919." Master's thesis, University of Wisconsin, 1949.

Gross, Edwin J. "A Political Grab Bag." Manuscript Division, State Historical Society of Wisconsin.

Harvey, Albert S. "The Background of the Progressive Movement in Wisconsin." Master's thesis, University of Wisconsin, 1933.

Huber, Henry. "War Hysteria." Manuscript Division, State Historical Society of Wisconsin.

Jackson, James E. "Wisconsin's Attitude Toward American Foreign Policy." Doctoral dissertation, University of Wisconsin, 1934.

McMurray, Howard J. "Some Influences of the University of Wisconsin on the State Government of Wisconsin." Doctoral dissertation, University of Wisconsin, 1940.

Meyer, Karl. "The Politics of Loyalty: From La Follette to McCarthy in Wisconsin, 1918–1952." Doctoral dissertation, Princeton University, 1956.

Olson, Frederick I. "The Milwaukee Socialist, 1897–1941." Doctoral dissertation, Harvard University, 1952.

Ralston, Craig. "The La Follette Dynasty." Manuscript Division, State Historical Society of Wisconsin.

Sayre, Wallace. "Robert M. La Follette: A Study in Political Methods." Doctoral dissertation, New York University, 1930.

Schmidt, Gertrude. "History of Labor Legislation in Wisconsin." Doctoral dissertation, University of Wisconsin, 1933.

Select Bibliography

Spellberg, William. "Wisconsin Reaction to the Versailles Peace Treaty as Revealed in Newspapers, Letters and Resolutions of Organizations." Master's thesis, University of Wisconsin, 1953.

Strange, John. "Autobiography." Manuscript Division, State Historical Society of Wisconsin.

Twombly, Robert C. "The Reformer as Politician: Robert M. La Follette in the Election of 1900." Master's thesis, University of Wisconsin, 1964.

Weissman, Norman. "A History of the Wisconsin State Journal" Master's thesis, University of Wisconsin, 1951.

Wilcox, Benton. "A Reconsideration of Northwestern Radicalism." Doctoral dissertation, University of Wisconsin, 1933.

Index

ABRAMS, Richard, vii
Adams, Henry C., 24
Adams County, 224
Agnew, D. W., 231
Aldrich, Nelson, 105
Allen, William Harvey, 165, 166
American Constitutional League, 246, 274
American Legion, 245, 246
American Protective Association, 160
Amerika, 27
Ameringer, Oscar, 158, 231
Anderson, John, 27
Anderson, Rasmus B., 27, 90, 231
Anderson, William J., 116, 126, 129
Anti-Catholicism, 159–162, 174, 190, 238, 242, 271, 285
Anti-Saloon League, 266, 268, 271n
Ashland, 181
Austrian-Americans, 224
Aylward, John A.: and La Follette, 66; candidates for governor, 125, 127, 149, 223, 278, 279; death of, 225

BABCOCK, Joseph: as La Follette ally, 45, 46; as anti-La Follette leader, 68, 71, 72, 75, 76, 81; opposed by La Follette, 77
Backus, James, 113
Bading, Gerhard, 156, 196
Baensch, Emil, 72, 181
Ballard, C. B., 249
Bancroft, Levi, 137, 231
Banks, Sam, 89
Baraboo, 166, 204
Barton, Albert O.: observations of, 8, 21, 38, 47, 53. 54, 59, 69, 74, 78, 80, 85, 94
Bascom, John, 19–20, 26n
Bashford, Robert M., 98
Beck, Joseph D., 171, 277
Becker, J. M., 195, 222
Beloit, 212
Beloit Free Press, 144

Bennett, J. H., 231
Bennett Law, 3, 16, 24, 30
Bentley, Frank, 233
Berger, Victor: as pre-war socialist leader, 67, 153, 154, 155; during war, 195, 197, 200, 209, 221, 227, 228–229, 233, 238, 241, 242; as postwar leader, 247, 259–260, 281
Black River Falls, 180, 205, 209
Blaine, John J.: 205, 273, 280; candidacies of, 125, 157–159, 234, 239, 241, 260–261, 262, 266, 267, 271, 272, 273–277, 278, 279
Bodenstab, H. H., 247
Bolens, Harry, 136, 138, 140
Borah, William, 105
Bosshard, Otto: candidate for governor, 1916, 180, 183, 184, 185, 186; as nationalist, 222, 227, 231, 257
Brandeis, Louis D., 132
Brayton, A. M., 205, 222, 256n
Brazeau, Theodore, 232
Bristow, Joseph L., 105
Broughton, C. E., 205
Browne, Edward E., 118, 176
Bryan, William Jennings, 33, 67, 127, 206, 286
Bryant, General George E., 4, 24, 286
Buffalo County, 123, 224
Burke, Timothy, 211

CALUMET County, 223, 224, 229, 232, 239, 278, 279
Cannon, Joseph, 6, 105
Cary, Charles P., 148, 161
Cary, William, 239
Casson, Henry, 23, 96
Chapple, John, 227
Chase, John, 231
Chicago and North Western Railroad, 47, 71, 128
Chicago, Milwaukee and St. Paul Railroad, 47, 71

301

Chilton, 232
Chippewa Falls, 231, 274
Churchill, Washington, 25
Chynoweth, Herbert W., 84
Clapp, Moses, 105
Clark, Champ, 128
Cleary, Michael J., 167, 169
Cleveland, Grover, 3, 4
Cochems, Henry, 113, 121, 156
Collier's Magazine, 139, 204
Columbia County, 223, 224
Comings, George, 272, 277
Committee of 48: 249, 252
Commons, John R.: and La Follette, vi, 131, 171, 203, 213; and primary, 102n
Concentration and Control, 132n
Congressmen (Wisconsin), 236, 239, 241, 272
Connor, William D.: 95, 114–115, 122, 123, 128, 283; candidacies of, 84–85, 99; and La Follette, 86, 104, 106; and Davidson, 88, 89, 92; and Wilcox, 231; influence of, 283, 284
Cook, Samuel A.: as anti-La Follette candidate, 72, 75, 76, 106, 114, 181
Cooper, George, 139
Cooper, Henry A., 113, 239, 277
Cooper, John G., 228
Cox, James, 226, 277
Crane, Charles R., 139, 225
Crawford County, 86, 276
Creel, George, 194
Crownhart, Charles: 178; aids La Follette, 171, 217, 254, 280; directs La Follette campaigns, 104, 112, 115, 181, 182, 190, 220n, 262, 267
Cummins, Albert B., 105
DAHL, Andrew: 186; and McGovern, 120, 122; candidate for governor, 1914, 125, 151, 152, 184; and Philipp, 158
Dane County, 6, 20, 26, 27, 28, 29, 33, 57, 67n, 86, 224
Davidson, James O.: as governor, 58, 59, 86; background of, 39, 86–87; elected governor, 1906, 86–99, 102, 110–111, 112n, 136, 223; in 1908, 103; in 1910, 105–106, 129; as threat to La Follette, 114, 123, 173, 217, 283, 284; and Philipp, 188n
Davies, Joseph E., 149, 225–228
Dawson, William, 199
Debs, Eugene V., 277
Democratic party: 81, 106, 109, 197; in late nineteenth century, 3, 8, 16, 29, 30; and La Follette, 50, 66–67, 73, 77, 79, 97, 126–128, 163, 171; pre-war campaigns of, 65, 76–77, 137–138, 148–149, 152; and war, 196, 202–203, 222–230, 240–243; after war, 247–250, 276–279, 288
Dennett, Fred A., 63
Dick, W. H., 218
Dithmar, Edward F.: favors conference, 179; in 1918 politics, 220, 220n, 228, 235, 236, 238–239, 241; in 1920 politics, 260–261, 263, 266, 271
Dodge County, 223, 224, 229, 235, 238, 261n, 278, 279
Doerfler, Christian, 180
Donald, John S., 150, 151, 162, 186, 256
Dunn County, 39, 239, 276

EASTMAN, Max, 213
Eau Claire, 199, 224, 230, 269, 276
Eau Claire County, 276
Eau Claire Telegram, 158
Ekern, Herman L.: 118, 123, 170, 178; as La Follette man, 87, 100, 101, 102, 103, 112, 117n, 121, 139, 160, 161, 168, 171, 179, 217
Election (popular): of 1888, 3; of 1890, 16; of 1894, 29–30; of 1896, 33; of 1898, 44; of 1900, 49–50; of 1902, 64–67; of 1904, 76–79; of 1908, 103; of 1910, 106; of 1912, 128, 137, 140–142; of 1914, 116–117, 121, 124, 125, 157–163; of 1916, 189–190; of April, 1918, 216, 227–230; of November, 1918, 239–242; of 1920, vii, 272–279; of 1924, 280. *See also* Democratic party, Republican party, Election (senatorial)

Index

Election (senatorial to 1911): of 1897, 35; of 1899, 45; of 1903, 64–66; of 1905, 84–85, 88; of 1907, 88, 99–100, 113; of 1908–1909, 101; of 1910–1911, 104–106
Eleventh Story League, 62, 63, 64, 66
Ellingson, C. K., 181
Ely, Richard T., 131, 203, 213
Emery, J. Q., 168
Equity News, 215, 218, 234
Esch, John J.: 180; and war, 177n, 189, 206; defeated, 1920, 264, 272, 277
Espionage Act, 194, 228, 241, 247, 258
Evans, Evan A., 166
Evansville, 206
Everett, Charles H., 24
Evjue, William T., 204, 216, 236, 271

FAIRCHILD, Edward T., 106, 168
Fairchild, Lucius, 4, 8
Falk, Otto, 246
Federated Trades Council of Milwaukee, 153, 154, 157, 260, 263, 280
Feise, Richard, 213
Fennimore Times, 62
Ferndale, 39, 201
Flint, Winston A., vii
Fond du Lac County, 223, 224
Fond du Lac Reporter, 138
Fox River, 13
Fraser, Cameron, 227
Frear, James, 140

GABRIEL, Ralph, 21
Gale, Zona, 166, 249
Gaveney, John, 233
George, Henry, 132
German-Americans: in politics, 3, 10, 49, 56, 63, 67, 79–80, 98, 106, 153, 176–177, 178, 181, 189, 196, 210, 222–224, 229–230, 232–233, 235–243, 245, 248, 253, 257, 258, 261, 266, 277–279, 280, 281; population in Wisconsin, 14, 67, 153, 197, 200, 279, 289; war views of, 176–177, 178, 189, 195–196, 200, 229–230, 242; wartime victimization of, 200, 202, 207–209, 229–230, 242, 282; postwar thinking of, 250, 251, 254, 265–266, 277–278
Germania, Die, 56, 222
Gettle, L. E., 262
Gilbert, Frank, 231
Gill, Thomas H., 47
Gittings, C. C., 181
Glynn, Martin, 160
Gompers, Samuel, 250
Goodland, Walter: as La Follette man, 116, 122, 184, 185, 186; as nationalist, 199, 205, 222, 231, 233
Grand Army of the Republic, 4–5, 30
Grange (Patrons of Husbandry), 8, 25, 234
Grant County, 239
Green County, 222, 239
Green Lake County, 223, 224, 229, 238
Gross, Edwin J., 89, 111, 112, 256, 257
Guardians of Liberty, 162, 174, 238
Gymnasium convention, 1904: 73–75, 84

HALL, Albert R., 39, 94
Hall, Elmer, 272, 277
Hambrecht, George P., 167, 169
Hannan, John J.: in Milwaukee, 62, 111; as spokesman for La Follette, 69, 120, 170, 233, 235
Harding, Warren L., 276, 277, 278, 279, 280
Harper, Samuel, 37, 60
Harrison, Benjamin, 3, 4
Hatton, William: views of, 21n, 159, 181; candidacies of, 101, 113–114, 122, 125, 152, 184, 186, 187, 188; opposes La Follette, 1920, 257
Haugen, Nils P.: as La Follette ally, 20, 22, 23, 26, 28, 29, 30, 31, 34, 286; opposes La Follette, 96; defends income tax, 140
Hicks, E. R., 75
Hicks, John, 66n
Highway Commission, 134

Hill, James J., 71
Hillis, Newell Dwight, 207
Hoan, Daniel, 196, 197, 200, 229
Hoard, William D.: as governor, 15–16; and La Follette, 24, 25, 31, 34, 96, 286
Holmes, Fred L., 217, 261, 262, 271
Houser, Walter O.: denounces McGovern, 107, 108, 120; 1916 delegate candidate, 180
Howe, Frederic C., v
Huber, Henry A.: 220; backs La Follette, 203, 212, 213, 280; attacks League of Nations, 254
Hudson, 209
Hughes, Charles Evans, 188, 189
Hughitt, Marvin, 47
Hull, Merlin: as progressive, 125, 139, 152, 175, 177, 181; as nationalist, 186, 205, 209; candidacies of, 234, 239, 266, 271
Husting, Paul O.: elected senator, 1914, 121, 149, 158, 162, 163; death of, 216, 225

INDUSTRIAL Workers of the World (I.W.W.), 245, 246, 272, 274, 281
Iowa County, 276

JACKSON County, 138, 181
James, Ada, 249
James, David, 231
Janesville, 21, 47, 144, 180
Janesville Gazette, 57, 138, 143, 255
Jefferson County, 223, 224, 235, 238, 261n, 279
Jeffris, Malcolm J., 180, 183, 187, 188, 189
Johnson, Henry, 140, 239
Johnson, Hiram, 254, 265
Jones, Granville D., 165
Jones, Jenkin Lloyd, 204, 205
Jones, Richard Lloyd; as pre-war progressive, 139, 151, 158; as nationalist, 195, 204–206, 210, 217, 225, 231, 246, 256

KEWAUNEE County, 223, 224
Keyes, Elisha: 100; observations of, 20, 21, 67n, 72, 73, 75, 112n, 116; opposes La Follette, 28, 56, 95–96
Kileen, E. F., 222, 231
Kirsch, William, 231n
Kirwan, Albert D., vii
Kletzsch, Alvin, 231
Knies, Karl, 131
Knights of Columbus, 161, 246
Knights of Labor, 13
Knights of Luther, 162
Kreutzer, Andrew, 55
Kronshage, Theodore, 42, 110, 115, 120
Krumrey, Henry, 249
Ku Klux Klan, 160

LA CROSSE, 180, 205, 217, 222, 276
La Crosse County, 224, 239
La Crosse Tribune, 158, 222, 256n
La Follette, Belle Case: observations and recollections of, 33, 40, 49, 64, 70–71
La Follette, Fola, 124n
La Follette, Philip, 280
La Follette, Robert M.: 145; as national progressive leader, v, 104–105, 107; as governor, v, 50–54, 57–59, 68–69, 84–85; and young and educated, 20–24, 286; and farmers, 24–26, 91, 193, 138, 201, 214–216, 218, 224–225, 234–236, 250, 257, 258, 262, 275, 276, 280, 286; and Scandinavians, 26–28, 79, 90–92, 129, 286; and German voters, 49, 56, 79–80, 129–130, 174–178, 189, 222–224, 235, 242, 253, 257, 258, 261, 278–279, 280, 281; and Democrats, 50, 66–67, 73, 79, 97, 126–128, 130, 158, 162–163, 180, 190, 222, 279; and Social Democrats, 67, 79, 152–157, 250–254, 259–260, 261, 273, 280, 289; pre-war ideas of, 5–6, 18, 36, 52–53, 82, 87–88, 93–95, 135–136, 174, 178, 201–202, 284, 286, 287; political strategy and techniques of, 18, 21–29, 35, 42, 44, 48–50, 52–53, 66, 69–71, 78, 80, 81, 82, 89, 93–95, 101, 102, 104, 118, 170–171, 178–179, 183, 233, 285, 288; attributes of, 18–19, 24, 33, 37–38; as young

Index

politician, 4–6, 20; falls out with Sawyer, 9, 16–17; wins Dane County, 1894, 28–29; 1896 campaign, 30–33; rejects office, 1896, 33–34; seeks patronage for backers, 34–35, 286; advocates primary, 35–37, 51–52, 53, 97–98; 1898 campaign, 42–44; elected governor, 1900, 45–50; antagonizes opponents, 51–60; renominated, 1902, 60–64; and Spooner, 64–65; re-elected, 1902, 64–67; renominated, 1904, 69–76; re-elected, 77–79; backs railroad taxation and regulation, 51–53, 68; elected to U. S. Senate, 84–85; opposes Davidson, 84–99, 103; and Stephenson, 99–100; renominated, 1910, 104–106; splits with McGovern, 106–123; defends progressivism, 1912, 149–150; attacks McGovern administration, 149–150; declines to run for governor, 157; opposes McGovern for Senate, 160–163; opposes Philipp, 1916, 170–171; seeks delegates, 1916, 173–183; and 1916 gubernatorial nominations, 178–180, 183–187; renominated, 183, 187, 189; and Philipp, 1916, 190; re-elected, 1916, 190; war views of, 193, 197, 201–202; condemned for war stand, 193–194, 197, 202–206, 209–214; survives war politically, 214, 241–243; campaigns for Thompson, 1918, 219–220, 226; and 1918 governorship, 233–237; postwar resurgence, 244, 252–259, 261–265, 271–277, 279, 281–282; attacks League of Nations, 253–255, 258; backs Thompson as independent, 273, 275–276; death of, 280; impact of war on, 282

La Follette, Robert M., Jr., 171, 280

La Follette's Autobiography, 52, 54, 164

La Follette's Magazine: founding, maintenance, and condition of, 139, 149, 170; positions taken by, 182, 186–187, 201, 217, 219, 253

Lancaster Teller, 158

Landis, Kenesaw Mountain, 247

Langlade County, 223

League of Nations, as political issue, 244, 250, 253–255, 258, 264, 265, 275, 276, 277

League to Enforce the Peace, 254

Legislative Reference Library, 132, 148, 149, 151, 168

Lenroot, Irvine L.: 110, 116, 117, 264, 284; candidacies of, 87–99, 100, 112n, 113, 216–217, 220–222, 224, 225, 227–228, 257, 264–265, 267, 268, 272, 273, 276, 278–279; and McGovern, 101, 111, 112, 113; differs with La Follette, 176; and Philipp, 240, 257, 272; and League of Nations, 254

Levitan, Sol, 217

Lewis, Evan, 74

Lewis, William M., 116

Liberty Loans, 194, 198, 206, 207, 209, 213, 220

Lincoln County, 239, 274

Link, Arthur, 282

Lockney, Henry, 231

Long, D. Weller, 251

Loyalty: issue of, 155, 156, 165, 168, 186, 196, 197, 215, 216–234, 238–243, 267, 268–269, 271, 272; campaign for, 193–201, 202–214, 244–247, 273–274, 281

Loyalty Legion, 198, 199, 204, 227, 240

McCarthy, Charles: 117n; observations of, 176, 181, 211, 215; as head of Legislative Reference Library, vi, 131, 132, 133, 134, 135, 139, 148, 151n, 159, 165, 167, 168; opposes primary, 102n; war service of, 197, 215; candidate for senator, 225, 226

McClure's Magazine, 78

McConnell, John, 186, 222

McCoy, R. B., 273, 276, 277

McElroy, William S., 111, 112

McGillivray, James, 97

McGovern, Francis E.: 199, 270; as Milwaukee leader, 42–43, 109–112, 122, 152, 155, 284; as statewide

candidate, 101, 102, 106, 115, 122, 140–143, 150, 152, 155, 160–163, 174, 179–180, 183–187, 221; split with La Follette, 106–119; as governor, v–vi, 121, 130–137, 143, 146, 156, 157; political impact of, 178, 283
McGregor, Duncan, 256
McHenry, A. C., 267–268
McKinley, William, 6, 18, 32, 33, 34, 47, 48, 49
Madison, 8, 19, 28, 64, 65, 66, 68, 72, 74, 86, 101, 103, 116, 131, 144, 149, 150, 178, 186, 187, 197, 202, 226, 234, 235, 251, 257, 262, 267, 270
Madison *Capital Times*: rise of, 217, 256; positions taken by, 217, 218, 219, 262, 265, 270
Madison Democrat, 147, 207
Mahon, Thomas J., 118, 199
Mahoney, D. O., 158, 231
Manitowoc County, 223, 224, 229
Marathon County, 223, 224, 227, 229, 261n, 276
Marinette, 165
Marquette County, 224
Marsh, Spencer, 118
Marshall, Rouget, 185
Marshall, Thomas, 226
Marshfield, 84
Mauston, 218
Maxwell, Robert S., 124n
Menace, The, 162
Menominee, 276
Merchants and Manufacturers Association (Milwaukee), 195
Merrill Herald, 158
Meyer, Balthasar H., vi, 131
Milwaukee: 5, 8, 9, 10, 30, 31, 47, 49, 62, 89, 101, 106, 107, 137, 138, 180, 256, 257, 258, 270, 275; pre-war economic development of, 13, 154–155; pre-war political situation in, 14, 32, 42–43, 54, 63, 67, 101, 109–113, 119, 122, 123, 153–157; population of, 67, 110; during war, 195, 196, 200, 203, 207, 229, 230, 241; after war, 245, 246, 247, 248, 251, 252, 271, 274

Milwaukee Free Press: under Stephenson, 62, 88, 89, 97, 120n, 130, 139; as organ of German-Americans, 177, 195, 222, 253
Milwaukee Journal: 38, 121, 171; pre-war comments of, 33, 37, 155; as nationalistic organ, 195, 226, 227, 229, 232, 245; after war, 255
Milwaukee Leader, 177, 210, 228, 253
Milwaukee Sentinel: 16, 38; as stalwart organ, 51, 62, 147, 196; backs neutrality, 176; during war, 195, 196, 232, 240, 241; after war, 253, 255, 265, 269, 276
Mitchell, Alexander, 8
Mohlenpah, Henry, 240
Monroe County, 224
Monson, Chris, 179
Morgan, William J.: 273; candidate, 1920, 264, 267, 268, 272; opposes Blaine, 272, 273
Morris, Thomas: 117, 118, 150, 174; opposes McGovern, 115, 116, 151, 160, 161, 162; and "Americanism," 186; as nationalist, 203
Mowry, George, vii
Munson, O. G., 117, 231
Murphy, Jerre, 60, 69
Myrick, H. P., 62

NAGLER, L. B., 195
National Security League, 193, 195, 202
Neenah News, 158
Nelson, Adolphus P., 246
Nelson, John M., 42, 139, 239, 277
New Deal, 146, 288–289
New Glarus, 151
New Nationalism, 105, 119, 131
New York Times, 210, 220
Nonpartisan League: 253; La Follette addresses, 201; as force in Wisconsin, 216, 234, 246, 250–251, 252, 253, 260, 262, 263, 264, 267, 272, 289; as political issue, 260, 261, 264, 268, 271, 272, 280, 281; outside Wisconsin, 262–263
Norris, George, 105
Norwegian-Americans: population

Index

in Wisconsin, 14, 90; and La Follette, 23, 26–28, 129; and Davidson, 86, 90–92, 103, 283–284; in 1920 politics, 267

ORDER of the Camels, 266, 267
Oshkosh, 40, 75, 267
Oshkosh Northwestern, 66n, 144, 158
Outagamie County, 223, 224, 276
Owen, Walter C., 182, 185
Ozaukee County, 223, 224, 229, 279

PAYNE, Henry C.: 24, 43; background of, 9–10; attacked as lobbyist, 15–16, 17, 25; and Cabinet post, 31, 34, 35, 46, 47, 48; as post-1900 stalwart leader, 61, 63, 76, 129, 164, 287; death of, 77
Payne-Aldrich tariff, 105
Peck, George W., 29, 76
Pederson, Eli, 26
Peterson, Alvin, 221, 231, 272
Peterson, Sewall, 23
Pfister, Charles F.: 43, 129, 164; rises to leadership, 30, 31–32, 46–47; as anti-La Follette leader, 32, 46–47, 51, 62, 72, 104; superseded as leader, 63, 71, 81, 169; and war, 195
Phoenix, J. J., 266n
Philipp, Emanuel L.: 59, 124, 242; as stalwart leader, 63, 71, 81, 104, 128–129, 144–145, 164, 179, 180–181, 188, 287; as governor, 164–173, 188, 191, 197, 198, 203, 216, 230–232, 245, 247, 248, 283; and La Follette, 46, 57–58, 236, 243, 256–259, 269–271, 281; and Lenroot, 222, 227; and Wilcox, 230–233, 238–239, 258, 269–271; and Dithmar, 260; campaigns of, 121, 122, 145–152, 157–159, 163, 187–190, 239–240; positions taken, 177–178, 254; characterized, 172
Pierce, Charles, 144, 145, 232
Pinchot, Gifford, 105
Plumb Plan, 249
Polk County, 144
Populism, 12, 154
Portage County, 276

Prairie du Chien, 276
Primary elections: 44; enacted, v, 68, 79; second choice vote in, 86, 103, 129, 134, 152; as political issue, 36–37, 40, 41, 42, 50, 51–52, 53, 55–56, 57, 58, 62, 68, 102, 145, 157, 184; as source of trouble for progressives, 57, 97–98, 99, 101–103, 129, 178–179, 185, 187, 233–234, 284. For contests, *see also* Republican party, Democratic party
Prohibition, 190, 232, 238, 239–240, 244, 247, 261, 266. See also Temperance
Progressives: attributes of, 18–24; pre-war thinking of, vi, 17–18, 27–28, 30, 93–99, 102, 130–136, 138–139, 159, 178, 206, 284, 285; pre-war arguments of, 21, 39–40, 42, 68, 71, 78, 104–105, 140–142, 146, 149–152, 157–158, 174–175, 182–183, 187–188; break with La Follette on war, 203–206, 231, 281. *See also* Progressive Movement, Progressivism, and La Follette, Robert M.
Progressivism: v; persistence of, 191–192, 280–282, 288; and New Deal, 146, 288–289. *See also* Progressive movement, Progressives, and La Follette, Robert M.
Progressive movement, nationally: v, 105, 106, 130–131, 141, 289
Progressive movement, in Wisconsin: fame of, v, 78, 81, 83; rise of, 10–82, 286–287; composition of, 12–18, 20–28, 41–43, 109–110; achievements of, v–vi, 68, 79, 82, 84, 134–135, 287, 288; political weaknesses of, vi, 79–82, 83–84, 92–99, 107–123, 124, 129–130, 136, 138–139, 146, 152–159, 163, 164, 172–173, 177–179, 181–182, 283–286, 288; political defeats of, vi, 68, 83, 86–99, 101, 102–103, 121–122, 124, 142–152, 158, 184; later victories of, 104–106, 187; and war, 214, 242–243, 244, 280–282, 285, 288–289; end of, 191–192. *See also*

Progressives, Progressivism, and La Follette, Robert M.
Progressive party (1924), 280

QUARLES, Joseph: elected to senate, 45; as anti-La Follette leader, 61, 63, 68, 75, 77, 81; displaced in senate, 84, 85

RACINE, 116, 181, 199, 205
Racine County, 271
Racine Times, 158
Railroads: 12, 13, 47, 84, 169; regulation of, v, 44, 50, 68, 71, 85, 93, 94, 113–114, 182; taxation of, v, 44, 49, 50, 51–52, 53, 55, 63, 68, 71; as force in politics, 7–8, 9, 47, 51, 68, 70, 71–72, 127, 164, 182, 287
Railroad brotherhoods, 249, 252, 253, 263, 280, 281
Ralston, Craig, 171
Reed, Thomas B., 6
Reedsburg, 114
Reinsch, Paul, 278, 279
Republican party (Wisconsin): strength and composition, late nineteenth century, 3–6; early machine control of, 7–11, 286–287; hurt by treasurer cases, 16, 29–30; hurt by La Follette-Sawyer clash, 16–17; decline of Old Guard in, 31–32, 46–47, 77, 81
Rhinelander, 246
Richland County, 276
Richmond, T. C., 144, 147
Rock County, 136, 172, 271
Roethe, Henry, 62, 125, 152
Rogers, Alfred T.: as La Follette adviser and spokesman, 87, 90, 101, 120, 121, 134, 178, 261; backs *Capital Times,* 217
Roosevelt, Franklin D., 146
Roosevelt, Theodore: as national progressive leader, v, 105, 119, 129, 146, 206; backs La Follette (1904), 77–78; and 1912 presidential election, 107, 119, 120, 121, 127, 141, 151n, 217; and preparedness, 175, 193; denounces La Follette, 210

Root, Elihu, 175, 193
Rosa, Charles, 158n, 171, 212, 217, 235, 237
Rose, David, 43, 65, 67, 109, 223
Rosebush, Judson, 266n
Ross, Edward A., 133
Rusk, Jeremiah, 155
Russell, Harry L., 165, 213

ST. CROIX County, 73, 209
Sanborn, A. W.: 246; favors organization, 102, 115, 178, 179, 181–182, 184; as progressive, 122, 139, 175, 180; as nationalist, 203, 222, 231
Sanborn, Walker, 246
Saugen, C. N., 237n
Sauk County, 87, 224, 238, 239, 261n, 276
Sawyer, Philetus: 45; as Old Guard leader, 7, 9, 10, 31, 34, 46, 61, 129, 164, 287; and La Follette, 16–17, 18, 30, 31, 32; death of, 46
Sawyer County, 239, 276
Scandinavians, 11, 14, 26, 79, 90, 160, 181, 286. *See also* Norwegian-Americans, Swedish-Americans
Schlitz Brewing Company, 46, 129
Schmitz, A. J., 137, 249
Scofield, Edward: 116, 173; chosen governor, 32, 33; and La Follette, 33, 35, 42, 43, 44, 48, 75, 76
Scott, George E., 140, 150
Seaman, Gilbert, 270–271, 273
Seidel, Emil, 67, 133, 154, 241
Shawano County, 223, 224, 229, 261n, 276
Sheboygan, 205
Sheboygan County, 223, 224, 229, 238
Sherman, James S., 104
Siebecker, Robert, 16
Skandinaven, 27, 90, 91n, 160, 161, 188n, 220
Smith, Adam, 131, 202
Social Democratic party: and La Follette, vi, 50, 67, 73, 81, 152–157, 163; in Milwaukee, 109–110, 119, 132–133, 152–157, 177, 196, 247, 285; during war, 177, 196, 197, 200–201, 202, 203, 209, 211, 213, 228–230, 232, 240–242, 282; after

Index

war, 245, 246, 247, 252, 259–260, 261, 273, 277, 278, 279, 280, 281, 289
Soldiers Grove, 86
Spooner, John C.: 28, 46, 58, 95; as senator, 10, 31, 64, 78, 99; as political leader, 10, 31, 48, 61, 63, 64–65, 69, 75, 76, 81; observations of, 47, 48, 55–56
Spooner, Willet M., 195, 232
Stafford, William, 176, 241
Stalwarts: 70, 71, 94, 211; grievances of, 50, 54, 63–64, 73, 74, 76–77, 80–81, 283, 287; character of, 54–60, 72–73, 76–77, 78–81, 164–170, 172–173, 283; campaigns of, 60–64, 65, 73–77, 88, 89, 95–96, 103–104, 105–106, 142–158, 163; as factor in progressive decline, 81–82, 126, 128–130, 283; arguments of, 64, 72, 105, 143–148, 164–165, 181, 188, 285; during Philipp administrations, 169–179, 172–173, 179, 181, 183, 188, 189–190, 221–222, 232, 237, 254
State Council of Defense, 197, 198, 207, 208, 244
State, The, 42, 48
Steffens, Lincoln, v, 78
Stephenson, Isaac: 106, 116, 123, 128; backs Payne, 34; and La Follette, 45, 46, 84, 85, 88, 92, 94, 95, 104; candidate for senator, 45, 84–85, 88, 99–101, 103, 113, 114; campaign investigated, 115, 260; influence of, 92, 139, 173, 283, 284, 285
Stewart, Charles, 169, 203
Stone, James A.: as progressive leader, 87, 88, 101, 114, 115, 120, 175, 178, 179, 184; as anti-La Follette nationalist, 203–204, 221, 231; postwar views of, 256, 264
Strange, John, 9, 96, 266n
Superior, 87, 276
Superior Telegram, 140, 158, 176, 210, 254
Supreme Court (Wisconsin), 76, 182
Swedish-Americans, 14, 90
Swenson, Magnus, 197

TAYLOR, George R., 13n
Taylor, Horace A., 28, 29, 56, 61, 63, 73
Taylor County, 223, 229, 276
Temperance: 80, 166, 279–280, 285; and Lenroot, 98; and Davidson, 106; and Philipp, 129, 238; in 1920, 266–268, 271. *See also* Prohibition
Thompson, James: 228, 229; as candidate, 180, 217–225, 238, 262, 267, 268, 273, 278–279; and 1918 governorship, 234, 235, 237; and League of Nations, 254
Thorkelson, Halston J., 167
Tittemore, J. N.: candidate for governor, 234–239, 260, 261, 271; opposes Nonpartisan League, 251, 260, 271
Trempealeau County, 87, 103, 123
Tumulty, Joseph, 194
Twesme, Albert, 103

UNIVERSITY of Wisconsin: 64, 109, 204, 270; serves state, vi, 92, 131, 133; enrollment at, 14; expenses rise, 143, 148; and La Follette, 24, 42, 66, 84, 213–214; as political issue, 137, 147–149, 151, 164–167, 285
Upham, William H., 29, 30, 31, 75, 116, 173
Usher, Ellis B., 144, 176
Utman, Bruce, 125, 152

VAN HISE, Charles R., 131, 132n, 166, 167, 213
Vea, F. J., 266n
Vernon County, 224
Vilas, William, 8
Vogel, August H., 195
Vogel, Fred, Jr., 254
Voigt, Edward, 241

WALL, Edward C., 8, 10, 43
Walworth County, 172, 222, 271
Warner, Hoyt L., vii
Washburn County, 239
Washington County, 223, 224, 229, 239, 278, 279

Waukesha County, 139, 239
Wausau Record-Herald, 144
Waushara County, 161
Weber, Frank, 278
Weisse, Charles H., 128
West, George, 180, 227, 257, 258
West Superior, 41
Whitehead, John M.: 66; in nineties, 21, 22, 46, 48; as stalwart, 55, 62, 169; and Wilcox, 232
Whitlock, Brand, 194
Whitman, Platt, 168
Whittet, Lawrence, 167, 169, 171
Wilbur, Harry C., 118, 119, 144, 161
Wilcox, Roy: 268; leads nationalists, 199, 242, 273; candidacies of, 230–232, 236–239, 240, 263, 266, 267, 268–271; for League to Enforce the Peace, 254
Wilcox Resolution, 212, 213, 238n, 263
Wiley, Alexander, 231
Williams, Burt, 190
Wilson, William, 226
Wilson, Woodrow: 157, 227; as national progressive leader, v, 132, 133, 141; as candidate, 189, 190; as wartime President, 193, 194, 198, 211; and Wisconsin politics, 128, 149, 175, 196, 206, 220, 226, 240, 249–250, 252, 253, 255, 256, 265, 276, 280
Winnebago County, 224, 239
Wisconsin, economic development of: 6–7, 11–14, 132n, 214–215, 284
Wisconsin Central Railroad, 47
Wisconsin Farmer, 25
Wisconsin Federation of Labor, 153, 154, 157, 216, 252, 253, 260, 261–262, 263, 280, 281
"Wisconsin Idea," 79, 131
Wisconsin Idea, The, 132, 139
Wisconsin Manufacturers Association, 136
Wisconsin News (Milwaukee), 253
Wisconsin Society of Equity: 125, 158, 253; during war, 215, 216, 224–225, 234, 248; after war, 251, 252, 261
Wisconsin State Journal: 28, 59, 204; as progressive organ, 139, 140, 141, 151, 158; and preparedness, 176, as nationalist organ, 195, 210, 217, 221, 227, 246; declines, 218
Wisconsin Vorwaerts, 153, 197
Wolfe, William, 190, 225
World War I: early reaction to, 174–177, 178, 183, 186, 189, 190, 195–197; impact of, 193–282

YELLOWITZ, Irwin, vii